Praise for *Hostile Environment*

'Maya Goodfellow's book could not be more timely. While politicians and pundits continue to peddle toxic myths about migration, Goodfellow dives into the details of the issue and exposes the way in which migrants have been vilified and mistreated in this country. The book is a brilliant exposé of the struggles faced by migrants and a rallying cry for the pro-migrant movement we desperately need'

Magid Magid MEP

'Maya Goodfellow has a sharp mind, a deep well of knowledge and a readable style. When she writes something I learn something'

Gary Younge, author of *Another Day in the Death of America*

'This is a hugely important first book from Maya Goodfellow. After a referendum debate dominated by anti-migrant rhetoric and falsehoods, it's vital that we reflect on how we got to this toxic place. The testimony from migrants in this book, and the examination of the policies under which people have suffered for so long, are a damning indictment of government policy on migration that has failed for years. Maya's voice in this debate is much needed and this book should be on every Home Office desk'

Caroline Lucas MP

'An informative and insightful account of the history and politics of modern migration to Britain that is also very readable. Ranging across the intersecting histories of class, race, nation and empire, Maya Goodfellow deftly shows how the contemporary demonising of migrants, including refugees and asylum-seekers, has a long and dispiriting national and global backstory to it – but there are also heartening stories of resistance and solidarity which point to the way forward'

Priyamvada G—   —nt Empire

LONDO   r

D1628052

'Maya Goodfellow provides a forceful narrative of the current state of British politics by placing anti-immigration at its centre. Goodfellow expertly tackles the consensus from left and right that immigration is a bad thing. In doing so, her book demonstrates the fundamental humanity at stake in critiquing and overturning that consensus. Now is the time to read this penetrating analysis'

Robbie Shilliam, author of *The Black Pacific*

'This is the book to read on UK immigration. It passionately makes the case that for too long lies, mistruths and institutional racism have morphed any conversation about immigration in the UK into something utterly demeaning. Maya Goodfellow's excellent reportage is impassioned, clear and filled with humane interviews with people from immigrant backgrounds at various stages of the process and experts on the front lines doing the necessary work to help them. This isn't a polemic. This is a human book that offers very clear and concise answers for how we have arrived at this point. A triumph of non-fiction writing'

Nikesh Shukla, editor of *The Good Immigrant*

'How immigrants became the scapegoats for injustices caused by the rich and powerful is one of the burning questions of modern politics. This masterful, wonderfully written, and vitally important book – written by one of the most powerful writers on race and migration today – more than does it justice. This book is essential to understanding the reactionary political upheavals which have swept the West'

Owen Jones, author of *Chavs*

'This is an essential study into the toxic discussion around immigration in the UK. It is as brilliant as it is necessary'

Nish Kumar

'A book to cut through the noise of toxic politics, the race to the bottom to demonise immigrants, and the ahistoric idea that a hostile environment is anything new. This book reveals the nuts and bolts of Britain's real immigration problem – the counter-productivity of its policies and the failure of its leaders. So important'

Afua Hirsch, author of *Brit(ish): On Race, Identity and Belonging*

'This book is a must-read if you are thinking of going into politics. It will highlight the trials and tribulations of political life and how the choices made at the very top of government can affect people in the harshest of ways. Maya enlightens the reader on both the decisions that lead to the pain and suffering inflicted through government immigration policies and Theresa May's legacy, which will no doubt be her fuelling of the hostile environment which she systematically designed to dehumanise a generation of legal citizens with devastating consequences. Maya brings to the fore in the most painful terms just how expensive it is to be poor'

Dawn Butler MP, shadow secretary of state for women and equalities

'*Hostile Environment* is a bold and, at times, brutal analysis. It raises many uncomfortable questions for those who sat at the table making this policy. An important contribution to an ongoing debate'

Sayeeda Warsi, Baroness Warsi

'*Hostile Environment* is a powerful reminder that the right has been weaponising the immigration debate to distract from the real causes of working-class dispossession. We need more writers like Maya Goodfellow, who so clearly and passionately outlines what is at work and at stake in battles for social justice'

Kehinde Andrews, author of *Back to Black*

Maya Goodfellow is a writer, researcher and academic. She has written for the *New York Times*, the *Guardian*, the *New Statesman*, Al Jazeera and the *Independent*. She received her PhD from SOAS, University of London. She is a trustee of the Runnymede Trust.

Hostile Environment

How Immigrants Became Scapegoats

Maya Goodfellow

VERSO

First published by Verso Books 2019
© Maya Goodfellow 2019

1 3 5 7 9 10 8 6 4 2

Verso
UK: 6 Meard Street, London W1F 0EG
US: 20 Jay Street, Suite 1010, Brooklyn, NY 11201
versobooks.com

Verso is the imprint of New Left Books

ISBN-13: 978-1-78873-336-6
ISBN-13: 978-1-78873-338-0 (US EBK)
ISBN-13: 978-1-78873-337-3 (UK EBK)

British Library Cataloguing in Publication Data
A catalogue record for this book is available from the British Library

Library of Congress Cataloging-in-Publication Data
A catalog record for this book is available from the Library of Congress

Typeset in Sabon by Biblichor Ltd, Edinburgh
Printed and bound by CPI Group (UK) Ltd, Croydon CR0 4YY

To Rambhaben Vallabhdas Tanna,
Vallabhdas Gordhandas Tanna,
Hedy Goodfellow and my parents

Contents

Introduction

An Honest Conversation

For Nazek Ramadan, the 2010 General Election brings back bad memories. She remembers how worried, unwanted and out of place people felt. To her and many others, it was as if immigration was everywhere you looked in the campaign, and so were the politicians who appeared to be competing with each other to be the toughest on immigrants. 'Things became very toxic,' she says.

Nazek is director of Migrant Voice, an organisation which works to encourage more migrants to speak for themselves in the media. When I meet her and fellow employee Anne Stoltenberg in their offices in London, she recounts tales of people she knew who were attacked and insulted by strangers on the street during the campaign. 'How can they hate us so much', she vividly recalls one person asking her, 'when they don't even know us?'

The answer is disappointingly simple: it was because they were immigrants.

The word 'immigrant' carries all kinds of ideas in its three syllables. It's weighed down by all the meanings it's been given. You know the kinds of things I'm talking about: 'low-skilled', 'high-skilled', 'contributor', 'drain', 'cockroach' or just, plainly put, simply 'a concern'. Not all of these terms are necessarily negative, but each of them is impersonal, clinical and cold.

As Nazek's experiences suggest, we live in a world where it is necessary to remind people that immigrants are not things, not a burden and not the enemy. That they're human beings. Insufficient doesn't even begin to cover how inadequate and clumsy this statement is when people's lives are devastated by the UK's immigration politics.

Almost every single person I interviewed for this book who had to move through the UK's immigration and asylum system could recount the exact dates their lives were uprooted or finally given security – when they were detained or deported, when they arrived and when they were given status. From anti-immigration politics come all kinds of policies: ones that ruin lives, leave people to drown at borders, treat them as subhuman or make their lives more difficult in a myriad of quiet and subtle ways. This book sets out to explain why this is not an inevitability; it will show how decades of restrictive policy and demonising rhetoric have created this system. And it will argue that it doesn't have to be this way. But to get to a different world, we have to understand how we got here.

The name 'hostile environment' is surprisingly appropriate for the raft of policies it refers to. It stands out from the dreary, opaque names governments give to those they'd rather stay under the radar. When the Conservatives changed the rules on social housing so that people living in properties deemed as having a 'spare room' had their benefits cut, they called it the 'spare room subsidy'. Campaigners renamed it the more appropriate 'bedroom tax'.

But when Theresa May unveiled her flagship immigration package as home secretary, she didn't even attempt to hide its cruelty. She flaunted it. The aim was to create a 'really hostile environment for illegal immigrants,' she boasted.[1] The plan was to make their lives unbearable.

And, so, the government began to create this hostile environment, stitching immigration checks into every element of people's lives. Through measures brought in by the 2014 and 2016 Immigration Acts, a whole host of professionals – from landlords and letting agents to doctors and nurses – were turned into border guards.[2] Regardless of how removed their profession was from the world of immigration policy, the threat of being fined or sentenced to jail time loomed over them if they failed to carry out checks to ensure people they encountered through their work were in the country legally. But they had it easy in comparison to migrants without the right documents, who could lose access to housing, bank accounts, healthcare and even be deported if they couldn't provide the 'right' evidence to show that they were 'allowed' to be in the country. 'I gave a presentation to a respiratory department,' Jessica Potter, a doctor and campaigner against immigration controls in the NHS recalls, 'and one colleague said they had a gentleman who had an early stage of lung cancer, potentially curable.' He didn't have the right documentation so 'he was shipped off to a detention centre for months and later came back into care. Now he has incurable lung cancer.'

Six years after May proudly announced her plans, and when I was in the middle of writing this book, some of the disturbing results of the hostile environment became national news. For weeks, the headlines were dominated by stories of black Britons who had every right to be in the UK suddenly being refused essential medical care or state support, losing jobs and homes and being left destitute. Some who had lived here nearly all their lives were deported and died before their deportation was revealed to be a mistake. What became known as the 'Windrush scandal' was an almost inevitable consequence of the impossible system the government had constructed to create the hostile environment.

The people whose experiences were plastered all over our newspaper front pages and who were being interviewed on the nightly news had arrived from colonies and former colonies decades ago, and they had come as *citizens*. By successive governments' own standards, they had come to and settled in the UK legally. Having first set foot in this country as small children or teenagers, many of them had never really known anywhere else; they had lived, worked and loved here for almost their whole lives.

The problem was that the hostile environment demanded they prove they had the right to be here, and for these people who had come as citizens under the Empire, the government had no record of their status or arrival. Landing cards, the only proof of when they arrived in the UK, were destroyed by the Home Office in 2010. This made it near impossible for them to show they were in this country legally.

Years before the story broke, the government had been repeatedly warned that these people were being caught up in the hostile environment's dangerous web. Caribbean foreign ministers raised the issue with the then foreign secretary Philip Hammond in 2016. And a high commissioner to one of the countries involved said the Foreign Office was told at least six times, since 2013, that there was a problem. But the government ignored these warnings and carried on regardless.[3] And so in spring 2018, for the briefest of moments, the issue of how the UK treats and talks about immigrants and people who are thought to be immigrants was a topic of national interest. Politicians earnestly committed themselves to humanising the 'debate' on immigration, pundits were aghast as to how this had happened and people in power promised tangible change.

Then the PR operation kicked into action. Home Secretary Amber Rudd resigned after saying she 'inadvertently misled' members of Parliament. The *Guardian* received a leaked letter she had written to Theresa May which included a reference to a target for removing undocumented migrants – this was after Rudd had told Parliament no such target existed. Rudd's replacement, Sajid Javid, promised a 'more compassionate immigration system'. The son of a Pakistani migrant, Abdul, who came to the UK with just a pound in his pocket, Javid drew on his family history to reassure the country that the Windrush scandal was personal for him, as if this would guarantee that any immigration policies introduced on his watch would make the system more humane.[4] He did this even though his parliamentary record showed he had invariably voted for stricter immigration and asylum laws, including those that made up the hostile environment.

The hostile environment was rebranded the 'compliant environment' and some of the associated policies were suspended. But most of them remained in place; ministers repeated they were necessary to deal with 'illegal immigrants'. Months after Windrush made headlines, the government still didn't know how many people had been deported thanks to their policies, and many of those who had been affected were still living in homelessness hostels, unable to work.[5] A year later, a compensation scheme was set up for the people who had been caught up in the whole affair.

The government was at pains to emphasise that the Windrush generation were here legally, and that the aim of their hostile environment policies was to tackle 'illegal' immigration. But the tag 'illegal' obscures more than it tells us. It carries with it an assumption of inherent criminality and immorality; if you are 'illegal', you are bad. You deserve, then, what you get, whether that be detention, deportation or having your access to housing and healthcare blocked.

But this fails to recognise that people can become undocumented for all kinds of reasons. Some, for instance, come here legally only to become 'illegal': the rules might change under their feet in our labyrinthine immigration system, leaving them without status but unaware that's the case; they might not be able to afford exorbitant fees to renew their documentation or they might simply lose their papers and be too scared to come forward in a country where politicians openly advertise the fact that they are working to create a hostile environment for undocumented migrants. Reliant on precarious work and having spent so much money to get here, some people will do what they can to continue sending money back home or to keep paying off the debt they accrued to be able to move in the first place. The Windrush affair – the visible tip of a nightmarish iceberg – was made possible by the system and by prevailing attitudes within the country at large, whereby it was deemed acceptable to treat people not as human beings but as problems.

Exemplifying this inhumane system is the government's immigration target. During the 2010 election, David Cameron pledged to reduce net migration (the difference between how many people come into the country and how many leave in a year)[6] to below the 'tens of thousands'. As well as the hostile environment, the obsession with numbers resulted in Operation Vaken, which involved Theresa May's Home Office sending vans reading 'Go Home' around diverse parts of the country and boasting about immigration raids on social media. At around the same time, the government issued over 100,000 visas for migrants from outside of the European Union (EU), suggesting that even as they talked and acted tough about reducing immigration they knew they needed people to fill labour shortages.[7]

And what of the Opposition? As the policies that went on to make up the hostile environment were being turned into law through Parliament, the Labour Party put up the most minimal resistance. Then Labour leader Ed Miliband attacked the government for failing to meet their net migration target, the party abstained on the 2014 Immigration Bill, effectively waiving it through; and they went into the 2015 Election selling Labour Party mugs that promised they would put 'Controls on Immigration'.

But there was some Parliamentary resistance. Sixteen MPs voted against the 2014 bill, six of them from Labour, including three of the people who would go on to lead the party a year later: Jeremy Corbyn, Diane Abbott and John McDonnell. When an inter-ministerial 'Hostile Environment Group' was set up so government departments could coordinate their efforts to make migrants' lives more difficult, then Liberal Democrat MP Sarah Teather, together with some of her colleagues, tried to make its existence and its name public knowledge through a Freedom of Information request. Years after they were introduced, former Head of the Civil Service, Bob Kerslake, said some saw the government's policies as 'almost reminiscent of Nazi Germany'.[8] Despite this, the hostile environment went ahead.

It's tempting to focus all the blame on the person or the party that cooked up and then rolled out this package of draconian policies. But Theresa May didn't create them all on her own, and intensely aggressive though it is, the Coalition government didn't introduce hostility into the immigration system. It's not some preordained destiny that brought the UK to the point where people can't get bank accounts or homes because of their immigration status, but it's not a wild deviation from the norm either. Instead, it is decades of exclusionary politics that have made it acceptable to treat migrants this way.

If there has been one point of consensus among the majority of politicians since 2010 it has been that we need to talk about immigration more, and more honestly. Labour MP and former shadow home secretary Yvette Cooper has claimed the UK has 'never properly had' a debate about immigration, former UK Independence Party (UKIP) leader Nigel Farage has said politicians 'betrayed' people on migration, and when he was prime minister David Cameron proclaimed that there needed to be a new approach to immigration – 'one which opens up debate, not closes it down'.[9] They have a point. But the candid discussion I'd like us to have isn't quite the same as the one these three had in mind. Though they'd be loath to admit it, when *they* talked about honesty, the subtext was that we needed to listen to people complain about immigration in whatever way they like, with an advance assurance that – regardless of what they say – they won't be accused of prejudice or racism.

Far from being a debate closed down, litres of ink, reams of TV footage and hours of debate have been dedicated to discussing all the reasons people want to reduce immigration. When I ask Diane Abbott, Shadow Home Secretary, whether politicians have shied away from talking about immigration, she baulks at the idea. After reeling off immigration acts introduced through the decades, she says, there has been 'a series of legislative measures, which were ill thought out . . . and that was all about pandering to anti-immigrant feeling . . . contrary to what everyone says [that has] always been very much close to the centre of political debate.' So it's not that we don't talk about immigration enough or that there's some kind of covert plan to shut down members of the public from airing their grievances about immigrants. The problem is that the 'debate' has run on mistruths, hysteria and racism for decades, if not centuries.

Garvan Walshe confirmed as much in February 2017. An adviser to the Tories during the 2005 election campaign, he tweeted that the party 'worked assiduously to ramp up anti-immigrant feeling' and few politicians – certainly not Gordon Brown, who would soon become prime minister – 'challenged the lies that immigrants took jobs, were here on benefits'.[10] The disinclination to confront myths, and indeed the eagerness to reinforce them, cultivated anti-immigration politics in the UK and would ultimately help produce the Brexit vote.

This book doesn't ignore the UK's vote to leave the EU, but it's not *about* it, and I wasn't motivated to write it as a consequence of the 2016 referendum. This might seem strange, not least because the winning side capitalised heavily on anti-immigration politics and in the process emboldened racists and xenophobes. But the immigration 'debate' was toxic long before David Cameron committed his party to holding a referendum on the UK's membership of the EU in the 2015 Conservative manifesto in a desperate attempt to keep together a Tory Party deeply divided over Europe. As one of the country's most ardent remainers, he had spent the years before the vote dismissing migrants as a 'swarm', blaming immigration for crumbling public services and implementing aggressively exclusionary immigration policies.[11] But despite having helped lay the groundwork for one of the central messages of the Leave campaign, Cameron seemed surprised by the result.

People who voted to Leave were more likely to dislike immigration than those who voted Remain,[12] but that doesn't mean it was the only reason they voted the way they did. Some South Asians, for instance, voted for Brexit after they were told it would mean more immigration from commonwealth countries, and it's not as though everyone who voted to Remain was enthusiastic about immigration. But the fallout suggested not every politician grasped that some of the problems thrown up by the referendum went far deeper than this one vote.

A 'hard Brexit', Labour's Andy Burnham warned months later, would 'turn Britain into a place it has never been: divided, hostile, narrow-minded'.[13] You have to wonder how much he knows about this country's migration histories. By that I don't just mean the many reasons people like my mum and grandparents migrated to the UK from India. Rarely discussed is the poisonous public discourse and suffocating racist legislation that met them when they arrived. Because of its vehemence in recent years, widespread anti-immigration politics seems a new addition to the national landscape. But it has old roots. In the UK's imperial history and present, there has too rarely been a prominent politician on the national stage who didn't engage in some form of anti-immigration politics.

If the vote to leave the EU reminded us just how overlooked these histories are, the aftermath showed how embedded anti-immigration politics is. Faced with the violent result of divisive anti-immigration politics in the form of a rise in the reported number of hate crimes, politicians continued to blame immigrants for the UK's problems as then Labour MP Chuka Umunna advocated for a 'muscular approach' to immigration.[14]

I wanted to write this book so I could not only question these ideas but also understand how they became commonplace; how it is so easy to talk about people as if they're not people at all, just because they were born in another country, and how politicians are able to build illustrious careers around denigrating immigrants and calling for stronger borders.

My aim isn't to document public opinion, but to take a look under the surface of, and challenge, the arguments made about immigration in politics and the media. Over the coming chapters, I will look at the realities of the immigration system and also pick apart the politics around immigration in the UK's recent and more distant past; looking at how the left and the right have helped create and sustain anti-migrant norms. And I will argue for an alternative to this politics.

This is a book about the immigration debate in the UK, the way immigration policies have demonised and racialised whole groups of people, and how ideas from the past rattle around the debates of the present, even if in altered forms, as race and class help decide who belongs and who doesn't. Ultimately, it is about why anti-immigration politics, not immigration itself, is one of this country's most serious problems.

1

The Cost of It All

What decadence this belonging rubbish was, what time the rich must have if they could sit around and weave great worries out of such threadbare things.

Sunjeev Sahota, *The Year of the Runaways*

An industrial estate on the edge of central Birmingham might not sound like the place to find out about the difficulties of migrating to the UK. But in a building nestled behind a car park and overlooking the network of canals that branch off to the nearby town of Smethwick, a group of around thirty people met up on a cold, rainy October evening to talk about their problems with the immigration system. Overstretched lawyers and immigration specialists were on hand to offer advice. As is typical of a winter's day in the UK, the darkness of evening descended far too early, and rain bounced off the pavement as we all made our way into the building, but the room was warm and buzzing with activity when I arrived. People were introducing themselves and getting to know each other while tucking into complimentary homemade samosas taken from a deep bowl that sat next to tea and coffee laid out on one side of the room.

Coming from all over the world, some of the people there that night had struggled alone to navigate disorientating immigration rules while others had to find a way through for their whole family. In the room were children of various ages – from curious babies to bored seven- or eight-year-olds. Some had been born in the country, others had migrated with their parents. But for all of them their future in the UK was uncertain. What united these people was the time, effort and money – often money they didn't have – they were spending to try to stay in this country. About fifteen minutes after I arrived, people took their seats, forming a circle in the middle of the room. As the meeting began, almost immediately their anger and worry spilled out of them. They shared stories of being fleeced by lawyers, going into courtrooms where the people they'd paid to represent them didn't even know the most basic details of their case, and explained the desperation they felt when their claims were repeatedly rejected.

For all the focus on the supposed importance of defending our national borders from outsiders and tales of immigration bringing problems to the UK, too few debates are concerned with how difficult it can be to be a migrant in this country.

One of the people I met in Birmingham was Diana.[1] She came from Zimbabwe as a visitor and began studying before going on to marry an EU citizen. But her marriage quickly deteriorated: 'I had to come out of the relationship because of domestic violence.' She says she left her partner to save her life. She knew nothing about the asylum process, but in 2013 she was told she could apply for refugee status. Diana quickly learned how many people are out there who are 'ready to mislead you'. One of her lawyers didn't give her the right information about applying for asylum, which meant that, when she went to court, she didn't present relevant facts that might have helped her case. Other lawyers she paid barely gave her any time and didn't go through her case properly. At each appeal, she was refused the right to stay in the country.

Understanding all the intricacies of what happened to Diana, and all the other people I talk to, takes time and requires countless follow-up questions. It's unclear how anyone manages to make sense of and navigate the disorientating process she describes. But she is still determined to secure refugee status, and she puts her lack of success at least partly down to poor representation. Still, she isn't giving up. 'One of the things I've found and that has encouraged me to be who I am today is you learn the hard way: ignorance is expensive – and ignorance is not bliss at all.'

Diana isn't alone. She and Kelly, another person I speak to, live in different cities and have had completely different lives, but their experiences of the immigration regime are remarkably similar. Calling the UK home since she was nine years old, Kelly came here after her dad brought the whole family – Kelly, her sister and her mother – from West Africa on a diplomatic visa. Ten years later, when Kelly was in the middle of her first year of university, he abruptly left the country and she was told she didn't have the right to stay in the UK. With her mum and sister, Kelly applied for a family visa, but when that was rejected, she decided to apply for the right to stay in the country alone.

'I went through three lawyers,' she says. The first one didn't understand her case and after he submitted her application, the Home Office said there was no cogent argument in the papers, so they had nothing to consider. That cost her over £1,000. 'At the time I didn't understand the case, so I was dependent on him to explain,' Kelly remembers, shaking her head. 'There was no communication . . . so . . . I was chasing him every second and then when the Home Office refused it there was not much done.'

Kelly waited three years for her appeals to be processed. With no right to work and unable to access state support, she had to resort to living between friends' houses and she nearly became homeless. 'It's ridiculous to be honest because you're not allowed to work, so where do you expect me to get the money from?' she asks. 'I think the cost is just to frustrate people to just give up and go back.' She asked multiple agencies for financial support and legal help. She was a 'novice' and had no idea 'what was going on'. It's not chance that makes Kelly's and Diana's experiences so similar. As well as exorbitant fees for visas and applications, support for immigration and asylum cases is almost non-existent unless you happen to have the money to pay for it, and when you're not allowed to work, for many people, funding legal representation is an impossible task. Even for those lucky enough to be able to afford it, there's no guarantee that the advice you get is going to be reliable.

'In the late 90s when New Labour came in, it was a sort of a golden age for legal aid . . . because there were a lot of asylum claims at that time the government was really throwing money at solicitors' firms to get them to open immigration departments . . . to get solicitors trained up in immigration law so they could take on all these asylum claims,' former immigration barrister Frances Webber remembers. The legal aid she talks about is money the state gives to people who need it to pay for advice or representation. It was available for people regardless of where they were born, so it could be used for people trying to regularise their status or claim British citizenship. But within about three years, New Labour started cutting back. 'It was like this great tidal wave of money was then retreating, retreating, retreating,' Webber says.

In 2007, the government introduced a flat fee for legal aid asylum cases, which meant lawyers were paid a fixed amount regardless of how many hours they worked on a case. 'If you did go over a certain number and if you could justify that . . . then you would get paid by the hour,' Webber explains, but getting to that stage was very complicated and difficult. These changes incentivised a factory-style process: encouraging 'rubbish firms who do no work or do very little work' and penalising those who took 'great care'. Firms were expected to subsidise work on asylum cases with money they received from more straightforward legal aid cases. Then the Coalition government cut legal aid in 2013, including the money available for most immigration and asylum cases.[2] 'When we talk about legal aid cuts and we talk about other aspects of austerity,' journalist Rebecca Omonira-Oyekanmi says, 'we don't also talk about immigration.'

New Labour had cracked down on fraudulent lawyers but, as costs spiralled and legal aid was hacked away, the chaos left people once again exposed to predatory lawyers. What has essentially been solidified is a two-tier justice system.

Reliable help is now extremely hard to come by. Two of the biggest not-for-profit immigration and asylum centres, Refugee and Migrant Justice (RMJ, formerly the Refugee Legal Centre) and the Immigration Advisory Service, closed in 2010 and 2011 respectively. Between them, they represented around 20,000 clients and employed hundreds of staff. The reason for their failure was massive cash issues; RMJ said this was brought on by changes to legal aid, which meant bills wouldn't be paid until a case was finished. When they went under, they were owed £2 million by the Legal Services Commission, which ran the legal aid scheme in England and Wales from 2000 until 2013.[3] 'You just don't have the bodies helping people, so you are going to see more rejections,' explains Alison Moore, director of Refugee Women Connect, an asylum organisation in Liverpool, which caters specifically for women. 'It's not an area where you shouldn't have a legal representative with you.'

But the issue is also the cost. 'Initially they were very modest,' Webber says of immigration fees. They were increased by a small amount when the Home Office claimed they weren't covering administrative costs. But then they skyrocketed to the levels they are now, and they're still soaring. In 2016–17, fees for settlement, residence and nationality increased by 25 per cent. They're constantly changing, but at the time of writing, if you want to become a permanent resident of the UK, it will cost you £2,389.[4] That's on top of £50 for a 'Life in the UK' test, which you have to take when you apply to become a British citizen or for permanent residency and, if you're required to take one, £150 for an English exam.

Playwright Inua Ellams had discretionary leave to remain and so had to refresh his status every three years, costing £900 each time.[5] Being able to stay in this country, he tells me, is 'expensive – it's thousands upon thousands upon thousands of pounds'. It's even gotten to the stage where the Home Office is charging £5.48 every time you require a response by email.[6] This inevitably impacts poorer migrants disproportionately, people who might not be able to pay to get the reply they need, which risks subsequently preventing them from successfully resolving their claim.

Having cash is not an automatic guarantor to frictionless movement, but money lubricates the whole system. As of 2010, if you have £2 million or more to invest in the British economy, you can apply for an 'investor' visa – and if successful, come to the country for three years and four months and bring immediate family members. The right to settle after two years has a £10 million price tag, and £5 million buys the same entitlement after three years.[7] For everyone else, the cost of it all can shape their whole lives.

While successive governments have extolled the virtues of family life, immigration controls have kept people apart. Since July 2010, migrants from outside the European Economic Area and their spouses in the UK have been separated by borders and the associated price tags. Under Theresa May's plans to 'get numbers down', a UK citizen or settled resident (someone who has the right to stay in the UK with no time restrictions) had to earn £18,600 per year before tax if they wanted their non-EU partner to join them. The cost rose by £3,800 if that included bringing a child, and an extra £2,400 for every additional child.[8]

For decades, non-EU spouses and family members have been treated with suspicion when all they wanted was to join their loved ones: couples are quizzed over the most intimate details of their relationship and asked questions often based on racist stereotypes; children's teeth and wrists are X-rayed to try to ascertain their age; and older relatives have been left continents apart from their closest family simply because they have a relative in the country they're in – even if that person isn't available, able or willing to look after them. It's virtually impossible for elderly non-Europeans, whether grandparents, aunts and uncles or siblings, to come to live in the UK.[9] And it's not always easy to visit either.

It's these strict, costly rules that left five-year-old Andrea Gada's family desperate. Walking home from school with her father and brother on a winter's day in Eastbourne, Andrea was hit and killed by a car. When her grandparents and aunt applied to come from Zimbabwe for her funeral, they were denied a visa. According to their local MP, then Liberal Democrat Stephen Lloyd, they were deemed 'too poor' to be granted a temporary visa to come to the funeral in the UK. The Home Office offered a more technical verdict: they hadn't previously left Zimbabwe, couldn't show they had regular incomes and therefore were considered at risk of absconding.

The three grieving relatives – Mona Lisa Faith and Grace and Stanley Bwanya – were desperate to be at Andrea's funeral. They tried every solution possible, from offering to wear electronic tags to saying they would report regularly to a police station while they were in the UK. Recognising how unfair the rules were, people rallied around their cause. Lloyd guaranteed that, if they were allowed to enter the UK, he would personally make sure they left the country after the funeral, and members of the community raised £5,000 to help cover travel costs. But the government rejected the application for a second time. Then slowly their case began to make headlines. The attention resulted in a petition asking the government to reverse their decision. Over 120,000 people signed it. Finally, the Home Office relented. Without public pressure and media attention, this could have been just one more story among countless others in which people are kept apart by uncaring and inflexible immigration policies. 'Anyone who has ever struggled with poverty', wrote essayist James Baldwin, 'knows how extremely expensive it is to be poor.'[10]

Worryingly and somewhat inevitably, the few organisations that exist to help people struggling with their status are over-stretched, laden with more responsibilities than they can manage and struggling to survive. But they are vital. 'It's become almost impossible for people with most kinds of immigration issues to get any advice,' says Benjamin, who gives assistance to destitute migrants. 'And it's become much more difficult for people who've got that legal advice to find routes to regularising their status.' And as successive governments have talked and acted tough on immigration, migrants – documented and undocumented – feel able to trust very few people. 'Just from the point of view of people who have jobs in the sector and get paid to do advice work it's really frightening. Caseworkers are burning out, and it's only possible to imagine that services are just going to become more and more strained than they already are,' Benjamin explains.

He calls charities that hold regular drop-ins for migrants, asylum seekers and refugees 'advice factories'; they're under immense amounts of pressure, people can't stay in the line of work for long and, as they leave, knowledge goes with them. This slowly depletes the level of experience within organisations, which is necessary to help people navigate what is an intentionally onerous and complex set of rules.

'It's hard not to feel like the government is doing it deliberately, not just to create a hostile environment for people who are here "illegally" but also to make it more difficult for people supporting them . . . and I think everyone anticipates that at some point there will be legislation deliberately aimed at the organisations that support, for example, undocumented people to make it more difficult for them to be accommodated and to make it more difficult for people to get advice.'

This advice is essential because it's hard to make sense of the UK's labyrinthine network of ever-changing rules and regulations. While politicians claim immigration is a taboo subject, one estimate suggests that, since the early 1990s, there has been, on average, a piece of legislation on immigration every other year.[11] Between 2010 and 2018, over the course of the Coalition and then Conservative governments, there were seven immigration bills containing all kinds of changes.[12]

'It's actually designed to isolate you, to bring you down, to make you want to give up and pack your bags and just go,' Diana, who has tried to claim asylum here, says. 'People have to really own their situation, you can't rely on somebody else. You have to know your rights and without that . . . you're headed for downfall.' She adds, 'I'm not really a bad person. You've [Britain] treated me so bad for just wanting to have a life to live.'

Diana isn't the only person I meet who feels like that. After applying multiple times for the right to extend her study visa and then being detained in the notorious detention centre Yarl's Wood, Christina agreed to go home. But when the day came for her to pack up all her belongings, take them to the airport and board a Nigeria-bound plane, she was left standing at the check-in desk without her passport. The Home Office was holding it hostage. Numerous emails, letters and meetings with her lawyer hadn't been enough for them to relinquish it. She was in a country that didn't want her to stay but that wouldn't let her leave. When I met her in early 2018 she was still struggling to either get papers that would enable her to finish her studies or to go home. 'I feel like I just want to talk to them face-to-face to ask them why they're not doing their job. I'm thirty-one, I came here when I was twenty-two; it's drained my years.'

As well as being at the forefront of giving advice and support to migrants, asylum seekers and refugees, support organisations see first-hand some of the biggest problems with the UK's immigration rules. Lindsay Cross runs West End Refugee Service (WERS) in Newcastle. Hidden among housing estates and beside a church in the west end of the city is a small detached house that WERS have turned into office space. When I first arrive in the middle of the afternoon at what looks like someone's home, I'm not sure if I'm in the right place. But I knock on the door and as soon as I'm welcomed inside, I see the appeal of having the organisation in what might be considered an unconventional building; it's a homely, unintimidating atmosphere and it's where WERS offer support and advice for people seeking asylum.

Like so many other immigration and asylum services, WERS struggle from year to year to make the money they need to support everyone that comes to them for help. They rely on volunteers giving their time and energy to stay in operation. As well as struggling to survive in a climate hostile to organisations like them, WERS have also witnessed what this environment has meant for asylum seekers. Some have been left destitute and hopeless, and many others have suffered thanks to private companies who provide asylum housing.

People who have been given refugee status or who have indefinite leave to remain have very similar housing and welfare rights to British citizens. But since the 1990s, people seeking asylum have had their rights stripped back through successive immigration and asylum acts, including the ability to choose where they live.[13] Introduced by New Labour, under the 'forced dispersal' policy, people seeking asylum are sent all over the country, usually to some of the poorest areas, regardless of whether they know anyone there or anything about the place.[14] 'It's not easy to start a whole life again,' says Diana, who was sent from Nottingham, where she had friends, a job in the NHS and a rented flat, to Birmingham, a place she didn't know at all. But the disorientation that comes with being shipped off to an area you don't know can be made even worse if you get to your new home only to find it damp, rotting or infested with insects, mice and rats.[15]

In 2012, estimated to amount to £620 million, six contracts shifted housing provision into the hands of three private companies, G4S, Serco and Clearel. It wasn't ever apparent what qualifications the first two had to be given this responsibility; only Clearel had any experience of providing housing.[16] When the new housing providers were announced, security firm G4S was probably best known for having been involved in the death of forty-six-year-old Jimmy Mubenga when, in 2010, three of the company's guards restrained him on board a flight to Angola. After seventeen years in the UK, Mubenga was being deported to the southern African country and in the process being separated from his wife and five children. One passenger claimed they heard him cry, 'Let me up, you're killing me. You're killing me. You're killing me. I cannot breathe. I cannot breathe.'[17] He died in seat 40E of the plane as it sat on the tarmac at Heathrow. A year later an inquest concluded that he had been unlawfully killed but a subsequent trial ended with the jury finding the three guards not guilty of manslaughter. Sixty-five racist texts found on two of the guards' phones weren't shown to the jury; defence lawyers argued they would 'release an unpredictable cloud of prejudice'. But a coroner's report that had been written three years after Jimmy's death said the texts were 'not evidence of a couple of "rotten apples"' but seemed to 'evidence a more pervasive racism within G4S'.[18] By the time the report was released, G4S had already been given the asylum housing contract.

Before the switch went ahead, a mix of local authorities, housing associations and private contractors had been responsible for the accommodation of asylum seekers. Cross says the shift away from local authorities was 'very obvious' and the private sector offered much lower cost contracts, but that came with 'absolute pairing down in the contracts'. Support for people was 'pretty much annihilated', putting more pressure on organisations like WERS. Though these private companies claim to take housing quality into account, there is a growing body evidence to the contrary.

In 2016, G4S – a company that paid no corporation tax in 2012, the same year it was given the contract – was fined £5.6 million for the low standard of the asylum housing it provided in 2013/14. In Middlesbrough, when G4S inspected housing provided by Jomast – a company G4S subcontracts to – they found urgent defects in 14 per cent of properties. Later, Home Office inspections found urgent defects in 91 per cent of properties. Jomast was reported to be taking £8 million from the taxpayer.[19] As asylum seekers were being sent to live in squalid conditions, the government was still handing millions of pounds' worth of contracts to the private housing providers.

The people I speak to aren't just victims of the immigration regime; they're much more than their immigration status. But they're angry about the way they've been treated; they talk about their experiences to expose the impact of the UK's immigration and asylum rules and to advocate for change. 'You know they're really brutal the way they treat people,' Kelly says. 'I've been here since I was nine years old. I feel like they treat me like some kind of alien. There's no sympathy or any form of understanding. They have to look at everyone as an individual, not just "you're a migrant, get out".'

Kelly describes the treatment she receives when she goes to sign in at the immigration reporting centre at London Bridge – part of the requirement for those waiting for a claim or appeal to be processed, so the state can keep track of them. She has been made to queue outside in the rain – 'When we told them oh it's raining, they're like "it's only water, do you not bathe?"' – and describes the policy proscribing phone use: 'Because they know that if you use your phone you can record something. If you use your phone, they'll kick you out.' One undercover report exposed an official at this same reporting centre telling a thirty-nine-year-old man,

We are not here to make life easy for you. It's a challenging environment we have got to make for people. It's working because it's pissing you off. Am I right? There you go. That's my aim at the end of the day, to make it a challenging environment for you. It's pissing you off. You're telling me it's pissed you off. There you go, I've done my job.[20]

It's become common sense to think too much immigration of a *certain kind* is bad for the UK in all kinds of ways – for wages, public services but also 'integration' and 'cohesion' – and that 'controls' are a solution. But look at what they do: force people to leave the country, even if it means being separated from friends and family, or stop them from staying long enough to make local connections if they want to. 'Controls' are making people's lives a misery; they are part of the problem.

To find an example of the inhumanity of migration policy in the UK, look no further than 'immigration removal centres'. This name works as a sanitiser, obscuring the brutal reality of these 'centres'. Andy knows this all too well.

Originally from Ghana, his family – made up of his dad and his younger siblings, two brothers and two sisters – moved around before they settled into life in the UK in 1997 when Andy was twelve years old. Andy never knew the specifics of his dad's job, just that he was often away on business: 'I remember my dad always travelled, no matter where we lived he always travelled.' One day, the woman who was looking after Andy and his siblings while his dad was away with work packed up and left: at the age of fifteen, Andy had to become the adult of the household. Without any means to contact their dad, he dropped out of school, got a job in a nearby market and looked after the family. His dad never returned. To this day, Andy still doesn't know what happened to him.

Before long, the circumstances of their makeshift family were discovered. With Andy still under the age of eighteen and trying to support his siblings single-handedly, his brothers and sisters were taken into care and social services told him he could go into accommodation provided by the council, but that he needed ID.

'Low and behold I get there and they say – first time in my life – "Where's your passport or birth certificate, where's your ID?" What? What's an ID? I don't know. They say, "Well unless you've got one of these things we can't help you". So, I went back to social services and they said go and search the house. I turned the house upside down. Nothing.'

Andy was left homeless. He got protection from, though never joined, a gang. But it was enough that he'd entered the gang's network. To survive on his own and find a way out, he left London and bought an ID from someone who specialised in identity fraud. Desperate to get a job and without any form of documentation – not so much as a birth certificate – he felt he had no choice.

A hard worker, he did well, but after one of many promotions, he was eventually found out. He went to prison for identity theft. His sentence was supposed to be ten months, then, out of the blue, the day before he was going to be released, he was told he was being put in immigration detention. But even that didn't happen straight away. 'I was supposed to be released from prison on 21 May 2010. That was the day. That was my release date. I stayed in prison until 13 June 2011, over a year.'[21] No one ever explained why.

After a year in Morton Hall, a detention centre in Lincolnshire, Andy was moved to Brook House, next to Gatwick airport. When he arrived, he realised what was in store for him: he was going to be quietly put on a plane and deported to a country he hadn't been to since he was a child; a place where he knew no family or friends.

Andy had already been encouraged by a volunteer in Morton Hall to apply for asylum: he is bisexual and could face persecution if he goes back to Ghana. To stop what he believed was a plan to deport him, he pointed out he was waiting on the asylum decision, so they could not deport him until he heard the outcome. This gave him more time. After applying for bail fourteen times, he was finally successful, and in October 2016 he was granted asylum by the courts, but the Home Office decided to appeal the decision. When we meet he's still in limbo, forced to carry around a biometric ID card – a policy introduced under New Labour – which is his only official piece of identification. He takes it out of his pocket to show me and the first thing I see is the words it has stamped across it in bold black writing: 'forbidden from taking employment'. Andy ended up being abandoned by the state because he had no ID; now he's made to carry one that marks him out as different. 'I've been out three years,' he says. 'I can't work, I'm not allowed to work paid or unpaid, I can't work but they expect me to survive . . . I don't get nothing.'

Between 2009 and 2016, 2,500 to 3,500 people were in detention at any given time. Most were held for less than a month, but some much longer. It's thought the longest someone has been detained for was 1,156 days.[22] In 2015, the Chief Inspector of Prisons noted in a report that high numbers of women put in Yarl's Wood detention centre were released, which, he wrote, 'raises questions about the validity of their detention in the first place'.[23]

Until the 1990s, the UK didn't have any permanent detention centres; people were put in prisons or held in a converted car ferry called the Earl William. Within two years of being in office, New Labour had dramatically increased the number of detention centres, and the country now has one of the biggest immigration detention estates in Europe. Almost as soon as they came into existence, these centres have been sites of hunger strikes and suicide attempts.[24] Andy says his experience of detention was worse than prison.

Fenced off from the rest of the world, presumably in the hope that no one would ever discover the mistreatment going on inside, there is one detention centre that has become a symbol of state cruelty. Alongside resistance and protest, report after report has made small holes in the bottle green barrier that surrounds Yarl's Wood, helping expose fragments of what goes on inside this notorious detention centre. This has been a collective effort. Channel 4 has sent investigation teams there. Women detainees on hunger strike inside have claimed column inches in the *Guardian* to explain their protest. Periodically, campaigners from all over the country have made the trip out to Bedford, surrounding Yarl's Wood, making as much noise as possible to show solidarity with people inside and demand its closure. And the *Independent* and the *Telegraph* newspapers have reported on the alleged abuse that goes on within its walls.[25]

But the coverage of what goes on inside Yarl's Wood can too easily become disconnected from the anti-immigration politics – the kind which presents immigration first and foremost as negative – that makes such an institution a reality, and that is perpetuated by our press and our politicians.

The former *Daily Star* journalist Richard Peppiatt describes to me the culture at the tabloid newspaper that helps make detention acceptable. When he was at the paper, there was a constant pressure, he says, to find stories that fit in with a particular anti-immigrant or anti-Muslim narrative. The *Daily Star* was no insignificant player. In December 2011, the Audit Bureau of Circulation (ABCs) figures showed that the *Daily Star* was the third most widely bought newspaper that month, below the *Sun* and the *Daily Mirror* and with a circulation figure of 616,498, almost double that of the *Financial Times*'.[26]

Peppiatt, who in a widely publicised letter to his boss, media mogul Richard Desmond, quit his job in 2011 after two years at the paper, recalls being sent to pursue a story about a family from Somalia who were seeking asylum in the UK and who had been put up in a luxurious townhouse in Chelsea.[27] 'These stories seemed to pop up every week', where the message would be 'asylum seekers are basically getting the absolute run of the pitch and being put up in expensive houses,' he explains.

When he got there, every other right-wing tabloid newspaper had a journalist camped outside the house. 'We could tell there was people in there,' he says. 'Quite an intimidating situation with photographers and journalists hanging about this house . . . putting notes through the door . . . the curtains would twitch occasionally and a photographer would try and flash off a shot to catch a picture of them.' Unsurprisingly with all these journalists on their doorstep, no one from the family came out of the house. So, despite intense pressure from editors back at the *Daily Star*, Peppiatt left, along with all the other reporters, as the night was drawing in. The next morning in the newsroom, Peppiatt's manager stormed over to him. 'What the fuck is this, I thought you said they didn't come outside?' he said pointing at the *Sun*, which had a quote from the father.[28] 'I said', Peppiatt recounts, 'they didn't come outside, 100 per cent, they didn't come outside!' The news editor responded, 'You know what, you need to be a bit more canny.' You can make your own mind up was what he meant by that.

Journalism that humanises migration or shows the realities of the UK's immigration rules – however harrowing, hopeful or challenging to the dominant discourse it might be – is not sufficient to entirely dislodge the public misconceptions about migrants. 'You get a lot of these biographical stories and stories of individuals or individual triumph or injustice,' Dr Gavan Titley, lecturer in media studies, says about coverage and understanding of immigration. 'And fine, we know all of that and how that operates in terms of empathy, but it's not necessarily *a* politics.'

This is what Charles Husband and Paul Hartmann found in their study from the 1970s, which showed how the media had covered the racism that migrants faced in the UK, in doing so, performing a 'valuable function'. But journalists of the day also depicted these people as a 'threat and a problem', 'a conception more conducive to the development of hostility toward them than acceptance'.[29]

Once in a while a news story does seem like it might rip apart a long-established narrative. When a photo of three-year-old Alan Kurdi's limp body, face down on a Turkish beach having drowned at sea, made front-page news all around the world, it seemed like there might be a shift. The boy and his family – his dad Abdullah, his mum Rehanna and his five-year-old brother Ghalib – along with nineteen others, had been making the trip from the Turkish coastal town Bodrum to the Greek island of Kos, which at the shortest route are separated by a stretch of water four kilometres long. Reportedly carrying twice the number of people it could hold, the boat Kurdi was on capsized five minutes into the journey, throwing all of its passengers – including Alan and his family – to the mercy of the unforgiving Aegean Sea. Alan, Rehanna and Ghalib were among the people who died that morning.

The attention Alan Kurdi's picture received sparked action in some countries, including the UK, Germany and Canada, who agreed to admit more refugees. But after momentarily softening their stance toward refugees, EU politicians competing with the far right wanted to show they retained a tough stance on refugees. Domestically and at the frontiers of fortress Europe they continued to reinforce and make sharper the many methods used to keep people out. Within months, if not weeks, tabloid newspapers that were outraged by Kurdi's death resumed normal service, running an endless stream of anti-refugee scare stories. Hostile coverage punctuated by compassion, positivity, pity or outrage – whether about detention or deaths – isn't going to fundamentally change policy or the myriad of negative ways immigration and asylum are represented, even if there is a shift in public opinion. A year after his son's picture became world news, Alan Kurdi's father, Abdullah, said, 'Everybody claimed they wanted to do something because of the photo that touched them so much. But what is happening now? People are still dying and nobody is doing anything about it.'[30]

Nora knows better than most about the brutality of the UK's immigration regime. Arriving in the UK at the age of just seventeen with her younger cousin, thanks to tickets their families bought by selling off their valuables, the two were helped out of a country in north-east Africa in 2001, escaping violence in the region with the aim of securing an education and with it a better life.

Nora's first asylum rejection was followed by another four. When her final appeal was refused, Nora, who by now had turned eighteen, was told she was no longer eligible for state support. 'They said I could go back . . . since I was an adult and they wouldn't help me anymore with my application . . . that was a bit confusing for someone who had just turned eighteen, not knowing what to do, where to go, how to get help.' Worried about disappointing her family back home and with no one to turn to, she was at a loss as to what she should do.

In 2005, while New Labour prime minister Tony Blair was claiming that the government was 'dealing appropriately with the issues in asylum and immigration', Nora was sleeping rough.[31] She would continue to do so for the first ten years of her adult life. 'I started hiding. Social services couldn't look after me anymore because I was an adult so I was kicked out of the hostel we were living in,' she explains. 'I started staying with friends, sometimes on a bus. I was jobless so I couldn't work because I didn't have a work permit and no forms of identification. So it was pretty tough, for ten years I lived that way, sleeping on streets and in tube stations.' Things got so bad that after nearly five years of being homeless, Nora decided to go back home. She went to the embassy of her home country, only to be told that with no proof she had come from there, they wouldn't let her go back. Nora was left in limbo.

Having to live on the streets for ten years took its toll. Sitting across from me in an almost empty coffee shop is someone who looks like they've got it together; Nora seems quietly self-assured. But as Christmas songs blare out from nearby speakers, she explains what happened after she eventually got her papers. 'I missed out on a lot, I mean without . . . documentation you don't have access to any form of higher education so after . . . I turned eighteen I couldn't apply for any university . . . I missed out on communication skills, on IT skills.' Nora got a job in retail, but she felt like she was at a disadvantage. 'You know you could overhear the managers: "A seventeen-year-old girl is so quick and really good at the till, she is quite slow." I know I am slow because . . . I haven't done so much . . . so I had that problem where I struggled to find work.' The whole process left her feeling insecure: 'I'm struggling . . . you have low self-esteem, you try . . . to catch up to people my age . . . they have degrees . . . and they've achieved so much and I'm just trying to catch up.'

When Nora arrived, the prevailing atmosphere within the country was hostile toward those trying to seek refuge. Anti-asylum seeker stories adorned the front pages of the UK's major tabloids.[32] In the years before, during Conservative prime minister John Major's time in office, then home secretary Michael Howard had warned of 'bogus asylum seekers', and their successors followed suit. Pitting the 'deserving' against the 'undeserving' and the 'legitimate' against the 'illegitimate', when Tony Blair talked about immigration and asylum, he littered his speech with toxic qualifiers. Labour were committed to 'fair' rules for 'hard-working taxpayers', 'those who genuinely need asylum' and 'those legitimate migrants who make such a major contribution to our economy'.[33]

In a 2004 by-election campaign – orchestrated by future deputy leader Tom Watson for the candidate Liam Byrne, who later became minister of state for borders and immigration – Labour attacked the Liberal Democrats as being on the side of 'failed asylum seekers'. 'Labour is on your side,' they claimed. The basis for this message was that the Liberal Democrats, along with some Labour MPs, had tried to challenge the government's plan to take away welfare support from asylum seekers with children after their claim had been rejected. Labour won the by-election by a margin of 460 votes.[34]

Fast forward just under a decade and a 2013 report that examined all of the content on migration in twenty British newspapers between 2010 and 2012 found that the most common word used with 'asylum seeker' was 'failed'.[35] This makes it sound like people are routinely cheating the system, when in fact, everyone has the right to seek asylum in another country.[36]

The UK is one of 148 countries signed up to either or both of the United Nations 1951 Refugee Convention and the 1967 Protocol, which are 'the centrepiece of international refugee protection'.[37] Under the terms of the Convention, a refugee is someone who is outside their country of nationality and who has a well-founded fear of persecution within that same country on the grounds of nationality, political opinion, religion, or membership of particular social group or race.[38] So this means that all kinds of sociopolitical factors – from fleeing climate breakdown to economic collapse – aren't covered.

Applicants for refugee status are classified as asylum seekers throughout the processing of their applications. Only once this is accepted does the applicant become a refugee, which under the Convention should confer certain rights – the right to housing, the right to work and immunity from prosecution for illegal entry. For the people whose application is rejected, the possibility of more uncertainty and distress is very real; they might be granted the right to appeal in country or they might be swiftly deported.

One of a number of drawbacks is that the Convention enables individual states to interpret who is a refugee. Contrary to what most people think about asylum, 'failed' applicants are not simply, automatically duplicitous liars, and not all decisions are fair or right, especially considering the prevailing culture of disbelief and the fact that evidence of eligibility – in a system that often demands you prove the impossible – can be difficult to provide.

Then there's the problem of movement. All refugees, by definition, have to cross a national border, yet countries including the UK have made that more difficult, with the introduction of increasing numbers of visas in the 80s, which makes travelling to a country to seek refuge hard. While tourist visas and work visas exist, for people fleeing war and persecution, there isn't a specific visa they can apply for.

It's a catch-22, Frances Webber explains. Until she retired in 2008, Webber worked as a barrister specialising in immigration, refugee and human rights law. If you come into the country on a visitor's visa, she says, you might be considered an 'illegal entrant' because you've lied to a visa officer about the grounds on which you've entered the UK. All of this can have an impact on the credibility of your asylum claim.

As Nora found out, as well as making it more difficult for people to get to the country, successive governments have made it harder for people to *live* here. The 1951 United Nations Refugee Convention means that people given refugee status are still supposed to be provided with basic rights, but there's been a concerted effort to reduce the resources available to people seeking asylum, and make it so that for some only temporary refugee status is offered until they can return home without fear of persecution – essentially leaving them in limbo.

'The big argument of the Blair years was that it was all about pull factors,' Shadow Home Secretary Diane Abbott says disapprovingly when we meet in her Westminster office. Politicians have operated on the baseless belief that jobs and social security are so-called pull factors – things that attract people to move to a particular country or part of the world. There's been a suggestion that either migrants are pretending to be refugees to get into the UK to access support or that people seeking asylum are coming to the UK rather than anywhere else because of what they'll receive. It was thought that 'only if you made it less attractive for immigrants and asylum seekers', Abbott says, 'would you be able to "bear down" on numbers'.

In 2014 the Coalition government withdrew its support for search and rescue operations in the Mediterranean. As people just like Alan Kurdi and his family made the journey across what had become a watery grave off the coast of Southern Europe, the then minister of state for foreign and commonwealth affairs, Baroness Anelay, justified the decision by saying the government had removed a 'pull factor' that encouraged 'more migrants to attempt the dangerous sea crossing'. When EU support for search and rescue was drastically scaled back, people did not stop coming, the crossing just became more treacherous – and more people died.[39]

Regardless of what politicians say, newspapers print or the public believe, there has never been any proof that significant numbers of people are coming to the UK to 'cheat the system' or claim benefits. A Home Office study from 2002 found that there was little evidence the people they spoke to 'had a detailed knowledge of: UK immigration or asylum procedures; entitlements to benefits in the UK; or the availability of work in the UK'. Eight years later, a Refugee Council report came to similar conclusions.[40] Almost everyone I talked to for this book who has experienced immigration rules first hand was confused by the maze they entered into. 'I had no idea what the laws were about different forms of entitlement, I was just scared that I was rejected so I had to hide in case I got caught,' Nora tells me. 'It can cost lives, I lost so much because I didn't even know what the laws were about an asylum seeker or a refugee or seeking refuge in different countries.'

The rules work against asylum claimants; they're forced to find alternative, dangerous and often unofficial routes to safety. Controls compel people to take risks; they can create 'illegality'.[41] 'I sort of fell through the system,' Nora explains. 'You hear the sirens and you're scared they're going to catch you and deport you because you don't have any form of documentation . . . you shouldn't feel like that at eighteen.'

'You live in fear,' she adds.

Being denied refugee status has proven unthinkable for some people. In 2001, twenty-six-year-old Iranian national Shokrolah 'Ramin' Khaleghi, who had been a political prisoner in his home country, was found dead in his room at the International Hotel in Leicester just one week after his asylum application was rejected. He had taken an overdose. Two years later, thirty-year-old Israfil Shiri, also from Iran, died after setting himself on fire in the Manchester branch of the charity Refugee Action. He had just been thrown out of his council flat and denied benefits.

Since 1989, the think tank the Institute of Race Relations has kept the most accurate record possible of all those who had passed through the UK's immigration and asylum system and subsequently died by suicide.[42] Robertas Grabys, Saeed Alaei, Nasser Ahmed, Souleyman Diallo, Shiraz Pir, Mariman Tahamasbi, Mohsen Amri and Sirous Khajeh are just some of the people who feature on their records between 2000 and 2002.

In 2010, ignoring the police who tried to talk him down from the railings of a seventh-floor balcony in Nottingham, and as others taunted him from below, Osman Rasul died by suicide after nine years of trying to get status. 'His life was governed by an interminable waiting', one of his friends said after he died, 'for meetings with solicitors, for correspondence with the Home Office, above all for an end to the paralysing uncertainty in which he had lived for the best part of a decade.'[43]

Borders seem as natural as day and night; firming up territories by demarcating where the nation state begins and ends. We tend to treat them as if they've always been there and always will be. But borders are created and recreated. They are policed and enforced within countries. Transcending the very things they seek to fortify, expand and sharpen, politicians work together across borders to make it more difficult for people to move, while capital is allowed to flow freely. The border you're born within can determine the conditions of your life and death; what rights and resources you can access and where you can go. If only we spent the same amount of time scrutinising borders as we do championing their importance, then instead of pandering to the demands of those who complain about people desperate enough to leave their home country to cross them, we might try to dismantle them.

Seen as representing strength and protection, they are, if you look at them more closely, violent and discriminatory in all kinds of way. Borders are not only where the lines on the map tell us they are. They are also drawn between people, with the use of words like 'migrant' and 'citizen'. By crossing a border, you can cease to be a human being to the people around you, becoming an ('illegal') immigrant or a ('bogus') asylum seeker. These words we use to talk about people aren't just descriptive or neutral categories; how they're used doesn't always and only coincide with their legal meaning; they're laden with other associations.[44] Just look at the term 'migrant'.

Twisted to apply to specific groups of people at particular times, there is no hard and fast rule of who is an immigrant and who isn't. In the public debate, 'immigrant' comes to mean all kinds of different things; messy and shifting, it is, at times, conflated with race or ethnicity, and it's applied to people seeking asylum or who have refugee status.[45] Immigrant has, then, become this catch-all term, referring to all kinds of things at once. In 2016, journalist Liz Gerard found two of the UK's tabloid papers ran 1,768 articles about migrants – which made 'an average of more than three per issue for the *Mail* and two for the *Express* (which has far fewer news pages)' – and according to Gerard, almost all were negative.[46]

For something talked about so much, there's a lack of clarity about what immigration refers to; between who falls or is pushed into the category 'immigrant', who resides on its edges and who, despite moving across borders, never comes anywhere near to it. Race, class and gender decide how so-called non-citizens are seen, because they certainly aren't all seen the same way. When people talk about immigrants, they aren't usually thinking of white, wealthy Americans.

There is no universally agreed-upon definition of who constitutes an immigrant. The UN describes a long-term international migrant as someone who moves to another country, which essentially becomes their residence, for at least twelve months. But even this explanation has its problems. 'The time frame of one year is arbitrary,' Professor Bridget Anderson points out, 'change that and you can drastically alter how we understand and measure immigration . . . If, for example, one chooses to define a "migrant" as a person intending to stay away for four years or more . . . Britain has been experiencing negative net migration for many years.'[47]

And despite definitions like this one, movement is complicated and so the distinction between refugees and migrants isn't always a straightforward one. Someone might flee war in their home country, arrive in another as an asylum seeker, and be granted refugee status. But after months or years of trying to find work or survive in this new country, they might decide to move somewhere in Europe, where they're told there's a chance of work, or where their family lives. Then they might be seen as a migrant.[48]

The ground is constantly shifting under people's feet; like a carousel, the debate moves from 'good refugee' and 'bad migrant' to 'bad refugee' and 'good migrant', as politicians reacting to and feeding global and national events determine who's acceptable and who isn't. Rarely is one category of people considered entirely welcome, and there aren't always unambiguous distinctions between asylum seekers, refugees and migrants, especially not in the public debate, where the potential differences and similarities between different people and their experiences are muddied; the sheer complexity of it all is lost.

Anti-asylum language feeds anti-immigrant narratives in an ongoing negative feedback loop, and regardless of their legal status, everyone who is seen as an 'illegitimate' outsider becomes a threat to the nation. Particular people are deemed undesirable, as the media and politicians conspire to give the impression that people who have come to live in the UK are undercutting wages, driving down conditions and diluting 'British culture'.

But often, amid all this complexity, liberal politicians, some of whom are relatively relaxed about advocating for more refugees to be allowed into the country, claim to have some kind of clarity: the real problem, they say, is economic migrants. Even some parts of the immigration sector have helped sustain a 'hierarchy of migrants', Fizza Qureshi, director of Migrants' Rights Network, says. Some organisations more comfortable with advocating for refugees have sometimes failed to tackle the stereotypes about migrants irrespective of what job they do, where they're from or how much they earn.

'Economic migrants' are thought to choose to move for better wages or a better standard of life, and it's according to this logic that they're problematised; it's assumed they are here to 'take' from the UK, out of no real necessity. Not in the country 'illegally', they're still considered illegitimate. But overlooked in the mix of hostility and hysteria about 'economic immigration' is an understanding of why people migrate to begin with.

Relocating all over the world, packing up their possessions, making journeys within countries, across oceans and whole continents, people are complex, there isn't always one single reason they emigrate. It might be for adventure, a new job, to be with family or a change of scenery. They are making these trips with their loved ones or leaving family behind to settle in countries entirely new to them or cities they've known only from news bulletins. Choosing whether to leave can be as much to do with where you are as it is with where you want to go.

Money in its most crude form of notes and coins isn't the only motivation for migration. If all movement were just a case of following the money, author and professor Arun Kundnani writes, 'everyone in Greece would have moved to Luxembourg where they could instantly double their wages'.[49] Many people can't scrape together enough money to move, and many others might not want to move in the first place. The frenzied discussion about 'mass migration' ignores that the vast majority of people stay where they are or move within countries. In 2016, estimates suggested only 3.2 per cent of the world's population were international migrants; in 1960 it was 3 per cent.[50] The world's population has grown substantially in this period, so although this amounts to more people moving, it's not a significantly higher proportion than in the past. What's also changed over this almost sixty-year period is that the countries people leave are more diverse and the number of destinations is far smaller. The EU, one of the richest parts of the world, is one of the most popular destinations.[51] But, even then, only a small proportion of the population of Europe are immigrants.[52] I don't write this to offer reassurance, as if movement is bad, but to provide context.

But as long as 4.2 billion people live in poverty and the income gap between the Global North and South is still growing, people will have to move.[53] 'What they've managed to do is create this idea that people are simply moving for economic reasons,' says Asad Rehman, director of global justice charity War on Want, when describing the term 'economic migrant'. 'And in people's minds that means you're moving from one wage to another, you're simply moving for a higher salary, rather than actually saying that people are survival migrants. What people are surviving is global inequality.'

We talk about poverty like it's natural. Global leaders hold grand summits where they lay out everything that needs to be done to reverse extreme inequality, as if extractive capitalist economies, colonial histories and racialised hierarchies of power haven't *produced* it.[54] Through crippling debt and colossal interest rates, unfair trade deals, war and global corporations being given carte blanche to plunder natural resources all around the world,[55] money flows out of poorer countries into richer ones. In 2008, Angel Gurría, secretary general of the Organisation for Economic Co-operation and Development (OECD), said poor countries lose three times as much to tax evasion as they receive in foreign aid.[56] When the world is designed this way, it's not surprising that some people feel the best option is to move.

Originally from the Philippines, Marissa Begonia ended up in the UK when she couldn't find a job that would give her and her three children a decent standard of living. 'It was the most difficult and painful decision to leave my family behind in search for a decent job in a foreign land where I was even unsure of what kind of life awaits me but this was the only way I could think of.'[57]

As a last-ditch option, Marissa became a domestic worker at the age of twenty-four. Trying to find decent employment, she shuttled back and forth between countries. First, she worked in Singapore, where her wages were so low it wasn't worth it.

Then she went to Hong Kong, where an abusive employer made her life unbearable. When she quit, she was so scared of what her employer might do that when she went to hand in her resignation, she did so holding a knife behind her back. She returned home to the Philippines, but nothing had changed; any work she could find paid so little she could barely afford to look after her children. And so she decided to try again. She went back to Hong Kong, and from there her employers moved her to London, where she still lives and where she is chair of the Voice of Domestic Workers, a grassroots organisation established in 2009 to empower migrant domestic workers to stand up to discrimination, inequality and abuse.

In the end, people like Marissa should have the right to stay and live a decent life in the country they are born in, as well as the right to move if they so choose. The problem is that, for some people, staying becomes an option they can no longer realistically entertain, even if moving, in a world hostile to migrants, can be dangerous. Many migrants, even if they only move temporarily, aren't poor as a result of laziness, stupidity or inability: they are trying to make a life for themselves in a global economy that is deeply unequal and that is destroying the places they call home.

Climate breakdown is increasingly going to make it impossible for people to stay where they're born, and it's likely people of colour will be disproportionately impacted. Set against a long history of decimating indigenous communities, who are imagined as unable to master the environment for profit as the 'superior', 'civilised' world can, extractive, growth-obsessed capitalism is destroying the planet. But under the legal definition of the refugee, written in the 1950s, people aren't protected: there are no internationally recognised rights for people who have to leave their home because of climate change.

Inequality and climate degradation meet in Bangladesh. The eighth most populous country in the world, it's thought to be one of the most vulnerable to climate change. But in 2014 it produced around just 0.44 tonnes of carbon dioxide per person, compared to the United States' huge 16.4 tonnes.[58] It's also a hotbed of global exploitation. Making cheap clothes for other parts of the world, people – predominantly women – have organised to demand better pay and conditions. But while the UK uses fossil fuels that destroy the Bangladeshi environment and buys clothes made by its citizens, the people from this country aren't exactly welcome to move here or welcomed when they do.

'I hate when the term "economic migrant" is assigned to us. Everyone moves around for economic reasons, not only us,' Ake says. He's been in the UK for over ten years, studying full-time at Kingston University when he arrived as well as clocking in thirty-five hours a week or more as a security guard. He used to be a union organiser, founded a group that protects migrants' right to work and, having completed a master's in international human rights law, is about to do a PhD. Well-acquainted with the disorder of moving, through his own experiences and his work, Ake points out that 'economic migrant' is applied selectively. People from 'Africa or developing countries' are 'economic migrants' but if someone leaves the UK and goes to Germany, they're likely to be called an 'expat'. 'They are people and we [are] less than human,' he says.

Making sense of terms like 'economic migrant' is not just about understanding how and why people move, but also how they're treated when they're here. As she talks to me in the café at the Unite the Union offices in Central London, Marissa doesn't hide her anger; it seems to drive her campaigning. Over the chatter of people milling in and out of the canteen during the lunchtime rush, she describes how her pitifully low salary, painfully long hours and controlling employers pushed her to join together with other domestic workers and fight back.

When the Coalition government came to power in 2010 domestic workers, who are predominantly women, were in trouble. At the end of the 1970s, visas for domestic workers were scrapped. For many, the proof that they were legally in the country consisted of a stamp in their passport that named their employer as the only person they had the right to work for. If they left their employer, they lost status and were classed as undocumented. After decades of domestic workers agitating, organising and campaigning, in 1997 the rules were changed. Under New Labour, domestic workers had the right to change employers without being deported. As a result, they could access a route to staying in the country and they were recognised as workers, entitled to workplace rights and time off. In 2008, the government threatened to strip away the rights workers had fought for, but were forced to abandon their plans because of the strength of resistance.

However, a new government in 2010 meant new ministers, with new resolve. In 2012, to widespread condemnation, the Conservative-led Coalition changed the rules so that domestic workers could only come to the UK for six months, had no right to renew their visas and were tied to their foreign employer. According to the *Guardian*, over 2016–17, the Home Office issued 18,950 Domestic Workers in a Private Household visas; if people brought into the country under one of these visas left an employer who was abusive or who was exploiting them, they became undocumented. This sat uncomfortably with that same government's aim to end modern slavery.[59] 'Theresa May is this great advocate for measures to protect people from modern slavery,' says former barrister Frances Webber, 'while at the same time her ministers are removing protection against extreme exploitation.'

Evidence shows that migrants are far more likely to be employed in lower paid, monotonous and dangerous jobs, with little or no trade union influence – yet they tend to be educationally and experientially overqualified for the work they do.[60] 'There are *reasons* behind why people are moving from their home land to Europe,' explains Ake, who came to the UK from the Ivory Coast via France. 'Like anybody else, we have dreams for ourselves and our families, and rights we are entitled to. And when you are denied these basic rights, your instincts switch onto the survival mode.'

While most of us are asleep, a multinational workforce is cleaning the expensive offices of people on six-figure salaries, doing shifts in high-end hotels all hours of the day or looking after older people in care homes.

'In this world, migrants have rights, but no or little way to make use of them or ask for their respect,' concluded one non-governmental organisation. 'They are legally voiceless.' The International Convention on the Protection of the Rights of All Migrant Workers and Members of their Families attempts to deal with this. It is concerned with protecting the human rights of anyone who crosses a border for work, regardless of their status – that is, whether they're documented or not. The treaty is designed to ensure human rights are applied to all migrants and to establish a minimum set of legal protections, which among other things requires states that have ratified the treaty give migrants and their families freedom of speech, the freedom to join trade unions and rights equal to citizens in terms of pay and working conditions. At the time of writing, only fifty-four countries have ratified the treaty; the UK is not one of them.[61]

When New Labour immigration minister Barbara Roche declared in 2000 that 'we are in competition for the brightest and the best', she was playing right into the framing that turns people into commodities.[62] Dividing migrants into 'the best and the brightest' vs. 'the rest' or 'skilled' and 'unskilled', as politicians still do, erases the complex, important work done by people who don't fit into the former categories. It creates a hierarchy of human value. 'There's a wholly artificial distinction between high-skilled people and low-skilled,' says Diane

Abbott. 'For instance, care workers are described as low-skilled, but they're vital. If Eastern European migrants stop coming here tomorrow, social care in London and the South-East would collapse because they can't get the labour.'

Even for people classed as 'highly skilled', the very immigration controls that governments claim are necessary for safety and security can produce precarity. If you're tied to your employer for your right to be here, as you might be on some visas, your status is essentially reliant upon their support. It's not that all employers who sponsor members of staff are out to actively and grossly exploit them; a licence could cost up to £1,476 (at the time of writing), depending on the size of the company and type of visa, and then they have to pay for each worker they sponsor. But there's a risk for employees: if you're struggling with a boss who is forcing you to work unpaid overtime and treating you badly, or you're just not happy in the job and you can't find another employer who will sponsor you, it might be more difficult to challenge mistreatment.[63] As Swiss writer Max Frisch once observed, 'We asked for workers and human beings came.'[64]

A global working class – the majority of whom are of colour – keeps the world economy going. Politicians in a number of countries know they need workers from all around the world and that an unfair, imbalanced global economy paired with climate breakdown means some people need to migrate. But that doesn't mean that everyone can do so, or that those who do then have freedom, choice or decent rights.

In 2001, twenty-one-year-old Mohammed Ayaz from northern Pakistan broke through security at Bahrain airport and launched himself into an opening on the bottom of a Boeing 777 headed for London. He had been working as a labourer in Dubai and, like so many others who feel like they have no better options but to take this same route, he got into huge amounts of debt to get there. But he wanted to make it to England. The combination of the cold and lack of oxygen had most likely killed him on the long journey and, early on Thursday morning, his body fell from the undercarriage of the plane. He was found dead in a Homebase car park near Heathrow. In the years that followed, two others – thirty-year-old Carlito Vale and twenty-seven-year-old José Matada – died in similar circumstances. 'He always spoke about going to work in America or England,' Ayaz's brother, Gul Bihar, said. 'But they don't give visas to poor people like us.'[65]

We like to tell ourselves a very particular version of the UK's past. One in which we've held the door open to people fleeing conflict and persecution, and welcomed others from all over the world. Whenever the brutal realities of this country's asylum system make newspaper headlines, the Home Office response almost always includes some variation of the following: 'The UK has a proud history of granting asylum to those who need it.'[66] But while there are tales of warm reception, and people from all over the world have made a life for themselves in this country, there are at least as many stories of doors slammed shut in people's faces and faceless walls of bureaucracy confronting those who arrive.

The asylum regime that became increasingly restrictive from the 1980s and through the 1990s and 2000s only got worse from 2010 on. Seeing that people were fleeing conflict, famine and political persecution, the Coalition barely squeaked the door ajar to asylum seekers; between 2010 and 2015 they resettled just 143 refugees who had escaped violent civil war in Syria. So far, well over 5 million refugees have left Syria. During the largest refugee movement since the Second World War, it was only under intense public pressure that Prime Minister David Cameron committed to take in up to 20,000 Syrian refugees over five years. But in comparison to countries like Germany, this was a tiny number, and when compared with the countries in the so-called 'developing' world, which host the vast majority of refugees, it looked even smaller.[67]

But when the Coalition government was put under the spotlight for failing to take in refugees from Syria, campaigners lobbied politicians to take in child refugees by drawing on national mythology. Conjuring up images of Jewish children arriving on the Kindertransport, they argued that the UK should not betray its history. This proved to be an effective campaigning tool that tapped into existing thinking; one 2011 poll found that 84 per cent of people said they were proud to be British and 82 per cent believed protecting the most vulnerable is a core British value.[68] But certain 'children were unaccompanied, and their Jewish parents left behind in Nazi Europe', Louise London reminds us, they were 'excluded from entry to the United Kingdom [and] are not part of the British experience, because Britain never saw them'.[69]

The shameful present, in which refugees are turned away, asylum seekers are left destitute on the streets, migrants are indefinitely detained and members of the so-called 'Windrush generation' are deported, is often compared to an imagined past, as activists and outraged politicians indignantly ask: What has this country *become*? The problem is, this is the kind of place it has long been.

2

'Keeping' the Country White

Not a single tea plantation exists within the United Kingdom. This is the symbolization of English identity – I mean, what does anybody in the world know about an English person except that they can't get through the day without a cup of tea? Where does it come from? Ceylon – Sri Lanka, India. That is the outside history that is inside the history of the English. There is no English history without that other history.

Stuart Hall, *Old and New Identities,*
Old and New Ethnicities

'Western society historically was white, that's how it works,' right-wing commentator Melanie Phillips told me during a 2017 BBC Radio 4 debate.[1] In the middle of a live recording, I'd been quietly brought into a small studio to talk to people I had never met but whom I sat with long enough during what was a brief segment for them to quiz me about so-called virtue signalling – a supposed phenomenon where people publicly and smugly say or do something 'morally good' for the principal purpose of demonstrating their rectitude. I hadn't been invited on the programme to debate 'race' or the history of 'the West', but that's where Phillips steered the conversation. Caught off guard, I explained why Phillips's statement wasn't true, but it seemed she had a point to prove; adamant that it was entirely logical that some people in the UK wanted to defend a Europe that she seemed to believe was once exclusively white.

Other people share Phillips's anger at the supposed disruptive change that has taken place in Europe. When a BBC children's cartoon used images of a multiracial family to explain life in Roman Britain, people on social media attacked it as historically inaccurate.[2] They seemed to believe it's common sense that racial and cultural homogeneity in this part of the world has been disrupted by migration. Except that has never been 'how it works': the UK, for instance, does not have a 'white' or monocultural history.

This is not a country unsettled by immigration, it is one *made* by it. Its first inhabitants came from Southern Europe, and by the time Roman troops and their auxiliaries landed on the southern tip of England in AD 43, this was already a place of diverse traditions and languages. The population was varied; made up of people from the areas that would come to be known as North Africa, Syria, the Balkans and Scandinavia. 'There were Africans in Britain before the English came here,' writes journalist Peter Fryer in the opening to his book *Staying Power: The History of Black People in Britain*.[3]

Throughout the 1800s, people like black radical Chartist leader William Cuffay, businessperson and nurse Mary Seacole and Wu Tingfang, the first Chinese barrister in the UK, were among many who lived in this country. 'There's a myth that . . . pervades the public debate that migration is something that happened in Britain after 1945 or that it's a modern phenomenon. Actually we have a long, rich and very diverse history of migration,' historian Sundeep Lidher tells me. She is one of the architects of *Our Migration Story*, a website that documents the generations of migrants who have come to and shaped the British Isles.[4]

Without detailed public knowledge of these histories, the UK's understanding of itself will always be narrow-minded, and as Lidher points out, mythical and inaccurate. With the history of migration 'comes a more accurate insight into our long-standing interactions and entanglements with the wider globe', Lidher explains. We talk nearly two years after the EU referendum, but the ill-informed debate that shaped the campaigns still hangs over us; she conveys a sense of urgency and frustration that the UK's migratory past is not better known. Imbued with nostalgia for a return to the Empire that was and is so rarely discussed in detail,[5] the simplistic calls to 'take back control' of 'our' borders during the referendum erased a much more complex past.

Britain has never been an independent country since it came into being in 1707, Professor Gurminder Bhambra points out. It has always been stitched together with other entities – the Empire, followed by the Commonwealth and then the EU. 'There has been no independent Britain,' writes Bhambra, 'no "island nation".'[6]

The UK's migration history isn't just about Empire, but the way we talk about immigration now can't be understood without looking back at recent UK immigration legislation and how it related to race and the colonial project. A cursory look at this country's past suggests that, if only this history were more widely known, people might think about immigration slightly differently. It might be seen as less of a problem and more as an understandable, neutral reality. Or at the very least, it may make it easier for us to understand anti-immigration sentiment for what it is: as less of a fact of life and more as a product of history.

Still, even when the UK's migration histories are recognised, they're presented as rose-tinted pictures that are predictably too celebratory an understanding of the past, fictions in which immigration plays a part, but without the resistance to and exclusions that accompanied it.[7] In 2013, then prime minister David Cameron did just that. 'Our migrant communities are a fundamental part of who we are and Britain is a far richer and stronger society because of them,' he said. 'This is our island story: open, diverse and welcoming, and I am immensely proud of it.'[8] We do not need to look back too far into history to find a very different picture of this country and its relationship with immigration.

In January 1955, Winston Churchill, generally lionised as a British hero, made a bold suggestion in one of his cabinet meetings. With a general election likely to happen within the year – one that he would not, in the end, contest – he tried to persuade his colleagues to adopt a campaign slogan that was similar to the rallying cry of the far right in the decades that followed. 'Keep England White', he suggested, would be a good message.[9] The prime minister, who had been heavily involved in the Boer War, Britain's bloody colonial adventures, and in creating the 1943 Bengal famine – which is estimated to have killed 3 million people – was adamant that restricting Caribbean migration was 'the most important subject facing this country'.[10] Objecting to people of colour coming to the UK, in 1954 Churchill told the governor-in-chief of Jamaica, Sir Hugh Foot, that their presence would create 'a magpie society', adding 'that would never do'.[11]

Churchill's views on matters of race and migration were hardly abnormal. Before and after the 1955 election, politicians from the left and the right complained that people of colour coming to the UK would threaten the very idea of the nation and undermine Britons' standard of living by taking jobs and housing. Immigration, how it was understood and the legislation that would be introduced to 'control' it, was inseparable from race and racism.

'Race is something we make,' philosopher Kwame Anthony Appiah tells us, 'it's not something that makes us.' Invented to control and govern populations, race has never had any biological basis; it's racism that gives it meaning.[12] Race hasn't always existed in the way we understand it now; it was a term used, for instance, to talk about class. Intended for a middle-class audience, one London weekly newspaper described 'the Bethnal Green poor' as 'a caste apart, a race of whom we know nothing'.[13] But over the late nineteenth and throughout the twentieth centuries, the racial hierarchy was solidified. Forming a justification for colonialism and slavery since the colonisation of the Americas in 1492, and then backed up by the scientific racism of eugenicist Frances Galton, as well as academics, politicians and thinkers – in other words, significant sections of the elite – it increasingly came to be believed that visible differences were a sign of much deeper ones. Humans have inherited a biological essence related to skin colour and bodily features, they said, and this biology decides our abilities. 'Race is everything: literature, science, art, in a word, civilization,' scientist Robert Knox declared in 1850.[14]

As they plundered, exploited and brutally controlled colonies and the people in them, all to enrich Britain as part of the growth of the capitalist project, colonialists swore by the racial hierarchy. Whiteness was not simply a descriptor; it was used to give anchor to the idea that Europe was the place of modernity and civilisation. White Europeans – in particular white upper-class men – were thought inherently modern and sophisticated; their black and brown counterparts, the opposite. The former, human; the latter, not. These ideas live on, subtly drawing a line between the developed and the developing, the advanced and the backward.

During Empire, the colonised needed to be civilised, and it was the responsibility of white Britons to do just that. 'Is it not strange to think, that they who ought to be considered as the most learned and civilized people in the world, that they should carry on a traffic of the most barbarous cruelty and injustice, and that many . . . are become so dissolute as to think slavery, robbery and murder no crime?' wrote abolitionist and philosopher Ottobah Cugoano in 1787.[15]

Yet, to this day, national myths abound of Britons nobly leading the charge against slavery. In fact, when slavery was abolished in Britain, slave owners were granted, using taxpayers money, £20 million in compensation, or the equivalent of around £17 billion today, the largest public bailout until the fall-out from the 2008 financial crisis.[16] Conveniently ignored are the facts that slaves and their descendants never saw a penny of compensation and the UK then played a significant role in forcing millions of people into bondage and indentured labour.[17]

As working classes at home agitated for and began to win democratic rights in the early twentieth century, the Empire was used to give coherence to a country deeply divided along class lines. People were told it wasn't just the elite that benefited from the imperial project, but also the country as a whole; white people's sense of self and of the nation was defined by their relation to the colonised. In one mass marketing campaign, which came in the form of posters, lectures, Empire shops and a library, the public were encouraged to 'buy Empire' and made to feel that as consumers they were helping keep the Empire alive. Racial superiority and all its ideas of differing humanity seeped into popular culture: adverts for household goods as mundane as soap or cocoa were marketed on images that showed black people as inferior to whites.[18]

But race was not only about skin colour or physical features. After visiting a Warsaw ghetto in 1949 and witnessing the treatment of Jewish people in Poland, the preeminent sociologist and author W.E.B. Du Bois concluded that the global colour line – which he'd understood at the beginning of the 1900s as the way black and brown people were segregated and treated differently because of their skin colour – was 'not even solely a matter of color and physical and racial characteristics'. 'No,' he explained, 'the race problem in which I was interested cut across lines of color and physique and belief and status and was a matter of cultural patterns, perverted teaching and human hate and prejudice, which reached all sorts of people and caused endless evil to all men.' The widely disseminated idea that there are ancestral differences between groups of people which determine people's abilities, instincts and ways of being, then, was not only denoted by skin colour.[19]

This thinking shaped the ways migrants have been perceived in recent history. Immigration hasn't always been top of the political agenda; neither has there been a single, uniform treatment of the diverse groups of migrants, but certain groups have been marked out and racialised as different, unwanted and even threatening. These ideas, targeted specifically at Jewish migrants, formed the backdrop of the UK's first modern immigration controls.

Escaping pogroms and riots in Eastern Europe and anti-Jewish policies in Russia, at the end of the nineteenth century, increasing numbers of Jewish migrants were arriving in England. Antisemitism has a long history in this country; Jews, along with Roman Catholics, didn't have the same rights as Protestants until the nineteenth century.[20] But these people, mostly orthodox in their views, were poorer and less anglicised than the existing Jewish population; with their arrival, the Jewish working class grew in size and the existing occupational and cultural profile of Jewish people in England radically changed.[21]

'Immigrant' and 'Jew' became interchangeable, and 'concerns' exploded about the supposed social ills that Jewish migrants brought with them to East London, one of the principal areas where they settled.[22] Politicians claimed the country's identity would be diluted by their presence, and *The East London Advertiser* attacked Jewish people as incompatible with the English way of life: 'People of any other nation, after being in England for only a short time, assimilate themselves with the native race and by and by lose nearly all their foreign trace. But the Jews never do. A Jew is always a Jew.' In 1906, one writer in the weekly socialist newspaper *the Clarion* described Jewish people coming into the country as 'a poison injected into the national veins'.[23]

Arriving during economic downturn, in language eerily similar to contemporary arguments that migrants undercut wages and change UK culture, Edward Troup, then Home Office permanent secretary, claimed that 'large numbers of aliens from Eastern Europe who had settled in east London and in other populous centres had lowered the wages in some of the unorganised trades to starvation point and their habits had a demoralising effect in the crowded areas in which they settled.'[24]

The UK's first ever substantial legislation to deal with immigration – the Aliens Act 1905 – was aimed at limiting the number of Jewish people, as well as the number of poor people, coming into the country. And, so, class and race met, as they so often do, in the reasoning behind immigration 'controls'. Foreign nationals were forced to register with the police and there were limits on where they could live. The British Nationality and Status of Aliens Act 1914 stipulated that people who wanted to become British citizens had to have 'good character' and 'an adequate knowledge of the English language'.

The British Nationality and Status of Aliens Act 1918 then gave the home secretary the right to rescind naturalisation certificates given to German citizens and barred any enemy from being naturalised in the ten years after the end of the war.[25] Restrictions that had been applied to certain migrants were extended during what would become the period between the two World Wars; the Aliens Restriction (Amendment) Act 1919 required all Jewish 'aliens' to carry ID cards that prevented them from taking certain jobs, made it illegal for them to promote industrial action, and dictated that they must tell authorities if they would be away from home for more than two weeks.[26]

It wasn't only Jewish people who were the focus of government attention. The 1919 Act also legalised different rates of pay for British seamen along the lines of race. Between the First and Second World Wars, the government tried to keep out Asian and black seamen arriving at UK ports. Fears of a mixed race population helped drive the restrictions introduced in 1925: British subjects of colour who landed in ports across

the country had to register themselves and clock in with officials if they were going to move; all the while the possibility of
deportation loomed over them.[27] This signalled what was to
come in the following decades; the racial categories created
during colonialism underpinned the debate and they would
continue to do so for years to come.

Desperate to retain global status as the British Empire was
crumbling in front of them and determined to continue an
economically exploitative relationship with colonies and
former colonies where possible, politicians embraced the idea
of the Commonwealth. Through this organisational vehicle
they claimed that the Empire was naturally evolving into a
multiracial collection of countries.[28] In this telling of history,
colonial independence could be cast not as a radical change
driven by anti-colonial movements but as a planned transfor-
mation that signalled the UK's benevolence and adaptability.
The 1948 British Nationality Act was part of this plan.

Clement Attlee's Labour government cobbled together the
legislation that would keep a semblance of imperial unity
through open borders. This, the first definition of British
citizenship, gave people from colonies and former colonies
British nationality rights; they could be known as either British
subjects or Commonwealth citizens. It didn't hand out any
new privileges, but wrote into law the rights these people
already had and created a check against any withdrawal of
them.[29] What the government really wanted was to make it
easy for people to move between the euphemistically named
'old Commonwealth' countries – otherwise known as the
'white dominions' – to come to the UK even if they were
developing their own forms of citizenship laws. That is, to
allow white people from Canada, South Africa, Australia and
New Zealand to move to the UK.[30]

And so despite the supposed 'open door' policy, people of
colour from the colonies and former colonies weren't welcome

in the UK. Politicians outsourced the border regime. Through the 1950s, Labour's official position was opposition to 'controls', but at the beginning of the decade, Attlee's government brought together a cabinet committee to look into how the immigration of 'coloured people from the British Colonial Territories' could be checked.[31]

By 1952, both Tory and Labour governments had implemented clandestine processes to keep out people of colour. They intervened in the market to raise the price of low-cost tickets on transatlantic crossings and they pressured colonial governments to limit who they issued passports to – a practice used even during the height of Empire, when the government was working with agencies abroad to make it harder for people to get the travel documents they needed to enter the UK.

When Jamaica refused to fall into line, the UK government made a film to be aired in the Caribbean, which took footage from the bitterly cold 1947–48 winter edited with images of out-of-work immigrants living in poor accommodation, to discourage people from coming. In India and Pakistan, the UK High Commissioner publicised the supposed difficult conditions of life in the UK in newspapers.[32]

So, when Empire Windrush docked at Tilbury, Essex, in 1948, eleven Labour MPs wasted no time in registering their unhappiness. 'An influx of coloured people domiciled here is likely to impact the harmony, strength and cohesion of our public and social life and to cause discord and unhappiness among all concerned,' they wrote in a letter to Prime Minister Attlee soon after the boat's near 500 passengers from the Caribbean disembarked on British shores. Neither brought nor invited by the government to work, the sight of this number of people deciding themselves to make journey to the UK alarmed some politicians. While some people welcomed new arrivals, who were able to carve out a life for themselves in the UK, these MPs demanded 'control': 'we venture to suggest that the British government should, like foreign countries, the dominions and even some of the colonies, by legislation if necessary, control immigration in the political, social, economic and fiscal interests of our people.'[33]

One of the reasons 'controls' weren't introduced in these years was that politicians and different parts of government were divided over the best policy to adopt. Some, like those in the Colonial Office, worried controls would undermine the idea of the multiracial Commonwealth and the remnants of Britain's imperial power along with it. But there were other parts of government, such as the Ministry of Labour, that kept advocating for overtly controlling immigration. Conservative MP Cyril Osborne was one of the most vehement in his opposition, claiming that people of colour coming into the country had a 'different standard of civilisation'.[34]

The Second World War had left the UK in economic decline; it lost one quarter of its wealth and plummeted from being the world's largest creditor to its largest debtor. Post-war reconstruction required workers, and the official line was that the country at the centre of the Commonwealth would take anyone willing and able to work, regardless of colour. This wasn't how it played out. Industrial giants like Ford, Vickers, Napiers and Tate and Lyle, in large part supported by the trade unions, implemented a colour bar.[35] But at the end of the 1940s, through the European Volunteer Workers (EVW) scheme, the government brought in Eastern Europeans, and though they were met with hostility, not least from some trade unions, they were thought to be racially suitable in a way that Jewish people, who were intentionally excluded, weren't.[36] An independent research institute declared in a 1948 population report 'the absorption of large numbers of non-white immigrants would be extremely difficult.'[37] Empire might have been caving in on itself, but its organising principles – race and its hierarchy of humanity – stubbornly persisted.

But as Windrush showed, people of colour who lived in colonies and former colonies decided to make the journey to the metropole anyway – and although most other Britons were not and might still not be aware, these new arrivals to UK shores came as citizens, not migrants. Some made the choice to take a chance and move with no definite job waiting for them; others came as part of certain company's recruitment drives, like the kind that existed in the NHS.[38]

Prior to the war, nurses and hospital workers from the Caribbean were recruited to work in the health service, and this policy continued when the NHS was established in 1948. Even Enoch Powell – Tory health minister from 1960 until 1963, who would become notorious for his virulently racist views – appealed to doctors in India and Pakistan to come to the UK as part of a plan to expand the NHS.

The catch was, they weren't necessarily expected to stay long. 'They thought we would come in, run the buses . . . do the nursing and all the other things that we did and we would go home at night,' former nurse Maria Layne-Springer, who came from Barbados, remembered. 'And somehow miraculously wherever we came from we would fly back in the following morning to continue our shifts . . . How we lived in the interim was of no concern to them.'

Sislin Hunte, a former district nurse who came from Jamaica, explained how badly she was treated. 'I felt like I was nothing, I was just a slave . . . just taken for granted, I felt low, very low, as if I was inferior, they make you feel like that.' Hunte was one of thousands of Caribbean and African women who were the lifeblood of the NHS; without them the country's beloved health service would have come to a standstill when it was in its infancy. Allyson Williams MBE, a former midwife from Trinidad, recalled the racism she experienced: 'They never prepared you for how the patients would treat you and you know they'd slap your hand away and say "don't touch me and you know your black is gonna rub off."'[39] When these women are remembered, it's often as part of a nostalgic celebration which overlooks the individual and structural racism they experienced; they were funnelled into low-grade posts, often with the lowest pay, the poorest conditions and most anti-social working hours.[40]

'When I had my daughter, that's when the scale of racism really hit me,' Amrit Wilson tells me. Wilson is a journalist and activist who first came to the UK from India as a student in the 1960s before settling here permanently. 'When you have a baby in a pushchair you feel incredibly vulnerable to racist attack on the street. But then there is the more subtle racism of welfare state professionals. The health visitors, for example the kind of advice they would give was unbelievable,' she explains. 'They would say "don't give your baby chillies to eat" . . . or "you need to make sure that your home is tidy", even if they hadn't actually seen your home. It was almost as if they thought nobody had had a child before they came to this country!'

'I knew Britain long before I came to Britain, as a matter of fact I knew more about Britain than I did my own little land. There were no books about us,' Alex Pascall, one of the founders of the Notting Hill Carnival in London, tells me in a quiet corner of the bustling British Library. Born in Grenada, where he lived until he was twenty-two, and like many children in the colonies, Pascall grew up reading Shakespeare and Wordsworth: he was raised on a quintessentially British curriculum. As groups of children on school trips trail past us and library-goers eat their lunches on tables behind ours, Pascall sits back and tells me about his first impressions of the UK. When he first arrived in the country after a ten-day trip across the Atlantic, he was shocked: 'they told us this was the mother country; oh, no there is no mother in this country.'

Britain had fashioned itself as the centre of an empire, in which those living in the colonies were its subjects – ones they ruled over, oppressed and exploited – so long as they stayed in their countries of origin or relocated only when asked.

'For hundreds of years, Britain has ruled the countries from which immigrants now come,' Avtar Jouhl, the secretary of the Indian Workers' Association wrote in 1961. 'The stand-ards of living there are appallingly low, partly due to the policies that Britain pursued. The high standard of living that the British worker today enjoys is partly because of a low standard abroad that makes it possible to import raw mate-rials at a cheap price from there. Under these circumstances, is it at all morally justifiable to disclaim all responsibility and close all doors to immigration?'[41] Poverty created and exacer-bated by Empire brought thousands of people to the UK; yet the racism of the mother country kept many destitute.

But people coming from the colonies didn't arrive naïve to the racism they would experience; some had been involved in dynamic anti-colonial struggle and understood the nature of British oppression. Radical black activists rejected the term 'migrant', calling themselves instead 'failed refugees', coming from independent countries that hadn't achieved transform-ative emancipation after formal colonial rule ended.[42] 'We're here because you were there' became one of the rallying cries of the movement against racism.

Decolonisation and anti-colonial movements had chal-lenged the supposed wisdom of the racial hierarchy, producing anxiety that the UK's mythical superiority was going to be exposed for what it was. To preserve these distinctions, differ-ence was continually being reasserted.

Racism was woven into the structures of British society. Instead of recognising this, politicians believed one way to achieve good 'race relations' was immigration control. In 1954, trying to find a justification for immigration legislation, a group of Conservative ministers circulated a questionnaire about black workers around labour exchanges. The report that followed claimed that, if immigration 'from the colonies, and, for that matter, from India and Pakistan' continued to grow at the same rate as it was, it could change 'the racial character of English people'. It argued that black workers were 'lacking stamina' and black women workers were 'slow mentally'.[43] Immigration was still seen as a sign of British decline. One journalist overheard a conversation between two people in a Bradford café: 'Once we were great,' one of them said. 'We had the most powerful navy in the world. We used to export to India. Now their blokes come over here, we train them, they go back and export to us.'[44]

But as people lamented Britain's waning power and as the government tried to hold together a rapidly disintegrating empire through the Commonwealth, it was also launching Operation Legacy. The exact date of when this programme of erasure began is unclear, but estimates suggest it started in the 1950s and lasted through to the 1970s. All around the world colonialists were expunging the country's bloody, genocidal colonial history from the record books by destroying or hiding files from former colonies, some of which were chosen because they were deemed too 'embarrassing' to be handed over to future governments.[45] In Britain, the elite refused to take responsibility for or accept the consequences of the racial categories that had been used to legitimate the colonial project.

And so, ten years on from the arrival of the Windrush generation, as summer was coming to a close, violence broke out after a series of racist attacks in Nottingham and then Notting Hill. One of the few areas where people of colour could get accommodation, the West London district was also a prolific area of recruitment for the National Labour Party, a precursor to the British National Party (BNP). White youths regularly prowled the streets looking for people of colour to harass. On 20 August, they hospitalised five black men, and over the August bank holiday an argument between a mixed-race couple drew the attention of people in the area and quickly descended into violence which lasted for days.

Some observers of the violence regarded immigration as the problem. 'The government must introduce legislation quickly to end the tremendous influx of coloured people from the Commonwealth,' Labour MP for Kensington North George

Rogers claimed. 'Overcrowding has fostered vice, drugs, prostitution and the use of knives. For years the white people have been tolerant. Now their tempers are up.'[46] His Parliamentary colleague MP Maurice Edelman demanded in the *Daily Mail* that now was the time for immigration controls. And Lord Salisbury, former secretary of state for Commonwealth relations and Tory leader in the Lords until 1957, chimed in, saying the violence showed controls should be brought in specifically to limit black immigration. Just over a month after they took place, pro-'control' Tory politicians got what they had long agitated for: the Conservative Party conference swung in favour of new immigration legislation to address the 'issue'.

Though for some the violence might have made the need for 'control' seem more urgent, others disagreed. Labour's ruling committee denounced the attacks, condemned racial prejudice and said they wouldn't support any restrictive immigration legislation. The judge who sentenced nine of the young people convicted of assault declared: 'Everyone, irrespective of the colour of their skin, is entitled to walk our streets erect and free from fear. This is a right which these courts will always unfailingly uphold.'[47]

Despite this criticism, it was said that police officers tried to play down the incident, as academics and politicians argued that any evidence of racism was a product of the behaviour of the same people of colour who were its victims – from living on low wages to engaging in interracial relationships, they were causing upset in the nation.

A year later, when thirty-two-year-old Antiguan immigrant, Kelso Cochrane, was murdered, this logic held. As Cochrane's blood dried on a street in Notting Hill, the police denied that it was a racially motivated attack, dismissing anyone who claimed to the contrary that they were making political capital out of it. A report issued months later described the behaviour of Britons towards 'coloured people' as 'restrained'.[48]

In 1950s Britain, when violence erupted, some people saw fit to perversely place the blame squarely at the feet of those who'd been attacked; their existence and presence depicted as the problem. This stance, combined with worries over the impact that automation would have on 'unskilled' jobs and the increase in the number of working-age Britons, meant that in the early 1960s the impasse that stopped immigration legislation being introduced was about to be overcome.[49]

When Conservative prime minister Harold Macmillan announced his plans to introduce the 1962 Immigration Act, he pointed to the numbers: 'knowing our difficulties, some Commonwealth governments have taken steps over the last few years to limit the number of people coming here by various methods, and we are very grateful to them. Several of them have used methods to discourage this mass movement.' That hadn't been enough, he added, 'the influx . . . can hardly continue uncontrolled.'[50] But it wasn't about how many people were coming; it was about *which* people. When he talked about an 'influx' he meant people of colour arriving from colonies and former colonies – they were the target of the 1962 Act.

Imagine you were a Commonwealth citizen. Before the 1962 Act you could, in theory, move as you please. Afterwards, if your passport was issued under the authority of a colonial government, you needed an employment voucher from the British government to come and live in the country.[51] Because of the very specific nature of the Act, it only affected certain people – in one fell swoop, the 1962 Act shut out voucherless people from Pakistan, India and elsewhere, many of whom were made British citizens by the 1948 Act. For the first time, the term 'immigrant' applied to British subjects.

If this had been about the *numbers* of people coming, like Macmillan claimed, the Act would have been directed at those arriving from Ireland too. In all but one of the seven years between 1955 and 1962, the numbers making the journey across the Irish Sea was greater than those arriving from the so-called new Commonwealth.[52] The treatment of the two groups was so different that Home Secretary Rab Butler looked to Ireland for help in reducing Commonwealth immigration to the UK.

But Irish people who mostly came to Britain at the end of eighteenth and beginning of the nineteenth century, initially to fill labour shortages, weren't enthusiastically welcomed. Catholics in a Protestant country and disliked because they were mostly working class, Irish migrants were discriminated against in housing and employment, and some pubs barred people with Irish accents. It wasn't uncommon for Irish people to be represented as racially inferior to white Britons. Before he became an MP, future prime minister Benjamin Disraeli said the Irish 'hate our order, our civilisation, our enterprising industry, our religion. The wild, reckless, indolent, uncertain and superstitious race have no sympathy with the English character.'[53]

This xenophobia, fierce though it was, waned as the years passed – though it continued to bubble under the surface of society and resurface at moments throughout recent UK history – and it never resulted in immigration legislation to address the 'problem'. Even after the country became a republic in 1949, Irish citizens were free to live in the UK, though the country was no longer part of the Commonwealth.[54]

The government wanted to make it more difficult for people of colour to come to the country. They were careful, though, to never explicitly mention race. But six years after it passed through Parliament, William Deedes, a minister at the time the 1962 Act was introduced, admitted candidly in a pamphlet on race and immigration that the aim had been 'to restrict the influx of coloured immigrants'. He elaborated: 'We were reluctant to say as much openly. So the restrictions were applied to coloured and white citizens in all Commonwealth countries – though everybody recognized that immigration from Canada, Australia and New Zealand formed no part of the problem.'[55] This obsession with racial purity drove the government to encourage white Britons to emigrate to places like Australia, New Zealand and Canada, even while there were labour shortages at home. But by introducing legislation that was not explicitly colour-coded, the government could maintain the idea of the multiracial Commonwealth, central to the UK's understanding of itself and the kind of image it wanted to project onto the global stage.

'The United Kingdom is one of the few countries in the European Union that does not need to bury its twentieth-century history,' soon-to-be Conservative minister Liam Fox said in 2016.[56] Significant numbers of people in the UK were – and remain – unwilling to face up to the racism embedded in the nation's history. There is a collective denial about the bloodiness of its empire and the embeddedness of the country's domestic history in global interdependencies. There would be no facing up to these realities in the years following 1962, and, again, it wasn't only the Conservatives that would attempt to bury them. Labour, the so-called party of equality, was wielding the shovel, too.

Most of the 1964 General Election campaign had been free from rain, but on 15 October, people trudged to polling stations through showers that drenched the country. Desperate to wrestle power out of Conservative hands, Labour's leader Harold Wilson could still be found out and about, touring London's marginals to whip up support in what would be a close-run election. Journalist Paul Foot recalled how he would shoot down anyone expressing anti-immigrant racism with questions such as 'Where would our health service be without the black workers who keep it going?'[57]

Two years before Wilson had been out on that rainy election day, Labour had opposed the 1962 Act when it passed through Parliament. Historian Dr Charlotte Riley tells me that when Wilson's predecessor, Hugh Gaitskell, spoke firmly against the UK's entry into the European Economic Community (EEC) in a 1962 speech it was at least partly because, she says, he thought 'it will be a way for the Conservatives to have more white immigration and less black Commonwealth immigration'. He applied the same judgment to the 1962 Act, describing the Commonwealth as a 'remarkable, multiracial collection'. Criticising the Conservatives for 'betraying the Commonwealth' through their restrictive immigration policy, Gaitskell could, to some extent, be put in with the people in Whitehall advocating the necessity of a Commonwealth citizenship to maintain Britain's imperial power. His stance on the Common Market prompted the *Daily Express* headline: 'EMPIRE FIRST – Gaitskell'.[58]

But even though Wilson was shouting down racism on polling day, Labour's stance on 'control' had changed well before then. While promising to legislate against racial discrimination, the 1964 Labour manifesto stated: 'the number of immigrants entering the United Kingdom must be limited. Until a satisfactory agreement covering this can be negotiated with the Commonwealth a Labour government will retain immigration control.'[59] Labour had given in; they agreed it was necessary to stop certain immigrants from coming into the country.

The wet weather didn't fatally damage Labour turnout – as the party so often worry it will – Wilson went on to narrowly win the election. Within the year, however, the country would see less of the man who firmly rejected racism on election day and more of the party that promised to limit immigration. When in power, they went on to introduce some of the country's most poisonous immigration legislation to date.

One turning point, remembers former general secretary of the Transport and General Workers' Union (TGWU) Bill Morris, was during the 1964 General Election campaign in the constituency of Smethwick, a small town in the West Midlands. Morris comes across as a gentle, affable and thoughtful person, he chuckles as he tells me about his life growing up in Jamaica and migrating to the UK in 1954. His speech is punctuated by moments of sadness, including the sudden death of his father, which ultimately resulted in him and his mother moving to join family in the UK. But his thoughtful recollections suggest he has fond memories of his childhood, moving here and becoming the first black leader of a major trade union in this country. Sitting under the grand glass roof in the atrium of Portcullis House in Westminster, Morris's light tone turns serious when he recalls living in Handsworth, a constituency near Smethwick: 'the whole thing was quite poisonous.'

In the 1964 General Election, Labour lost what was considered a safe seat in the Midlands; it had been in the party's hands since it was created in 1918 but fell to Tory control by a margin of 1,774 votes. What happened in Smethwick became so well-known that a year after the election and just days before he was shot dead, black power icon Malcolm X visited the area because he was disturbed by reports that people of colour were being treated badly.

'If you want a n***** for your neighbour, vote Labour.' Now infamous, this was the slogan associated with the Conservative campaign. It never appeared in any of Griffiths's electioneering, but he refused to denounce this violently racist message. 'I should think that is a manifestation of popular feeling. I would not condemn anyone who said that,' he told *The Times*. 'I would say that is how people see the situation in Smethwick. I fully understand the feelings of the people who say it. I would say it is exasperation, not fascism.'[60] He denied that there was any 'resentment in Smethwick on the grounds of race or colour'. But he drew on racist tropes of people of colour as unclean and disruptive, black men as sexual predators, who would make the country's streets unsafe, and claimed 'voters in turbans and saris' decided Smethwick's future. Labour's position was to 'build more houses and let 'em all come', he claimed, 'surely if more houses can be built they should go to British people first ... In any case, would more houses end the nuisance and filth? Would more houses end the knife fights? Would more houses make the streets safe for young women and girls?'

Griffiths wanted tighter immigration control and floated potential voluntary repatriation schemes for unemployed migrants.[61] In contrast, his Labour opponent and party grandee Patrick Gordon Walker opposed the 1962 legislation. Rumours circulated about his private life: 'Gordon Walker had sold his house in Smethwick to blacks. Gordon Walker went out to the West Indies to recruit blacks for Smethwick industry. Gordon Walker's wife was black. So was Gordon Walker!'[62]

Labour hadn't expected Griffiths to win, but Smethwick bucked the general trend. After thirteen years of Conservative government, Labour scraped into office with a majority of four. What was nevertheless a significant triumph – with the Tories losing sixty-one seats and Labour winning fifty-nine – was marred by this loss; the national swing away from the Tories was just over 3 per cent, yet there was a 7.2 per cent swing in the opposite direction in Smethwick. 'It's an election they win overall, [but they lose] in a seat they had thought was safe, so it's frightening,' Dr Riley tells me. 'It's unusual basically quite a key MP in an area that's supposed to be a safe seat ... and really early they start to use the language that we see now, like "Labour is losing its core working class support."'[63] The reason for this loss of support, Labour figures decided, was immigration.

'Looking back on the original Act which limited the entry of Commonwealth citizens into this country, I feel that the Labour Party of that time should have supported it,' Roy Hattersley admitted in the Commons chamber in 1965. Applause broke out from the Conservative backbenches. 'I make this point with no great joy,' he added, 'because I was a passionate opponent of the Act.' Powerful anti-control politicians seemed to fall like dominoes. Hattersley, Wilson and Labour MP Richard Crossman went from opposing the government's bill to accepting it as a necessity. Crossman said immigration could be 'the greatest potential voter loser' if Labour is 'seen to be permitting a flood of immigrants to come in and blight the central areas of our cities'.[64]

Still, the party tried to have it both ways. While Labour MPs were making these statements in Parliament, Wilson threatened Griffiths would be treated like a 'Parliamentary leper'.[65] They were at once denouncing Griffiths's racism while simultaneously accepting the premise of his campaign that people of colour entering the country were a problem to be controlled.

Labour didn't necessarily have to shift to the right on immigration. In an election they won, Smethwick went back to Labour in 1966, when the Conservatives made a pledge to 'deal with the problem of immigration'.[66] The candidate, Andrew Faulds, though hardly on the left of the party, was said to have been inspired to join Labour by civil rights activist and iconic singer Paul Robeson and to have campaigned on an anti-racist platform.

While many people might have regarded Walker as Griffiths's opponent on immigration, former MP Denis Howell gave a slightly different version of events. Nearby Gordon Walker in Birmingham Small Heath, Howell claimed similar racist campaigning was used in his constituency. The difference was, he said, in the way the two approached the issue. He remembered during the election that both Labour candidates were at a factory gate meeting where Gordon Walker essentially blamed the Tories for letting immigrants into the country in the first place. 'If you are a person who is worried on the race issue, why vote for Patrick Gordon Walker', Howell said, 'when you can vote for Peter Griffiths and have the full Monty.'[67] Months after he had supported Gaitskell in opposing the 1962 Act and well before the 1964 election, Gordon Walker, who would be appointed foreign secretary by Wilson, declared,

> I think there is a case for restricting or controlling immigration in certain circumstances when it gets too big . . . I don't think that at the moment the rate of immigration of coloured people, which is, I think, what most people are worried about, had reached the point where there should be this sort of control. But I would not reject the idea of control as such.[68]

What Labour figures also overlooked in their assessment of why they lost Smethwick was that Griffiths – a primary school headmaster cum Conservative local councillor since 1955, who went on to become leader five months before the general election – was a formidable campaigner. Gordon Walker lacked the same fire. One *Washington Post* reporter commented that, although he might have been a 'decent man', as a campaigner, he 'has about the political sex appeal of a turtle'.[69]

As for Labour's other concern, it was true they were losing some of their working-class support, but not necessarily just because of immigration. 'The reason is the rise of affluence in the 1950s,' says Dr Riley. 'Working-class people don't identify as working class anymore, the Conservatives in the 1950s got really good at the politics of affluence: "You've never had it so good." The Conservatives sell ambition and what's seen as a modern consumerist future to the working classes. Whereas Labour in the 1950s are perceived as still the old Labour politics of Attlee.'

All of this aside, even if Labour figures were right about anti-migrant sentiment in Smethwick, instead of challenging it, they encouraged it.

But it wasn't just what happened in that one constituency during that one election that shaped the party's position. As is often the case with anti-immigration politics, this can't just be narrowly understood as a response to public opinion, which they had a hand in creating. The clandestine controls Labour had implemented in the '50s, the content of their manifesto and the ease with which they accepted the 1962 Act suggested that some MPs and people high up in the party hierarchy already believed people of colour should be deterred from coming to the UK.

The Labour Party, and the wider labour movement, have a chequered history when it comes to migration and Empire. There is a strain of internationalism in the left that understands solidarity as being inherently cross-border and is concerned with the power of a worldwide movement for emancipation. In the early 1900s, activists such as Arthur MacManus and John MacLean saw the working-class struggle as part of a global effort, and people organised against xenophobia and racism. Just under twenty years later, in the wake of racist attacks, a group of women married to black sailors demanded justice for people of colour. And in those early decades of the century, the Communist Party of Great Britain mounted organised campaigns against racism and imperialism.

But there was also a brand of nationalistic politics in the left that remains to this day. Typical of this standpoint was Ben Tillett, the dockers' leader and himself the son of an Irish migrant. Referring to the Jewish workers engaged in collective action, he reportedly declared, 'Yes, you are our brothers and we will do our duty by you. But we wish you had not come to this country.'[70]

According to Professor Satnam Virdee, some of the most well-remembered forms of working-class resistance were accompanied by intense racism and antisemitism in all social classes.[71] Egged on by people like socialist leader Manny Shinwell – whose British Seafarers' Union banned black members – in one of many outbreaks of severe violence at port towns and cities between January and August 1919, a group of white men chased black sailors through the streets of Glasgow, blaming them for the rising unemployment and housing shortages that met them when they returned home from war. That same year, in bouts of racist violence, Chinese laundries in Cardiff and London were destroyed. This had been preceded by virulent anti-Chinese sentiment in the union movement. Key figures campaigned against what they called the 'Yellow Peril', meaning the Chinese people employed on local ships, who they accused of undercutting wages. Many of the people they attacked had left China after British imperialism had helped cripple the economy, but an internationalist approach that would have factored this into analysis mattered little to the people spreading this racism. However, it wasn't just economics that drove violence; rumours circulated about the dangers of miscegenation and the threat people of colour posed to the country.[72] It's against this history, and not just Smethwick, that we should understand the labour movement's engagement with immigration.

In office, Labour didn't just uphold the immigration policy led by the Tories; they extended it. In 1965 they reduced the number of vouchers available to migrants, extended powers to deport people deemed 'illegal immigrants', issued a time limit on student visas and imposed restrictions on who could be classed as dependants.

Under Labour and the Tories the state carried out virginity tests on women from South Asia. Regardless of who was in office, the government seemed to see these women as props to be used for their own ends. They were exempt from needing a visa because politicians thought their presence good for 'race relations' if it made it less likely that South Asian men would marry white women, but they first wanted to 'prove' whether these women coming into the country were already married or not.[73] Humiliating, invasive and mainly practised by male doctors, journalist Amrit Wilson – who reported on this at the time and covers it in her book *Finding A Voice: Asian Women in Britain* – describes these tests as amounting to 'sexual harassment'. Though they were eventually stopped in 1979 thanks to vibrant community campaigns from groups like the Indian Workers' Association, AWAZ, the Organisation of Women of African and Asian Descent (OWAAD) and Southall Black Sisters, that they colluded in implementing this practice gives an idea of how weak-willed and dangerous Labour's approach to migration and race could be.

Darryl Telles is frustrated that these histories are not better known in the labour movement, and he's particularly vexed that the Commonwealth Immigrants Act 1968 is not more regularly talked about. 'It's a much-forgotten episode,' he tells me, explaining that people 'remember [Enoch] Powell but they won't remember this'. Only four years old when he came to the UK from Kenya, he still recalls the detrimental effect this piece of legislation, crafted by a Labour government, had on his family. Since the country gained independence in 1963, Asians in Kenya – who were mostly, Darryl explains, 'from India's Gujarat, Punjab and, like my parents, from Goa', but who had 'settled in Kenya since the end of the Second World War, as Britain encouraged immigration from the subcontinent' – had been feeling the brunt of 'Africanisation' policies. But it was the change to citizenship laws that had one of the biggest, most damaging impacts. Under the new rules introduced after independence, people of African descent were automatically granted citizenship. For anyone who wasn't, including East African Asians like Darryl and his family, they had to apply within two years to qualify. Few Asians did; they had the security of a British passport.

After Kenyan independence, Asians in the country got their documentation straight from the British and not, as was previously the case, the authority of the colonial government. That meant because of the changes brought in by the Commonwealth Immigrants Act 1962 back in the UK, they had the unencumbered right to enter the country. And they did so, in increasing numbers from 1967. That year, 'Africanisation' measures tightened even further. Asians were sacked from the civil service, were only able to work in certain sectors and the Kenyan Immigration Act required anyone who wasn't a citizen to get a work permit.

Then in early 1968, panic spread among Asians in Kenya. Their British passports, which were supposed to be their pass out of the country should they so need it, were made essentially useless. 'I can vaguely recall that in the Goan community and in the East African Asian community everyone was meeting and talking and saying what should we do,' says Darryl.

Rushed through Parliament in three days, partly in response to a rancorous campaign from Conservative MPs, it was the Commonwealth Immigrants Act 1968 that created this chaos. It dictated that any citizen of Britain or the colonies would be subject to immigration controls unless they had one parent or grandparent born, adopted, naturalised or registered in Britain as a citizen of Britain or its colonies.

From 1 March, planes full of Asian people leaving Kenya and trying to make it to the UK were turned away; others were forced to spend weeks on end in airports because even though they were British citizens, they couldn't come into the country. Some would spend months or years trying to get to the UK. With the prospect of the Act being introduced looming over them, Darryl's mum went ahead to the UK to secure them a route out of Kenya. Darryl, his brother and his dad joined her a few months later. His gran wasn't so lucky. She was separated from her family for four long years before she was allowed to come to the UK. Darryl's father, who worked for the British civil service, was furious at the way they had been treated by the government whose payroll he was on.

'My dad was adamant that we were British . . . despite on paper being told this is the mother country, that you worked in the civil service, that you built the railways, as some Goans did, that you're Christian,' Darryl explains. They were told: 'You're not British actually, you're immigrants.' A few years after arriving in the UK, his father tried to kill himself. Darryl says there was likely a lot of reasons for this, but this period of their lives was hardly inconsequential. 'The trauma of '68 and "the exodus", as we called it, played a part, and since then I understand that a lot of people did have mental health problems because of it.'

This Act was the beginning of a British citizenship explicitly demarcated by race: it was Asians – not white settlers – who were impacted.[74] But Callaghan refused to accept the legislation was about race. 'I regret the need for this bill,' he said in Parliament. 'I repudiate emphatically the suggestion that it is racialist in origin or in conception or in the manner in which it is being carried out.' Though he kept up the façade in public, the home secretary's private words exposed him.

'It is sometimes argued', Callaghan wrote in a memo six weeks after the bill passed through Parliament, 'that we can take a less serious view of the scale of immigration and settlement in this country because it could be, and currently is being, more than offset by total emigration. This view overlooks the important point that emigration is largely by white persons from nearly every corner of the United Kingdom, while immigration and settlement are largely by coloured persons into a relatively small number of concentrated areas. The exchange thus aggravates rather than alleviates the problem.'[75]

His concern was not whether there was sufficient infrastructure and planning to accommodate shifting numbers of people living in different areas of the UK – if it was, then why would he need to mention race? His problem was people of colour coming to the UK: this was, quite simply, racism.

The bill made it through the chamber, though not without opponents from across the Tory, Labour and the Liberal benches, mass protests and a challenge in the European Court of Human Rights. One Conservative, Lord Gilmour, told the *New Statesman* years later, 'If it had been the case that it was 5,000 white settlers who were coming in, the newspapers and politicians who were making all the fuss would have been quite pleased.' Even as it claimed limits were necessary, when Parliament passed the bill, an editorial in *The Times* called it 'probably the most shameful measure that the Labour members have ever been asked by their whip to support'.[76]

As the decades have passed, it's not been uncommon for Labour folk to look on Wilson's government fondly, as one that despite its faults, cared about people, and Callaghan as a kindly figure who badly mishandled the Winter of Discontent.[77] Another side of Labour history came to the fore in 1968. One of the most reactionary immigration acts that has ever passed through Parliament was brought forward by a Labour government.

But in line with the left's tradition of radicalism and anti-imperialism, there were people fighting back. The Movement for Colonial Freedom (MCF), for instance, was an anti-colonialist organisation that included among its founding members strong anti-imperialist voices like Labour MPs Fenner Brockway and Tony Benn and some national trade unions, as well as constituency Labour parties and trade union branches. Established in 1954, for years they advocated for decolonisation, attempting to raise questions in the Commons and influence Labour policy.[78]

There was an array of anti-racist activity in the '60s, '70s and '80s that came in different forms and with different aims:[79] mass anti-racist gatherings in the form of Rock Against Racism and radical organising, some of which was done exclusively by women, in Southall Black Sisters, OWAAD, the Institute of Race Relations, the Notting Hill Carnival and the Black Power movement, through which the notion of political blackness evolved. There were anti-racist initiatives introduced by Labour councils in the '80s, and in the decades before people organised within the Labour Party, through black sections, as well as outside it. Local unions actively tried to recruit people of colour and printed their leaflets in different languages; from the mid-1950s, the Nottingham Trades Council set up a liaison committee for migrants and produced booklets welcoming them to the city.[80]

'Classically there was a wing of the Labour Party that quite liked black people as long as they were far away,' Labour frontbencher Diane Abbott recalls. 'They were devout anti-apartheid campaigners some of them, but once you were a person of colour and you were actually here in the UK that was different.' Nonetheless, anti-racist campaigners made significant and important gains inside and outside institutional frameworks by securing support for minority ethnic children in schools, increasing the numbers of people of colour in Parliament and helping pressure a Labour government to bring in the 1965 Race Relations Act.

With no law to prohibit it, in the 1960s it wasn't uncommon for estate agents and employers to deny people of colour jobs or homes. Opposed by the long-fickle Trades Union Congress (TUC) who allied with the Confederation of British Industry (CBI) to argue that the government's plans interfered with industrial relations, the 1965 Act made it illegal to discriminate along the lines of race, ethnicity or nationality.[81]

The Act itself was toothless, applying only to public spaces but not to key areas of public policy like education, employment or housing. As one academic pointed out, because of the way it worked, the burden of proof was so high that 'no prosecutions were brought.'[82] In 1968 it was strengthened and in 1976 it was extended such that housing, employment, education and services were brought into its remit, and prohibitions were placed on discrimination on the basis of nationality. It wasn't until 2001 that it was extended to the police force.

Insufficient though they were, the Acts – each of which were introduced by a Labour, never a Conservative, government – marked a significant symbolic and educative change because overt racial discrimination became far less acceptable than it once was.[83] Writing on the 50th Anniversary of the

1965 Act, Professor Iyiola Solanke outlined the importance of the legislation. 'As a black British woman I have come to think of the Race Relations Act almost as a soundtrack to my life,' she wrote. 'Without the norms that it (to some extent successfully) introduced into British society, my life would not have been the same.'[84]

A benevolent Labour government didn't simply gift this legislation; the passing of every progressive law has a hidden (and often long) history of struggle to bring it about. In the years before the Act, while most of his party were blaming people of colour for the racism they faced, one MCF member, Fenner Brockway, put forward nine bills in an attempt to prohibit racial discrimination.[85] Each one failed. People like Dame Jocelyn Barrow, the first black woman to be a BBC governor, who helped found the Campaign Against Racial Discrimination (CARD) which agitated for the legislation, and the lawyers who committed to it being introduced were vital protagonists in this history.

But the very same year the 1968 Race Relations Act was introduced, so too was immigration legislation. The former stated that people of colour should be treated equally; the latter, based on the premise that people of colour were a problem to be dealt with, implied 'too many' of 'them' shouldn't be allowed here in the first place. The two main parties arrived at some form of compromise on immigration and racial justice; the Tories gave a small amount of ground to protecting people of colour, as Labour abandoned their defence, flawed or not, of immigration.[86] Large sections of the Labour Party were heavily embroiled in a political imaginary that expressed anxiety over race, immigration and the country's lost empire. Anti-racist movements refused to accept the terms of this debate, but the battles were far from over.

Three days ahead of the second reading of Labour's 1968 Race Relations Bill, the Tory Shadow Secretary of State for

Defence stood in front of just over eighty people on the second floor of the Midlands hotel in Birmingham. This event might not have been the grandest of occasions, but what was said on that Saturday afternoon in April would be picked over by historians in the years to come.[87] Talking to the Conservative Political Centre, Enoch Powell's words dripped with contempt:

> As time goes on, the proportion of this total who are immigrant descendants, those born in England, who arrived here by exactly the same route as the rest of us, will rapidly increase. Already by 1985 the native-born would constitute the majority. It is this fact which creates the extreme urgency of action now, of just that kind of action which is hardest for politicians to take, action where the difficulties lie in the present but the evils to be prevented or minimised lie several Parliaments ahead.[88]

The second in a series of three racist speeches on the same theme that year, Powell's shift on immigration had come in the mid-1960s. He had gone from recruiting Caribbean workers who kept the NHS afloat to giving a hate-filled sermon, conjuring up dystopian images of the 'River Tiber flowing with blood'. His main concern: 'they' were undermining British social cohesion and through the race relations acts would soon be a powerful majority. This was racist fear of the 'other' writ large.

There was an outpouring of support from sections of the public for Powell. A Gallup poll following the speech found a nation that was broadly of the same opinion as him, with 74 per cent saying that he'd got it right. Historian Amy Whipple sifted through the letters he received in the months after the 'rivers of blood' speech, finding that many people saw immigration 'as a sign of Britain's postwar descent from global, or even European, pre-eminence'.[89]

That year at the Conservative Party conference, eighty constituency resolutions were sent on immigration, and

Powell, who had his eye on the leadership, made a speech about more immigration controls that was received with a standing ovation.[90] In the days following the speech, 'knock, knock, we want Enoch' could be heard ringing through the streets of Westminster as far as Downing Street, as London dockers and meatpackers from Smithfield came out in support of him.

The reception from his colleagues was chillier; Powell's racism and xenophobia was too transparent for the Conservatives. The dockers had been out in front of Number 10 because then Tory leader Edward Heath swiftly dismissed Powell from the shadow cabinet. Recruits to the far-right National Front skyrocketed.

Like Heath, contemporary politicians often look on Powell with disgust and denounce his intense racism, though as happened periodically since he gave this speech, in recent years key figures have begun to question whether his anti-migrant premise had some truth to it. Powell's career ended in failure, but his ideas endured and endure.

Not long after firing Powell from his shadow cabinet, Edward Heath and the Tories were back in power, and they didn't waste any time in consolidating the racist basis of UK immigration policy. The previous Labour government had already done most of the groundwork for the infamous Immigration Act 1971, but on the day the country became part of the European Economic Community (EEC), the tie between entry into the country and Commonwealth citizenship was completely severed.

Ending the idea of Commonwealth 'subjects' or 'citizens', the 1971 Act made a significant change by replacing them with the categories 'patrial' and 'non-patrial'; the former didn't carry with it any restrictions on entry, the latter did. This was another piece of implicitly colour-coded legislation. Patrials were people born or naturalised in the UK, or who had a parent or grandparents born or naturalised in the country. Primary immigration had already been reduced; one aim of the 1971 legislation was to halt it altogether while also making family reunification much harder. The Black People's Alliance, led by Jagmohan Joshi, marched against the Act, but, faced with only lukewarm opposition from the Labour Party, it made it through Parliament. Like so much of the legislation preceding it, the Conservatives made it easier for white Australians, Canadians and New Zealanders to enter the country than people of colour from other parts of the Commonwealth.

But there was one particular moment where the Heath government resisted what had become an anti-migrant norm of UK Parliamentary politics. Echoing what had happened in Kenya four years earlier – albeit concerning smaller numbers of people, the policy parameters and rights of movement were remarkably similar – on 4 August 1972 Ugandan President Idi Amin gave Asians just months to leave the country. The *Daily Express* responded by warning on its front page of a 'New Asian threat', telling readers, 'Britain was threatened yesterday with a flood of Asians from East Africa.'[91]

Desperate to find a solution, Geoffrey Rippon, Chancellor of the Duchy of Lancaster, flew to Uganda to talk to Amin but was snubbed by the president.[92] The government was forced to try to persuade over fifty other countries to 'share the burden' by taking in migrants, which some did, but it was not enough. To the fury of people like Powell and the ultra-right-wing Conservative pressure group the Monday Club, Heath, believing he had an obligation to the people who would be expelled by Amin, 'allowed' in 25,000 Ugandan Asians.[93] The National Front exploited the unhappiness that flowed from this decision; in the '70s their membership, at one point, grew to around 14,000 people.[94]

At the same time, the Opposition was reflecting on its own policies. One study into race and immigration conducted by the Labour's ruling body, the National Executive Committee, concluded that it wasn't accurate to say, as many politicians did, that restrictions on immigration would reduce hostility to immigration.

When they came back into office in 1974, Home Secretary Roy Jenkins announced an amnesty for undocumented Commonwealth citizens or people from Pakistan who were impacted by the retrospective nature of the 1971 Act, and they raised the quota for passport holders from 3,600 to 5,000. But the same toxic ideas persisted. In 1976, Jenkins admitted that he believed 'there is a clear limit to the amount of immigration which this country can absorb and . . . it is in the interests of the racial minorities themselves to maintain a strict control over immigration.'[95] This demonstrates the stubborn staying power of some of the most pernicious ideas about immigration. Labour was still buying into and repeating racialised immigration narratives – but this kind of thinking, and the restrictive policies that flowed from it, certainly wasn't going unchallenged.

On a sweltering hot Friday in August 1976 Jayaben Desai strode off the Grunwick Film Processing Laboratory factory floor in Willesden, London. 'A person like me, I am never scared of anybody,' she is said to have told her managers before leading a walkout. Working long hours for little pay, workers – who had to ask permission to exercise their basic rights, like using the toilet – had finally had enough. With no union representation to speak of, they made the decision to strike. Three days later, the Grunwick dispute had begun.

The heat of the summer passed, but resistance didn't fade with it; strikers saw out a dull, wet autumn and a chilling winter, as the number of people on strike swelled to 137, largely East African Asian and female. By the time summer rolled back around again, there were regular marches through the streets of North-West London, the biggest of which was estimated to be made up of around 20,000 people. The crowd was an eclectic mix, the strikers won the backing of the National Union of Miners leader, Arthur Scargill, and striking miners and trade unionists, who travelled from across the country to stand in solidarity with the Grunwick workers. Uniting this disparate group was no small feat given the racism that ran deeply through the trade union movement. The dockworkers union that had ten years prior come out in support of Powell could now be found at Grunwick.

But the atmosphere surrounding resistance was febrile and deeply dangerous. The same summer Grunwick workers walked off the factory floor, there was a spate of separate racist murders: nineteen-year-old Dinesh Choudhri and twenty-two-year-old Riphi Alhadidi were stabbed to death by a group of white youths in Essex. In June, teenager Gurdip Singh Chaggar was stabbed in Southall – where Blair Peach was killed, almost certainly by the police, three years later during a demonstration against the National Front – and in September, sixty-year-old Mohan Dev Gautam was dragged from her home in Leamington Spa and murdered.[96] Two years later, Altab Ali, a textile worker who was born in Bangladesh, was murdered in East London in a racist attack. The response to Ali's death was powerful – people of Bangladeshi, Indian, Pakistani and Caribbean heritage joined together to protest what had happened. There were demonstrations and sit-ins near the spot Ali was murdered to challenge the National Front who organised in the area. On the day of Ali's funeral, 7,000 people marched behind his coffin chanting, 'Black and white, unite and fight.' The procession snaked through Central London, stopping at Downing Street and demanding something be done about the racism that had led to this killing.[97]

The Grunwick strike continued until a little over two months after Ali's murder. But its conclusion was not a happy one. After two years of resistance, the TUC, pressured by James Callaghan's Labour government, effectively withdrew their support for the strike. The Grunwick strikers were sold out, let down by the movement that was supposed to have their backs.[98] Despite this sour ending, Grunwick remains a significant moment in labour history. But Dr Sundari Anitha, whose work focuses on South Asian women's participation in the Grunwick strike, is sceptical of how it is remembered. Grunwick, she says, shouldn't be thought of, as it often is, 'as an exceptional moment in South Asian women's militant history because there were many other disputes where they were active before. They aren't in our consciousness because they weren't supported and therefore they failed, not for want of trying and so it's not an exception that they stood up to fight for their rights, they'd been doing it a long time before and they've done it for a long time since.'

When people celebrate Grunwick as a rare moment of migrant resistance or fetishise the women involved as 'strikers in saris',[99] they reproduce the stereotype of Asian women as submissive, passive bystanders in history. But the UK's history of racist legislation and exploitative working conditions is, it should always be remembered, also one of resistance.

Three years before Grunwick, in 1973, there was a three-month strike formed by Asian workers at the Imperial Typewriters plant in Leicester. Like Grunwick, it was ultimately unsuccessful in achieving its immediate aims, but unlike its successor, it didn't gain the support of the trade unions. Kept out of bonus schemes, paid less than white workers, forced to use separate toilets and disciplined for the most minor of infringements, Asian workers, including many women, challenged the relentless racism on the shop floor and in their pay packets by going on strike. But the TGWU representative, George Bromley, dismissed them, saying the strikers 'have got to learn to fit in with our ways'.[100]

'There was real racism from the company, but on top of that they were completely screwed by the unions,' former trade union organiser and researcher Ben Sellers explains.

'The union branch in the region would have nothing to do with them, they only saw them as a threat, and they also colluded with the management to keep them out of bonus schemes and keep them on lower pay. So there was real resentment about the union.'

Together with fellow academic Professor Ruth Pearson, Dr Anitha argues in the book *Striking Women* that one of the possible reasons the union movement supported Grunwick workers was because, unlike the Imperial Typewriters strike, there weren't any pay differences between white and black workers to challenge. In Grunwick, the workforce was divided along race lines: most of the factory floor workers were people of colour; the drivers were black men and the managers were white. 'It wasn't that people were across the different races working on the same shop floor and were being paid differently. So that solidarity within factory was probably possible because of that,' Dr Anitha says. Like many others, the Grunwick strike was about racism, but it could also be cast as concerning trade union recognition and collective bargaining. 'It became . . . easier for trade unions to mobilise to defend workers who wanted to join the union rather than workers who were critical of the way the union was functioning.'

Alongside the Imperial Typewriters strike, people were laying down tools in Woolf's rubber factory in Southall, Courtaulds' Red Scar Mill in Preston and Mansfield Hosiery Mills in Derbyshire. Part of the reasons for these worker-led strikes was that with an unofficial colour bar in operation, people of colour were concentrated in low-skilled, insecure and dangerous jobs in sectors where there were labour shortages and unsociable working hours. By the mid-1970s black and Asian male workers remained disproportionately represented in semi- or unskilled roles compared to white male workers.[101] One Indian man who settled in Birmingham in the late 1950s remarked years later, 'I didn't know any schoolteachers at that time, I didn't know anybody working in bank or office jobs, even those people who have graduated who worked as teachers back home, they were working in the factories or foundries.'[102]

As well as protesting against and resisting racist murders on the country's streets, racism in the workplace and flourishing far-right politics, working-class people of colour set up initiatives to support each other when they were racially harassed, making sure everyone understood their rights. Migrants were regularly accused of segregating themselves, but it was racism in all its different forms that kept people apart. Perhaps no one knew this better than Anwar Ditta.

Born in Birmingham in 1953, in 1962 Ditta went to live in her father's country of birth, Pakistan. When she returned back to the UK thirteen years later, married and with three children, immigration law split her family apart. Although her British passport was an automatic pass into the country, her children, who had been born in Pakistan, had to apply for the right to enter the UK. Ditta and her husband remarried when they arrived in the UK, thinking their Islamic marriage wouldn't be recognised in the country. But when they applied for their children to join them, the two marriages led the Home Office to conclude there might be two Anwar Dittas. And so, their children were denied entry and the family split apart. This is a mere glimpse of the impact successive pieces of immigration legislation have had on people's lives.

Distraught and unsure what to do, she went to an anti-deportation meeting in Manchester. There she found support for what would become the Anwar Ditta Defence campaign. The Asian Youth Movements in Manchester and Bradford, The Indian Workers' Association, Rochdale Labour Party and many other anti-racist groups supported her as she appealed the decision. Even after it was rejected, resistance continued. Her case became a cause célèbre; campaigners created so much noise that Granada TV made a documentary about

Ditta. Following all this public pressure the Home Office decision was eventually overturned.[103]

People of colour coming to the UK were being discriminated against and mistreated, yet they were by no means the pliant subjects they are often portrayed as, bending to the will of UK government. Many played influential roles in strikes across the country; challenging the UK's immigration regime and the racist, exploitative labour market as few others did.

'People are really rather afraid that this country might be rather swamped by people with a different culture', Margaret Thatcher told current affairs programme *World in Action* shortly before she became prime minister, 'and, you know, the British character has done so much for democracy, for law and done so much throughout the world that if there is any fear that it might be swamped people are going to react and be rather hostile to those coming in.'[104] The National Front had reached what would be the peak of their success at this time, but Thatcher likely knew what she was doing by using this kind of language: making more respectable their racist, anti-immigrant politics. But though her word choice was more explicit than many other politicians', it wasn't entirely out of step with how migrants were portrayed in the Palace of Westminster and beyond.

When Thatcher was in power, much of the architecture of the country's restrictive immigration policies was already in place. By 1980, visitors from the new Commonwealth and Pakistan were thirty times more likely to be refused entry into the country than people from the old Commonwealth.[105] The process to be granted permission for one's spouse to come from India took years; by contrast, the equivalent application for those from New Zealand and Canada was resolved without problem.

As she moved the whole country to the right,[106] Thatcher tightened this system further. Between 1962 and 1983, there were people all around the world who had British citizenship but not the automatic right to enter the country. The British Nationality Act 1981, which came into force two years later, fundamentally changed this – being born in this country didn't automatically entitle you to citizenship; instead, at least one parent had to be born or settled in the UK. This was, again, about race: white South Africans, for instance, were much more likely than people from all over the new Commonwealth to be able to keep citizenship because of their ancestral connections.[107]

Echoing the Conservative rhetoric on immigration, in the 1980s, people of colour – regardless of where they were born, but black people in particular – were constructed in newspapers as the enemy within. So-called 'sus' laws (also known as stop and search) were originally introduced in Victorian times to grant law enforcement the power to arrest people on the suspicion they were going to commit a crime. During the Thatcher years they resulted in the disproportionate harassment of black people by the police. This was justified by a society plunged into moral panic. Black people were characterised as being responsible for muggings, as threatening to social order in the UK, and for the country's economic decline as unemployment rose.[108] Watered down and made more 'respectable', this thinking filtered into Conservative Party literature. In a manner remarkably similar to attacks on Labour's shadow home secretary Diane Abbott in the 2017 election, in 1987 before and during the election, Conservative advertisements and newspaper reporting suggested that activists organising as part of the Labour party's black sections and two of Labour's black Parliamentary candidates – Abbott and Bernie Grant – were extremists.[109]

Thanks to decades of organising and struggle within the party, the Opposition was at the forefront of ensuring people of colour and women had seats in Parliament. But they continued to offer a confused message on immigration. Labour's

1981 manifesto still declared immigration 'controls' necessary, but said the party would repeal the 1971 and 1981 Acts because they were discriminatory. In July 1985, Shadow Home Secretary Gerald Kaufman reiterated that Labour would maintain immigration controls, but said that they would be applied in a non-racist manner. They didn't explain exactly how that would work.[110]

Racism was still rife in the UK. In 1981, an uprising broke out in Brixton, an area suffering from crippling levels of unemployment among people of colour. In 1986, as he tried to defend another Bangladeshi student from racist bullying, thirteen-year-old Ahmed Iqbal Ullah was murdered in the playground of Burnage High School by a fellow pupil.[111] Instead of trying to make sense of the racism they were creating, repeating and sustaining with their damaging narrative on crime and discord, most Conservative politicians offered nothing more than a momentary, disinterested glance. Instead, before and during Thatcher's time in office 'multiculturalism' – lambasted by anti-racists as saris, samosas and steel bands, or the three S's – meant there was more focus on superficially encouraging 'cultural' practices than on the depth and destructive power of racism in the UK.

Two terms in as prime minister, Thatcher showed little sign of letting up when it came to immigration. When there was a rise in the number of people seeking asylum, particularly from Sri Lanka, a former British colony in the midst of an intractable civil war, the government responded by bringing visas into effect. This was the first time that visas had been used for former Commonwealth countries, and the next year when staff at Heathrow Airport threatened to strike over the number of passengers coming into the country, the government brought in visa requirements for the countries from which the majority were arriving – India, Pakistan, Nigeria, Ghana and Bangladesh.[112] By 1987, ship and plane owners could be fined £1,000 for each person who came into the UK on their vehicles without a visa or valid documentation.

After Thatcher left office in 1990, the clampdown on asylum intensified. Acts passed in 1993 and 1996 increased the use of detention, which led to the building of more detention centres. Private contractors were brought in for the first time, and the government required employers to check the immigration status of every job applicant that crossed their path.[113] It was in that final Act, just before the Conservatives lost office, that the 'white list' was created. Comprising countries the Home Office said presented no real risk of persecution, the implication was that people from countries on the list did not have well-founded reason to claim asylum; they were among some of those fast-tracked through the appeals process.

Who was coming can explain why restrictive legislation was introduced from the '80s onwards. With the rise of affordable air travel, an increasing number of people were coming to Europe; in the UK the number of asylum applications went from around 2,500 to 4,000 per year in the 1980s to 84,000 in 2002. But they were also coming from different places than before. Previously in Europe, the most commonly recognised figure of the asylum seeker was a white man fleeing Communism; by the end of the century and beyond, this began to change.[114] From civil war in Sri Lanka and unrest in Somalia through to economic degradation in Zimbabwe and the US-led invasion of Afghanistan, all around the world people were fleeing conflict and persecution. There have always been significant numbers of people seeking asylum in the Global South – as a mere glance at the disaster wrought by the British partition of India shows – what changed was their destination, they increasingly were arriving in Europe.

'What was different was that they were from the Global South, usually from former European colonies. This made them undesirable,' writes political sociologist Lucy Mayblin. The legacies of colonial discourse, which classed black and brown people as somehow less than human, still survive and thrive, even as they have changed. Asylum seekers from the Global South came to be seen as 'other'. 'It is not the fact that they are marked as different as a consequence of their difference,' Mayblin says, 'but that the colonial discourses marked them as such.' This shaped successive governments' asylum policies.[115]

At the end of the 1980s, the UK had one of the strictest border regimes in Western Europe.[116] Produced by a mix of political hostility, imperial legacies and public opinion, from the 1960s, and before, both Labour and Conservative governments had made concerted efforts to limit the number of people of colour entering the UK: at its core, the nation's history on immigration legislation is a history of racism. It's in this context that the Conservative's 'hostile environment' policies can be seen for what they are – not a deviation from the norm, but well aligned with the UK's approach to race and immigration over several decades.

3

New Labour: Things Can Only Get Better?

In a society where the good is defined in terms of profit rather than in terms of human need, there must always be some group of people who, through systematized oppression, can be made to feel surplus, to occupy the place of the dehumanized inferior.

Audre Lorde, *Age, Race, Class and Sex: Women Redefining Difference*

No one had anticipated it would cause the stir it did, but when *The Future of Multi-Ethnic Britain* was published one Tuesday in early October 2000, the right-wing press were apoplectic. The *Daily Telegraph* claimed that then home secretary Jack Straw, who spoke at the report's launch, 'Wants to Rewrite Our History', and the *Sun* declared, 'Now it's racist to use the word "British."'[1] The report was the outcome of a three-year long commission, established by the race equality think tank the Runnymede Trust, which examined the changing diversity of the British population. Flawed though it might have been, the final document offered one particularly important warning, which it turned out politicians should have listened to.

'England, Scotland and Wales are at a turning point in their history,' explained the report's authors. 'They could become narrow and inward-looking, with rifts between themselves and among their regions and communities, or they could develop as a community of citizens and communities.'[2] Their words would turn out to be prophetic: Britain might not have yet splintered into its constituent parts but, sixteen years later, the UK would vote to leave the EU, triggering a sharp rise in hate crimes, and there was an increasingly rabid tenor to the political and media conversation on immigration. With renewed vigour, politicians talked about the need to control UK borders and blamed immigration for the country's problems. If the authors of this report were right and the country was at a crossroads in 2000, looking back, it seems we chose the path of further insularity.

When New Labour came to power in 1997, there was hope of change. Eighteen years of Conservative rule had sidelined, shrunk and in some cases neutralised anti-racist activities. To the tune of D:Ream's 'Things Can Only Get Better', and with the Cool Britannia campaign, New Labour fashioned themselves as a modern, 'multicultural' force that would create an inclusive vision of the country.

In the years of *Goodness Gracious Me*, Zadie Smith's *White Teeth* and *Bend It Like Beckham*, that is, the late '90s and early 2000s, it might have felt like such a transformative project was indeed taking place. New Labour were the party who introduced the 1998 Human Rights Act and the Race Relations (Amendment) Act 2000 and thanks to tireless campaigning from the family of murdered teenager, Stephen Lawrence, formed the government who commissioned the long-overdue inquiry into his death.[3] But for all the promise, one academic argued in 2008, New Labour didn't move sufficiently beyond 'a superficial notion of equal opportunities'.[4]

The UK was hardly pro-migration or a post-racial country before New Labour's time in office, but when they were in power there was an undeniable shift; immigration climbed up the list of public concerns. When I speak to Bhikhu Parekh, who was the chair of the commission that produced the prescient *Future of Multi-Ethnic Britain*, and who is now a member of the House of Lords, his explanation of what happened on the day the report was published offers to shed some light on why immigration became the issue it did.

The New Labour response was 'very strange', Parekh recalls. 'We were not quite sure how they would respond, so we had kept them in our confidence; we in fact shared the penultimate copy of the draft report with them. Jack Straw was pleased with the penultimate draft, but then some bits were leaked out and received adverse publicity, which put pressure on New Labour to change its position and it became slightly hostile.'

What seemed to be responsible for the upset among tabloid editors and journalists was the report's restrained recognition that Britishness and whiteness were still assumed to go hand-in-hand.[5] Forged during colonialism, it's as if the connection between the two is made of the groundbreaking material graphene: not possible to see with the naked eye but unbelievably strong. The academics, journalists and public figures who made up the commission appeared to agree that if politicians wanted to avoid the country becoming more insular, they needed to challenge and change this link between white identity and national identity.

Spurred on by the right-wing papers, Straw flipped the report's narrative on its head; it was the unpatriotic left, he declared, who were 'narrow, exclusionary and conservative'.[6] He leapt to the defence of patriotism; glossing over any implication that ideas of whiteness might be lurking in many peoples' understanding of who belonged in the UK.[7]

When I ask Parekh if in the years following the report the government took on board the suggestion to construct a more inclusive idea of the nation, he replies, 'The answer is yes. But what kind of national narrative came of it? There I was disappointed. The kind of Britain they aspired for is not the kind of Britain I had hoped for.'

There were some early signs this might be the case. In 1995, as the debate about the UK's borders and about Europe raged in the Conservative Party, the weekly politics magazine the *New Statesman* reported that Shadow Home Secretary Jack

Straw had told members of the European Parliament that on immigration and the EU it shouldn't be possible 'to insert a cigarette card' between Labour and the Tories.[8] Just over two years later, Labour were in power.

'I was working in government at the time (in 1997) and I was really excited,' Naaz Rashid, now a lecturer in media and cultural studies, remembers. 'Straight from the offing I was disillusioned and I think because historically Labour has always been seen as weak on law and order, weak on immigration, so it just seemed they overcompensated.'

If you look a little closer at the Race Relations (Amendment) Act 2000, you see the kind of thing Rashid means. Amid the positivity was buried a key exclusion: it was possible to discriminate on the grounds of nationality or ethnic origin when administering immigration, asylum and nationality law, but not on those of race or colour. It wasn't clear how, or if, the distinctions between those different categories could be made; there was little apparent consideration or concern that this might end up being racially discriminatory.[9]

New Labour had a huge and increasingly diverse Parliamentary majority with a young, well-polished and enigmatic leader in Tony Blair. As the Parekh report had suggested, they had space to at least begin redefining the terms of the debate on immigration, race and the nation, after decades of its being poisonous, ill-informed and racist. But their reaction to that very report suggested that wouldn't be the case. For all that was achieved, too much of New Labour's hopeful shine quickly lost its lustre; they entered Downing Street saying and doing some of the right things, but failed to deliver or seem to want to make some of the widespread, systemic change that would be required to fundamentally transform the country for the better.

Assessments of the reasons behind the notable rise in fractious, anti-migrant feeling that came in the wake of New Labour tend to overlook this Janus-faced brand of politics, which undoubtedly played a part in the way immigration is talked about and understood to this day. Instead, most analysts focus on the hard statistics on immigration, arguing that it became such a big issue because New Labour relaxed the system too much and let too many people in. In 2009, Andrew Neather, former adviser to Tony Blair and the Home Office, gave succour to this line of argument when he wrote that Labour had an intentional policy to 'open up the UK to mass migration'.[10] An article treasured by the far right, this is taken as proof that Labour were part of an elite group colluding to change the country right under the noses of 'ordinary' people but without their consent.

The facts seem to be on their side. Between 1993 and 2011 the number of people in the UK who were born abroad doubled from 3.8 million to over 7 million. And when ten new countries joined the EU in 2004, the UK was one of three member countries that didn't impose transitional controls. The number of people arriving rapidly exceeded government forecasts; the prediction was that 5,000 to 13,000 people would come to the UK, but in the end, over 1 million did – although these figures only reflect the numbers of people entering the country and don't include those who left during that time.[11]

At the same time, immigration once again became a political lightning rod; in 1999 only 5 per cent of people thought it was a priority, by December 2007 that had increased to 46 per cent.[12] Parties who traded in anti-immigration sentiment grew in popularity – the overtly racist, far-right BNP increased their number of votes from 25,832 in 1997 to 192,000 eight years later. At the 2010 election they were left with no seats, yet they briefly became the fifth biggest political party in the country. This would turn out to be the peak of their success, but, as support for the BNP declined, the anti-EU, anti-immigration UKIP grew from being the fourth largest party in vote share in 2010 to the third in the 2015 General Election, when it won 4 million votes. These two parties have different ideological foundations; unlike the BNP, UKIP didn't grow out of fascist or Nazi ideology, but they are bedfellows when it comes to the indiscriminate peddling of anti-immigration ideas.[13]

It's easy to look at this picture and accept the popular account where Tony Blair's government was too accommodating and open to migrants and where numbers of people who came in to this soft, welcoming system were too much for the public. But it's the perception of migrants, asylum seekers and refugees as undesirable 'others' and the UK as better off without them that gives immigration figures, which have no meaning in and of themselves, their significance. This meaning has been created and sustained by parties and people across the political spectrum, and that includes New Labour.

For the Roma asylum seekers who arrived in Dover on 20 October 1997, the wave of negative media coverage that day might have been distressing. Many of them had left the Czech Republic and Slovakia, fleeing persecution and potential attacks by neo-Nazi skinheads or escaping high unemployment levels and a state unwilling to protect them from systematic discrimination. They sought political asylum in Canada and then the UK.

Arriving by coach in the coastal town known for its chalky white cliffs, some having sold all their possessions to make the crossing, they waited while their applications were being processed. In the two years preceding 1997, the people seeking asylum received a mixed welcome from local residents but when the national news picked up on the Roma presence in Dover that day in mid-October, the tone was nothing short of hostile.

The *Daily Mail* invoked natural disaster language to declare: 'THE DOVER DELUGE: Pleas for action as port is flooded by gipsy asylum seekers', and the *Daily Mirror* implied that their arrival was a cause for concern: 'CRISIS TALKS ON GYPSIES'. But it wasn't just the tabloids who issued hysterical warnings about the Roma people arriving in the UK. The *Independent* focused on the supposed greediness of the people seeking refuge, announcing, 'Gypsies invade Dover, hoping for a handout'. Other papers focused on numbers: *The Times* declared, 'Dover overwhelmed by Gypsy asylum-seekers,' and though the meaning was vastly different from the *Daily Mail*, an article on page five of the *Guardian* used similarly dehumanising language: 'Tide of Gypsy asylum ebbs'.[14] A glance at the headlines in some of the UK's national newspapers on this day would have suggested inordinate numbers of undeserving and freeloading 'others' were coming to take over the country.

Though certain journalists tried to dispel the myths surrounding the Roma, they were soon dubbed 'bogus' asylum seekers, as particular papers homed in on a Czech documentary that showed one Roma family moving from eastern Slovakia to the UK. The *Independent* implied it was 'the lure of promised lands' that encouraged people to take the arduous journey to Dover.[15] Labour immigration minister Mike O'Brien did little to challenge these ideas: he told the *Daily Mail* he wanted to make it clear the UK was not a 'soft touch' for 'gypsies' who were 'seeking an easy life'.[16] An editorial in the *Dover Express* described asylum seekers in the town as 'a nation's human sewage'.[17] Almost everywhere you looked were images of Roma as greedy and out for what they could get, while the severe anti-Roma racism they were trying to escape was sidelined.[18]

Throughout history, Roma communities have been oppressed and harassed: driven from their homes in the late fifteenth and early sixteenth century, targeted with sterilisation programmes in twentieth-century Scandinavia and killed in gas chambers by the Nazis.[19] In England, a series of laws were passed between the sixteenth and eighteenth centuries that limited Roma freedom and, until 1793, you could be imprisoned or expelled from the country just for being Roma.[20] 'The Romani community is very diverse, some of us are migrants . . . but our family has been here for 500 years,' Jake Bowers, a part Romani journalist, tells me. 'As soon as we try and enter a community the reaction is exactly the same, which is "Oh, god, the gypsies are coming."'

Commonplace and often considered socially acceptable in all kinds of political circles, anti-Roma sentiment could still be found at the heart of government two years after scare stories about Roma asylum seekers were on national newspaper front pages. 'There are relatively few real Romany gypsies left, who seem to mind their own business and don't cause trouble to other people, and then there are a lot more people who masquerade as travellers or gypsies . . . but who seem to think because they label themselves travellers that therefore they've got a licence to commit crimes and act in an unlawful way that other people don't have,' then home secretary Jack Straw told BBC regional radio in 1999. 'Many of these so-called travellers seem to think it's perfectly OK for them to cause mayhem in an area, to go burgling, thieving, breaking into vehicles, causing all kinds of trouble, including defecating in the doorways of firms and so on, and getting away with it.'[21] From the most unimaginative stereotypes to the most ridiculous and offensive, Straw unquestioningly regurgitated all the old scare stories about Roma.

The particular racial stereotypes used to attack the Roma stemmed from a long history of anti-Roma prejudice. But this was also part of a broader anti-asylum narrative that New Labour deployed almost from the day they took office.

In 1998 Straw claimed there was 'no doubt that large numbers of economic migrants are abusing the system by claiming asylum', fuelling both anti-migrant and anti-asylum narratives at the same time. After stigmatising asylum seekers through a voucher scheme that denied them access to money in excess of £10, in 2001, he admitted to the *Observer* that no matter what the government's international obligations, 'There is a limit on the number of [asylum] applicants, however genuine, that you can take.' Once he had taken over as home secretary, David Blunkett channelled Margaret Thatcher to declare asylum seekers' children were 'swamping' schools while he was defending a bill that would give the government the right to take asylum seekers' children out of the mainstream education system.[22] New Labour also embraced detention centres – previously championed by Ann Widdecombe – by vastly expanding the number of them in the UK.

By 2003, Blair was announcing that asylum applications would be cut in half within the space of seven months. Neil Gerrard, who was a Labour MP at the time, remembers this claim and describes it as 'ludicrous' and former immigration barrister Frances Webber recalls being shocked by such a statement. 'It's like saying we've got to get the numbers of primary school children down – how? People have needs, they're there, what are you going to do, cull them?'

The punitive policies came thick and fast. Asylum seekers no longer had the right to work, and for people who applied for asylum in-country, access to support was limited to those who could prove they had submitted their application 'as soon as reasonably practicable'. It was in this hostile system that, according to some reports, in the eighteen months before July 2008, the number of refused asylum seekers and refugees who were destitute doubled and the number of people forced to sleep rough significantly increased.[23] This was a significant part of New Labour's asylum policy: dehumanising asylum seekers while cutting support to the bare minimum.

Blair's former adviser Matthew Taylor tells me that New Labour wanted to appear credible when it came to enforcing borders. But striving for credibility in an area that requires humanity led Labour to vilify asylum seekers, pushing the national conversation deeper into xenophobic territory. Polling in 2002 found that people thought there were ten times the numbers of refugees in the UK than there actually were.[24]

By constantly depicting asylum seekers' motivations as disingenuous and implying they were taking advantage of UK hospitality, New Labour just strengthened anti-immigration politics. 'You can't tell someone you're an asylum seeker,' Nora, who came to the UK trying to seek asylum, remembers. 'When we used to live in a hostel to get weekly subsistence, you sort of hide it from people. We went to college for about six months, you would hide from your classmates that you were an asylum seeker and that you're actually going to social services. So you would hide because you're ashamed that you're poor.'

'The real story was a sense of pessimism that they would be able to make this [immigration] a popular policy,' recalls Don Flynn, former director of Migrants' Rights Network, in a soft Liverpudlian accent when I meet him in Central London. Now retired, Flynn is a mild-mannered man who worked in the migration sector for most of his career. He seems to have an encyclopaedic knowledge of immigration policy under New Labour and is candid in his analysis.[25]

'The immigration minster . . . I remember cornering him at a conference within six months of Labour getting elected,' Flynn explains as he takes a bite out of the croissant that is sitting on the wooden table between us, 'saying, "This is really your opportunity, you've got a completely fresh start . . . You could do something that nobody has ever done before, which is at least get people to understand immigration, if not make it popular." And he looked at me and said, "That will never happen. Everything that we know about immigration is that it is a complete no-no."'

The distinction between asylum and immigration is blurred and fluid but there was a difference in New Labour's approach to the two. Unambiguously anti-asylum, their relationship with immigration was more complex. Their policies seemed to vacillate between forging a new, more flexible system – though for many of the people moving through it, this was still riddled with thorns – and sticking with the old, albeit reformulated, restrictive script. And as Flynn's encounter suggests, one of the core problems was that they never fundamentally broke with the idea that some of the people coming into the country posed a problem to the UK.

In a relatively distinct break from what had come before, New Labour rejected attempts to reduce the number of people coming into the country with no justification and focused on the economic importance of immigration. In 2000, Barbara Roche, the immigration minister at the time, gave a speech symbolising this shift, announcing that immigration had a 'very positive impact' on countries like the UK.

Prior to New Labour coming to power, many were looking to migrants from the Global South as well as Eastern Europe (whose home countries weren't then in the EU) as a potential and often cheap labour supply to remediate acute shortages in various sectors. Under what the government called 'managed migration', which was supposed to refer to immigration policy that was based on evidence, Blair vastly expanded the ways people could get into the UK from outside the EU and reformed the systems that had been developed in an uneven way. New Labour broadened existing schemes and launched new ones for 'low-' and 'high-' skilled migrants, increased the number of international students and relaxed the criteria for work permits.[26]

Some of the more hostile aspects of the immigration system were also softened. When they came into office, New Labour quickly scrapped the long-hated primary purpose rule. Introduced by Thatcher's Conservative government in 1980, this made the near-impossible request that people who were married to British citizens had to prove the main reason for their marriage wasn't to obtain British residence. Thousands of couples were separated in the process. New Labour granted leave to remain to around 70,000 people who were waiting for their applications to be processed and brought in reforms to enable same-sex partners of British nationals to qualify for residency.[27]

But Flynn recounts how New Labour's strategy was to communicate to the public that, even if large numbers of people were coming into the country, the government would manage resources effectively to cope. So while they did shift the narrative a bit by pointing out the economic benefits of migration, albeit in a fairly muted way, they were focused on making the system 'efficient' rather than changing it altogether.[28]

Worried that people already thought of them as out of touch on issues like borders and immigration,[29] Blair and his team flexed their muscles. They would say, Flynn remembers, 'we've got it all under control, we know each and every one of them, they're being allowed into the country on the understanding that they would be contributing positively as workers and if they stepped out of line we have the enforcement capacity to grab hold of them and whisk them out of the country as quickly as possible.'

To make more sense of how this approach was understood, I ask someone who was heavily involved in the New Labour project. When we meet in a small church café in Cambridge, Charles Clarke, who was appointed home secretary in 2004, wastes no time in talking me through New Labour's thinking on immigration. 'The core way to solve the migration issue is to have a regime for governing migration, which is rational, is accepted and which people can then support,' he tells me, 'and then for that to be fairly and reasonably administered and run. And that remains the way through, not closing the borders, not putting in numbers.' When I leave our meeting, I feel like I've been New Labour–ed. Clarke is to the point and he sounds convincing; his rationale appears reasonable and he even frames it in such a way that makes it appear fair.

But on the walk back to the train station, I think about what he told me and begin to focus on the detail. The 'regime' he talks about was far from even-handed. 'Managed migration' didn't substantively change conditions for migrants but created a flexible migrant labour force, and in a deregulated jobs market, that included bringing in cheap, disposable labour, people who would do the '3Ds': jobs that were dirty, dangerous and difficult.[30]

Flexibility didn't flow both ways. While people in high-level migration schemes could bring their family with them, settling and moving between jobs with relative ease, some of those on 'low' schemes were bound to their positions. Their ability to reside in the country was dependent on their employer and they couldn't always easily access the same rights. One particular scheme only allowed residency for one year, making it almost impossible for some people to recoup the money they spent migrating in the first place. Faced with the prospect of returning home in debt, many stayed on without papers. Others who were able to stay for longer worked in low-paid, unpleasant jobs, enduring bad working conditions and having little access to rights.[31] People were functioning more like commodities than human beings, being instrumentally managed to fill jobs and boost the UK economy.

'New Labour was about reducing everything to pounds and pennies. That's why, in a way, the New Labour project is actually the antithesis of the left,' Stewart Wood, former adviser to both Gordon Brown and Ed Miliband, argues, 'because it tries to solve everything in terms of more money. You know Marx didn't get out of bed to defend public spending, he got out of bed because people were being exploited at work and alienated from their labour, those are philosophical concerns.' With their economy-focused messaging on managed migration, an assiduous focus on the 'pounds and pennies' helped frame New Labour's immigration policy. The reason many of the people who came into the country were able to do so was, as Roche seemed to suggest, that they would be good for the economy.

Although not every single decision New Labour made was part of a grand, calculated plan – their approach to immigration was a mixture of ideology, triangulation and reaction – the people who came into the UK did so on the basis that they would slot into a specific economic model. 'I always thought my job was to build on some of the things she had done rather than reverse them,' Tony Blair said when Margaret Thatcher died in 2013. 'Many of the things she said, even though they pained people like me on the left . . . had a certain creditability.'[32] New Labour inherited an economy over-reliant on the financial system and riven with poverty.

Instead of recognising the fundamental flaws of this economic model and intervening, the government pursued the 'Third Way' – a political ideology that borrows ideas from the right and left – and under the cover of modernisation, embraced neoliberalism. New Labour blunted some of its sharpest edges, introducing tax credits and a minimum wage (although this was set at the meagre £3.60 an hour), but they also slashed business taxes, deregulated the market, refused to build council housing and upheld what Blair called 'the most restrictive trade union laws in the Western world'.[33] Inequality increased and a low-wage labour market left many workers vulnerable. At the same time, public services continued to be overstressed as state support – which mitigated some of the worst effects of the system – was attacked. Bringing people into this system through 'managed migration', with the aim of creating a more pliable workforce, was hardly the hallmark of progress, and eventually New Labour's claims that immigration was good for the economy would look like a lie when wages began to stagnate and right-wing politicians placed the blame at the door of the newcomers. This message was even more convincing given how migrants and minorities had, at times, already been singled out as a threat to the country.

These strategies of blame, which have deep historical roots, had never been sufficiently challenged by New Labour. They refused to confront the deeply held, racialised belief that certain immigrants were a threat and that strong borders were the only way to keep the public happy – instead reinforcing these ideas in their own way.

In 2003, the home secretary at the time, David Blunkett, told BBC political programme *Newsnight* that there was 'no obvious limit' to immigration.[34] But in the space of just over a year between 2003 and 2004, immigration and police officers conducted an estimated 235 immigration raids in public spaces in London, stopping and questioning people suspected as 'immigration offenders'. In April 2003, the government made public their decision to deport twenty-one people to Afghanistan.[35] And months before, Blunkett was dismissing institutional racism as a mere 'slogan' which 'missed the point'. Doreen Lawrence, campaigner and mother of murdered teenager Stephen Lawrence, said the government had 'lost interest' in race.[36]

New Labour acted as if their policies had entirely decoupled immigration and race, and yet they weren't willing to challenge some of the inveterate ideas on immigration which had stubbornly been created and recreated in the preceding decades. 'They kept on conceiving a national narrative, except that the narrative was not sufficiently inclusive, not sufficiently probing. They never came to terms, for example, with colonialism and imperialism or with a class divided society,' chair of the Commission on the Future of Multi-Ethnic Britain, Bhikhu Parekh, says. Refusing to recognise the country's past, Chancellor Gordon Brown said of Empire: Britain 'should celebrate much of our past rather than apologise for it'.[37]

The government's reaction to violence in post-industrial towns in the north of England, in places like Burnley, Bradford and Oldham, in the spring and summer of 2001, confirmed how fraught their engagement with race and immigration was.

Not a single party leader visited Oldham after violence broke out in the middle of the General Election campaign.[38] The BNP had been campaigning in the area and tensions between white and Asian people were continuing to grow, so when the police responded to white racist gangs in Oldham by arresting Asian as well as white people, violence ensued. But this was also a sign of decades of economic and social exclusion. Young Asian people clashed with the police because they were tired of being ignored by government officials who would only listen to individuals selected as 'community leaders'. Having seen how their parents – many of whom had come from Pakistan and Bangladesh – had been funnelled into low-paid jobs or forced into unemployment after factory closures shrank job opportunities, they had little hope for the future. This was a common story across the country; people of colour were still being discriminated against. Asian people and white people in northern towns, forced to compete for jobs, retreated into their own communities.[39] Economically disenfranchised and attacked by racists, violence was one of the only options for young Asian people to make themselves heard.

This was almost entirely lost in the government response. Home Secretary David Blunkett treated people of colour as if they were outsiders. Focusing on the 'integration' of people newly entering the country, as well as of those so-called 'established' migrant communities,[40] he argued that, to achieve harmonious community relations, 'people should have the wherewithal, such as the ability to speak English'. 'We have norms of acceptability,' Blunkett said shortly before two reports into the disturbances were released. 'And those who come into our home – for that is what it is – should accept those norms just as we would have to do if we went elsewhere.'[41] Though more nuanced than Blunkett's assertion, one of the reports – the government-commissioned Cantle Report – reproduced these ideas, treating 'ethnic groups' as homogenous and suggesting British Asians weren't sufficiently 'integrated' into British society. Just two months before, then Conservative Party leader William Hague had warned that the country under New Labour would become a 'foreign land'. Now the Labour home secretary was calling for citizenship classes and language lessons, as though none of the people involved were British. This response exposed what a group of scholars called New Labour's 'white heart'.[42]

'We saw the underside of the Labour policy, they called it "Fairer, Faster and Firmer"' (the name of the government's 1998 white paper on immigration and asylum), former barrister Frances Webber recalls, 'but what we saw . . . was very tough.' This seemed to be their strategy: deportations paired with clampdowns gave off the impression that the country was being protected from threatening people who didn't belong.[43]

From as early as 1997, New Labour had begun whittling away civil liberties, but 9/11 and the unfolding 'War on Terror', along with the 7/7 bombings in London, precipitated rapid expansion of the surveillance state. Muslims in particular were marked as racialised outsiders who endangered the nation. And though the groups are often conflated in public debate, migrants and asylum seekers were singled out too; controlling immigration of the 'wrong' kinds of people was part of New Labour's tough approach to law and order. A string of ministerial resignations and Home Office scandals in the early to mid-2000s made the need to appear in control seem urgent.[44] In the party's 2005 manifesto all proposals about immigration were included under a section titled 'Crime and Security'. By the time of the 2010 General Election, they had a manifesto section called 'Crime and Immigration', as if the two fit together hand and glove.[45]

This was part of New Labour's liberal politics: some inclusive rhetoric peppered with a smattering of socially progressive policies but weighed down with social authoritarianism. A pro-economy immigration regime that expanded the number of routes into the country was set against a backdrop of exploitative working conditions, racialised immigration rhetoric, deportations, raids and 'assertive' border controls. Looking back on twenty years since New Labour won power, Blair's former speechwriter and strategist Peter Hyman said he admired that his boss 'never pandered on immigration', claiming 'it was the best time to be British'.[46]

~

The anti-racist movement in the UK wasn't what it used to be, but when nine detainees from Campsfield House immigration detention centre were arrested, they weren't alone. The Campsfield Nine Defence Campaign was established to support the detainees, and it called for all of those on trial to be freed and granted refugee status and for Home Secretary Jack Straw to resign. Resistance still existed, and it came in all kinds of forms.

The struggle for justice began in the early morning of 20 August 1997, when detainees in the Campsfield House removal centre were woken by cries of pain as two West African asylum seekers were violently taken out of their cells by guards who worked for Group 4, the private company that ran the facility and that would later become G4S. They were going to be deported without warning. Distressed by what was happening and wanting to show their support for their fellow detainees, people held inside the centre began to protest and unrest broke out. Parts of the building were damaged and set on fire, and a handful of those alleged to have been involved were arrested.

When the case went to trial, it became clear that the detainees weren't the only people to have caused damage. Security camera recordings contradicted statements from Group 4 staff. One staff member said that detainees had smashed phones on that day in August, but the video appeared to show that he was responsible, while another who denied strangling one of the people who was being deported was seen on the footage with his hands around the detainee's neck. It had been expected to last three months, but after seventeen days of trial – held an arduous ten months after the incident in which time four of the defendants attempted suicide – the case against the nine accused fell apart. Throughout this long process, the movement behind the nine did all they could to support them and try to lobby for their release.

Immigration detention mushroomed under New Labour and opposition grew along with it. Hunger strikes and campaigns were staged within the walls of the centres, and protesters organised outside them. Some were backed by trade unions, many of which themselves had a national policy of closing all detention centres. Publishing newsletters and organising meetings, the National Coalition of Anti-Deportation Campaigns (NCADC) fought against deportation, as well as to defend migrants' rights more widely.

Local migrant and refugee groups sprang up across the country, including Dover Residents Against Racism, which campaigned against attacks on asylum seekers in the town. Black-led organisations like the National Assembly Against Racism (NAAR) focused some of their campaigning on supporting refugees and undocumented migrants, and when Labour's Asylum and Immigration Bill in 1997–98 passed through the Commons, the NCADC and the NAAR established the Campaign for Asylum and Immigration Rights (CAIR) as other groups tried to lobby behind the scenes.[47]

The indispensability of resistance was apparent from the early years of New Labour's first term. At the start of the new millennium, the government tried to implement a new system for asylum seekers whereby people waiting on their applications who needed state support weren't given money but paper vouchers that could only be used in specified shops. The rules were so stringent that, if their weekly or daily shopping amounted to less than the value of their voucher, they weren't allowed any change. Bill Morris from the TGWU called it 'degrading and inhuman' and John McDonnell, a backbench Labour MP at the time, attacked it as 'outstandingly reactionary' and 'racist'.[48] It was eventually stopped when protests led by asylum seekers at supermarkets in the North-East turned into a national campaign supported by the Refugee Council, Oxfam and TGWU, but the fact the government tried to get away with it at all spoke volumes as to the depths to which they would sink on asylum.

McDonnell was part of a small but organised group of Labour MPs who resisted the government's punitive asylum measures. Another was Neil Gerrard, then MP for Waltham-stow. When we meet at his home in east London, Gerrard explains the difficulties of organising resistance, as his fluffy tabby cat prowls around his living room, eventually settling on a warm radiator under the window as a suitable spot to nap. 'There wasn't a big number, but there were enough Labour MPs concerned to provide opposition to some of . . . the bills that went through. Both Tory and Labour sometimes. Just one or two bits of the bill or sometimes it was the whole bill.' There was support from groups beyond Parliament but, he says as he takes a sip of tea, 'It felt like an uphill battle at the time.'

Amnesty International, the Refugee Council, the Immigration Law Practitioners' Association, lawyers and advocacy groups picked over each government policy when it was announced and tried to stop some of the most pernicious pieces of legisla-tion making it through Parliament. This shows how legal processes can act as a counterweight to violent, restrictive policies. When in 2004 New Labour tried to make it near impossible for asylum claimants to have decisions on their applications reviewed by the courts – they wanted to create a system whereby people would only have had a single appeal to a newly created asylum and immigration tribunal – refugee groups, lawyers and the lord chief justice came together to stop them.[49] Although the government was contributing to a toxic environment for those seeking safety, instilling in the public a sense that asylum seekers and certain migrants weren't to be trusted and implementing regressive policy, they were not an unstoppable force given carte blanche to do what-ever they wanted. Relatively small though it might have been, there was opposition and it did make a difference.

By the time of the 2005 election, immigration was *the* Tory election issue. 'Immigration must be brought under control. It is essential for good community relations, national security and the management of public services,' Conservative leader Michael Howard declared. 'Only my party has the courage to tell the truth about immigration and the courage to act.'[50] Famous for arguing it wasn't racist to be concerned about immigration, Howard, with the rest of the Conservative Party in tow, created a patchwork campaign stitched together by xenophobia. This was the first of many times that Australian strategist Lynton Crosby, well-known for spearheading divisive campaigns, would be on the Conservative payroll.

Inflammatory messages were splashed across candidates' local leaflets. 'What bit of "send them back" don't you understand Mr Blair?' one demanded; another claimed their constituency had 'unlimited immigration'.[51] As the Tories were honing in on immigration and thus giving more credence to far-right messaging, support for the BNP and UKIP was increasing. In the 2004 European elections, UKIP received 2,650,768 votes and picked up another ten seats to add to their existing two. The BNP received just over 800,000 votes in those same elections.[52]

Meanwhile turnout had been falling since 1992 and Britain's two main parties were witnessing long-term membership decline. The invasion of Iraq – which went ahead despite hundreds of thousands of people marching through the streets of London against it, me, as a young teenager, included – long-term deindustrialisation, wage stagnation and lack of affordable housing left many feeling disconnected from what they saw as an out-of-touch elite. With not much hope or faith in a democratic system that offered the political equivalent of different shades of the same colour, a lot of people simply stopped voting altogether. Though they comfortably won the 2005 election, New Labour lost fifty-eight seats in the process; it was clear they were rapidly losing support. Having abandoned the party's long-term class analysis, the government appeared relatively content with chasing the biggest slice of an ever-shrinking pie. Far-right parties like the BNP sought to capitalise on this mood, and they did so with some success. In Barking and Dagenham, council housing had been sold off under Thatcher and no real replacements had been built, creating an acute housing shortage. Hijacking class grievances, the BNP blamed migrants and people of colour for the lack of housing.[53]

In 2006, Labour minister Margaret Hodge and MP for Barking fed these ideas, blithely claiming that in her constituency white people were no longer supporting Labour because 'they can't get a home for their children, [there are] black and ethnic minority communities moving in and they are angry.' This carried echoes of the BNP; in the 2005 election they circulated a leaflet that read 'Africans for Essex Scheme', claiming people from the African continent were incentivised by Barking council to buy houses in the area. A year later, Hodge modified her message slightly, saying her constituents 'feel that they've grown up in the borough, they're entitled to a home, and that sense of entitlement is often overridden by a real need of new immigrant families who come in'. When she was criticised by colleagues and the GMB union, who called for her resignation, the BNP came out to back her.[54]

It wasn't just ministers turned seeming outliers like Hodge who were trying to manage anti-immigration politics – Blair was doing it in a different and somewhat subtler way. 'Tony was watching it like a hawk throughout the campaign, to decide whether we needed to deal with it as an issue in the election campaign,' Charles Clarke recalls of immigration during the 2005 General Election campaign, 'and he finally decided that the way to do it was to do a speech in Dover.'

On 22 April 2005, Blair went to the seaside town where years before Roma people seeking asylum had arrived hoping to find safety, only to be met with hostility. It was here that he delivered one of the main speeches of the 2005 election campaign. He did so smoothly and self-confidently. 'Concern over asylum and immigration is not about racism. It is about fairness. People want to know that the rules and systems we have in place are fair.' When the time came for the photo op after the speech, the audience behind him was entirely white.

When I ask Matthew Taylor about this, he says it wasn't intentional.

'I was pretty heavily involved in that campaign. It would have to have been a pretty big secret if there was an attempt to say, "Let's do it with a kind of subliminal message of whiteness." I'm pretty confident in saying if that was the case it was insensitivity rather than in any sense deliberate.'

Intentional or not, the location, the optics and the sea of 150 white faces – all of whom were loyal activists or councillors – read like a clumsy attempt to appeal to exclusionary English nationalism.[55] Labour messaging still reflected the supposed importance of protecting British borders from outsiders and did nothing to address the connection between national identity and white identity that the *Future of Multi-Ethnic Britain* report had identified and been criticised for five years earlier.

Not everyone remembers the 2005 campaign this way. Charles Clarke, home secretary at the time, recalls a sensible Labour government standing against an unreasonable Conservative Party. They had 'a completely incoherent position', he says. 'They had what we called a fantasy island, which they were going to deport people to – it became a joke.' Matthew Taylor tells me in a matter-of-fact way that during that very election campaign – which Labour stood a very possible chance of losing – the Tories mobilised 'dog whistle politics', showing 'they were not fit for office', whereas Labour's approach showed that as 'progressives' they understood that 'people have concerns' and that 'we share that concern', but they wouldn't 'pander to any notion that migration is . . . bad for the country or that diversity is problematic'. Such claims conveniently ignore the fact that, with their response to the unrest of 2001 and their programme of deportations and citizenship tests, New Labour had already accepted that the 'wrong' kind of immigration was unacceptable, that certain people were a threat to the nation, and that embracing nationalistic messages was key to maintaining support.

Faced with the prospect of the BNP winning three seats in local elections in Burnley in 2002, New Labour advisor Philip Gould said the party should accept voters' concerns on migration and asylum.[56] In the five-year plan laid out in a White Paper months before the 2005 General Election, Blair appeared to do just that. He spoke of contributions that successive generations of migrants had made to the UK but said 'traditional tolerance is under threat. It is under threat from those who come and live here illegally by breaking our rules and abusing our hospitality.' This fed the idea that people entering the country were out for what they could get, and that they might destabilise the nation. As part of the government's focus on 'integration', in a 2006 speech, Blair made a somewhat farcical proclamation: 'Our tolerance is part of what makes Britain, Britain. So conform to it; or don't come here.'[57]

There was a hardening consensus among New Labour politicians that immigration could be bad for the country in ways they had not previously considered and that government needed to vastly reduce the number of people coming in, or at the very least, reassure the public by implementing harsher control measures and nationalistic messaging.

In 2007, Home Secretary John Reid, who was known for taking an overtly tough stance on immigration, showed that he had few qualms about pitting people against each other. He claimed that it was 'an underlying reality that we have not been tough enough in policing access to such services as council housing, legal aid or NHS care'.[58] The year before, with public discourse increasingly focused on European freedom of movement, he had announced that the British labour market would be closed to Romanians and Bulgarians when their countries joined the EU in January 2007. That same year, the government extended the length of time immigrants had to wait to become eligible for residency from four to five years and the year before that they abolished a scheme that let non-EU graduate doctors work in training posts without a permit; to get one would mean proving there was no British or EU graduates who could fill the post.[59] There was a human cost to these policies.

Dr Imran Yousaf left Lahore to finish his training. He came to the UK thinking that the NHS was in desperate need of staff. Two years after he arrived, he was still unable to find a post, despite having applied for countless positions, and when the changes to the training scheme were announced in 2006, he was left desperate. When the British Association of Physicians of Indian Origin (BAPIO) took the Department of Health to court, he joined the suit – but he wouldn't live to see the verdict. In 2007, he killed himself. There was no suicide note, but next to his body sat a letter from immigration officials informing him that he couldn't have any more extensions on his visa.[60]

Chuba arrived in the UK when New Labour were in power. He didn't have much knowledge of how the immigration system worked, but he quickly learned just how forbidding it could be. Twenty years after he first set foot in this country, hoping it would be a place he could seek asylum, he is still in debt from court fees and administration charges. 'I have a full-time job, but I sometimes do part-time jobs just to keep me going because I ended up in so much debt through the process . . . I don't know how bad it would be if I didn't have people helping me.'

I met Chuba in a crowded coffee shop not long before Christmas 2017. Already dark outside, it's the kind of bitter evening people hurry home to escape from, but we're in no rush. Sitting in a spacious but bustling café, surrounded by

people laden with shopping bags and others working dili-
gently on their laptops, Chuba explains what happened to
him. He was hurriedly helped to leave his home country in
North Africa at the age of twenty-two by family concerned
that his involvement in student politics would put him in
danger, and came to seek asylum in the UK in the early 2000s,
by which time, New Labour had already played their role in
creating a poisonous climate for asylum seekers. More likely
to be seen as statistics than human beings, people like Chuba
were an inconvenience for a government determined to reduce
asylum numbers at almost any cost. His application was
denied. When he was waiting for the verdict on his appeal, he
was detained out of the blue, and from the inside of a detention centre, he was told he was going to be sent back home.

Chuba spent the next year in his country of birth trying to
get back to the UK, which he eventually did with help from
his friends, family and his local Labour MP. But when the time
came for him to apply for permanent residency, the Home
Office sat on his paperwork for two years. 'I kept chasing, I
even at some point thought the solicitor didn't send the
application. I kept waiting, waiting, waiting.' With a stable
job in the NHS, a young son born in the UK and network of
friends, almost all of Chuba's life was in this country. One
day in the middle of January he was called into a meeting and
found out that the Home Office had refused his application.
The message was clear: 'I couldn't carry on working, so I had
to go home.' After contemplating an appeal, he eventually
applied for the right to stay in the country and won – but not
before he had lost his job in the UK's health service. On paper,
everything that happened to Chuba might seem straightforward; the setbacks he experienced can be explained in a
couple of paragraphs, the status problems he had for years
resolved in one page. But what he had to endure was long-
drawn-out waiting periods, uncertainty hanging over him as
his anxiety about whether he'd be able to stay in the country

grew and he was forced to struggle to get by on what money he could scrape together in the meantime.

While Chuba was fighting to stay in the country, Gordon Brown, who had recently become prime minister, was in Brighton telling the TUC conference he wanted 'a British job on offer for every British worker'. At Labour Party conference that month, he repeated the same slogan, and later in the speech, followed it up: 'Let me be clear: any newcomer to Britain who is caught selling drugs or using guns will be thrown out. No-one who sells drugs to our children or uses guns has the right to stay in our country.' The BNP capitalised on Brown's words. 'British jobs for British workers,' they declared. 'When we say it, we mean it.'[61]

When power changed hands from Blair to Brown in June 2007, there was no obvious reflection on the impact that anti-immigration politics or policies were having on the UK; no thought for what it meant for people like Chuba when the government of the day peddled anti-migrant messages or pushed through aggressive legislation.

Then the 2008 crash happened. Resentment towards an out-of-touch political class and an economic system that didn't deliver on the fairness it promised had been building for decades. But the crash seemed to confirm how disconnected those in power were from the people they were supposed to represent; parts of the population that had been promised change, opportunity and a decent future were faced with a rotten but still intact status quo. The 2009 MPs' expenses scandal only hardened the idea that politicians in Westminster formed part of a distant and unconcerned elite.

As this was all unfolding, Labour continued to stick with Brown's 'British jobs' line. When Home Secretary Jacqui Smith tightened the points-based system that had been introduced in 2008 – which targeted recruitment of higher skilled workers while reforming the eighty different entry schemes in the UK by importing them into a new, five-tier system – she argued, 'It is right in a downturn . . . to do more to put British workers first.'[62]

Irrespective of the xenophobia that politicians touted, people everywhere were struggling, migrants included. Finding himself unemployed right in the midst of the financial crash, Chuba had to look for ways to get by. While he was still waiting for status, he was forced to take cash-in-hand jobs in restaurants for just £2 an hour because he wasn't allowed to work and, since there was almost no state support for him, his vulnerability could be exploited. Chuba looks at the positives and becomes particularly animated when he talks about all the people who helped him, including the friend who loaned him £2,000 for immigration fees. But even now that he has a job and papers, the debt he's racked up has had long-term effects. He says he was lucky to make it through the whole process: 'If you have to be struggling like that, it's just easy to find yourself in a place where . . . you've got nothing to lose . . . and that's the reality of it. For me at forty-two, I kept thinking . . . I probably would have gone to university . . . it's something that I still aspire to but I have to be realistic. I have huge debt so I can't just go off and study again.'

As Chuba was struggling to stay afloat, Labour continued to read from the same script. During campaigning for the 2010 General Election, which Labour would go on to lose and which Brown had waited three years into his premiership before calling, they were promising to 'control immigration' through their points-based system. Though they rejected Tory calls for a quota, they promised a rise in employment and wages, 'not rising immigration', while boasting that net migration and the number of asylum claims had fallen. This proved, they proudly said, that they were acting on people's 'concerns about immigration'.[63]

As had become normal for New Labour, recognition of those concerns included a focus on the material and the 'cultural'. While they were promising 'British jobs for British workers', as part of a broader authoritarian pressure to embrace Britishness, and bearing some similarities with their response to the 2001 disturbances, Brown devised a citizenship strategy with the aim of 'increasing public confidence' in immigration policy.[64] He planned different stages to citizenship, including a series of tests and requirements that would determine the right to stay in the UK. Brown, who had in 2006 suggested creating a 'national day' to celebrate Britishness, continued to oversee an agenda that treated particular people coming into the country as a threat to both security and fabled ideas of national identity.[65]

Then, just over a week before people went to the polls, New Labour's hypocrisy on immigration was put on show for an already-disenfranchised public to see. Surrounded by journalists, photographers and aides, Brown was on the campaign trail in Rochdale, a satellite town in Greater Manchester, when he had a brief conversation with lifelong Labour voter Gillian Duffy. She told Brown she was worried about education, the health service, and our ability to look after the vulnerable but she was also worried about 'immigrants'. 'You can't say anything about immigrants . . . All these Eastern European what are coming in, where are they flocking from?' she asked.[66] This showed the way the debate had changed shape or expanded, in that, it wasn't people of colour who she focused on, but migrants from certain European countries, people who many might automatically imagine as white. What remained the same was a familiar political response: avoidance. Brown replied by pointing out that British people migrate to Europe as well as Europeans coming to live here, before swiftly changing the topic to healthcare and education.

As he left, not realising he was still wearing a microphone, he climbed back into his car and turned to his aides to tell them that his conversation with Duffy was a 'disaster'. Then he uttered two of the words that would come to define this interaction: she was a 'bigoted woman'.

The leader who had embraced the fascistic phrase 'British jobs for British workers' wasn't willing to robustly challenge anti-immigration sentiment in his political campaigning, instead reinforcing it and saving any critical thoughts that he might harbour – regardless how crude – for behind closed doors. Brown's mistake was telling, and in some ways encapsulated the problem contained in New Labour's six immigration acts, raft of secondary legislation and reams of hostile rhetoric. Like so many politicians and journalists before him and countless who would come after him, it was as if he believed people's views to be entirely unconnected to the political climate around them that he had helped create.

One Saturday in March 2015, with a general election just months away, I was working the weekend shift for LabourList, a website that covers news and comment from across the labour movement, when a piece of election merchandise went on sale on the party's online shop. By the next morning, it had become the subject of multiple news stories. For £5, party supporters could own a mug in characteristic Labour red imprinted with a slogan in bold white lettering: 'controls on immigration'. A cascade of criticism followed online, with people questioning what such a vague phrase even meant. Diane Abbott, a backbench Labour MP at the time, tweeted a picture of the mug, branding it 'shameful' and an 'embarrassment'. Images of it still crop up on social media as a symbol of Labour's capitulation to the right on immigration under Ed Miliband.[67]

Elected as Labour leader in 2010, as a representative of the soft-left, Miliband was supposed to signal a change for the party. Having taken part in fifty-two nationwide hustings with him during the leadership election, Abbott has a particularly novel insight into the Miliband years. A candidate herself, she witnessed leadership hopefuls talking tough on immigration during the 2010 leadership race. 'I would be saying something different [from the other candidates]: "I'm a child of immigrants . . . they make a great contribution to the economy." And what they saw was that in front of actual Labour Party members their line wasn't flying because you don't join the Labour Party to hear how immigrants are the source of everyone's problems,' she says. 'So gradually by about half-way through they stopped talking about immigration because it just wasn't working with their audience.'

Because they got to know each other over this time, once he became leader, Abbott says, Miliband wanted to hear her views, 'I remember one of Ed's first speeches on immigration, he asked me to look at it.' She says she was straight with him: his approach was wrong. One of the main issues was that he was accepting immigration as a problem. 'After a bit he stopped sending me his speeches because we clearly didn't agree. But I don't think Ed in himself believed a lot of that stuff.' Having been elected on a promise to move the Labour Party to the left, Miliband – who had briefly flirted with an anti-immigrant, so-called traditionalist group within the party, Blue Labour – never seemed willing to directly challenge anti-immigration politics.

It has often been suggested that there are two options for the left in the immigration debate, either ignoring anti-immigration views or capitulating to them. But there is a third choice: listening but also seeking to persuade people that immigration is not the problem. Miliband wouldn't do that. 'He thought he couldn't change the British public's view of it, that . . . the way to change the British public's view of it was to restore a healthy economy where job security was gradually restored and then as a function of that, people's concern about immigration would wane,' former adviser to Miliband, Stewart Wood says. And so Miliband used his first party conference speech to declare: 'You wanted your concerns about the impact of immigration on communities to be heard, and I understand your frustration that we didn't seem to be on your side.'[68] We got it wrong on immigration, he would repeatedly say as leader, implying New Labour let 'too many' people in.

As Labour was pandering to anti-immigration sentiment, the Tories were charging ahead with their own agenda. Implementing austerity, cutting public services and overseeing a fall in living standards, the Conservatives also zeroed in on immigration. Under Theresa May and David Cameron, the government pledged to get immigration down to the tens of thousands. With this target in mind, May, as home secretary, oversaw the chilling 2014 and 2016 Immigration Acts, which aimed to create a 'hostile environment' for undocumented migrants. Rather than attack the government for their policies, Miliband used opportunities like Prime Minister's Questions to criticise the government for failing to meet their own immigration target. The message, yet again, was that immigration was a problem.

Labour was worried they would appear out of touch with people who had issues with immigration. Miliband adviser Harvey Redgrave believes the spectre of Brown's 'totemic' Gillian Duffy moment hung over them. He said, 'It revealed a truth that people already believed about us which is that we [think] . . . anybody who raises a concern about immigration is a racist.' So he thought, 'Labour needed to demonstrate – visibly demonstrate – that we'd got it wrong on immigration.' But this ended up reinforcing anti-migrant politics, helping breed further discontent and strengthening their political rivals.

As Miliband was claiming, New Labour had let too many people into the country, UKIP were becoming a significant political force. Initially established as an anti-EU party in 1993 by academic Alan Sked, UKIP had been struggling for nearly twenty years to influence UK politics. Marred by infighting and dealing with cash-flow issues, until 2010, the party had only seen patchy success at European elections and was mostly 'a southern English, middle-class vehicle for ex-Tory voters'.[69] But by the end of 2012 there had been a five-fold increase in support for UKIP – from just under 2 per cent to over 10 per cent, and by the 2014 UK European Parliament election, UKIP won 26.6 per cent of the vote to Labour's 24.4 per cent.[70] UKIP's leader Nigel Farage positioned himself as a man of the people and the party as anti-establishment, working against a political class that had overseen the 2008 crash and decades of a managerial, unrepresentative form of politics. But when it came to it, UKIP were far less bothered about economic disenfranchisement than they were about the number of immigrants living in the UK.

Farage helped to popularise the party's agenda by turning every political issue into a debate about migrants or the EU, often with a heavy focus on the former. He repeatedly pointed out that free movement – one of the 'four freedoms' of the EU's single market – was ruinous for the country. Free movement of workers had been around since the EU's precursor, the EEC, was set up. In the 1990s, free movement was guaranteed for everyone, although with specific caveats, such as the rule allowing EU nationals to stay in the country for three months, any longer than this was conditional on their being in work, having the prospect of a job or otherwise having 'enough' money to live in the UK without employment. It was then formalised in the Maastricht Treaty, which created the EU and the concept of European citizenship.

Free movement had become a central part of the immigration debate over the New Labour years and remained so during the entire time Ed Miliband was leader, with a particular focus on people from certain countries in Eastern Europe. UKIP reinforced and capitalised on that by tapping into the idea that people's evident lack of control over and say in their lives was somehow related to or produced by free movement in the EU.

With no BNP-style 'Rights for Whites' slogan, Farage made somewhat sophisticated attempts to distance the party from race – pointing out, for instance, that EU immigration is unfair because people from the Global South, many of whom are of colour, should be able to come in on the basis of skill. The party's 2015 manifesto declared: 'Immigration is not about race; it is about space.'[71] But between UKIP member of the European Parliament Godfrey Bloom saying UK aid should not be sent to 'bongo bongo land' and Farage announcing he would be concerned if people from Romania moved in next door to him, the repeated declaration that UKIP did not engage in racism was risible. And although free movement was often in UKIP's line of fire, the boundaries of the debate were and remain blurred; the differences between EU and non-EU migration, for instance, is not always clearly understood. And so against the backdrop of the 2011 'riots' and grooming cases, UKIP focused its policy on immigration and British Muslims, claiming to be representatives of the 'white working class', while blaming low wages and crumbling public services in an austerity-riddled UK on migrants.

Between 2010 and 2015, some claimed UKIP were a threat to Labour as well as to the Tories, pointing out how Farage's party appealed to the 'left behind' or the 'white working class'. This panicked Miliband and his team. There was some truth to the idea that UKIP made a concerted effort to make inroads in Labour territory. But commentators and some academics overemphasised this threat and the underlying implication was that Labour – the party that had been hardening its line on immigration for years – needed to be 'tougher' still on the issue.

'Because the polling kept coming back in the run-up to the election saying you're weak on immigration, you're weak on immigration, what you've got doesn't cut the mustard . . . so we had thoughts about lots of different things, and in the end he went for a rhetorical device: the idea of just saying "controls on immigration,"' Stewart Wood explains. 'We were extremely policy-light because Ed didn't talk about it, because he [Miliband] didn't want to fall into the UKIP-lite trap, and when it came to the campaign, he just ramped up the rhetoric to assert he had control when he didn't. So, it was the worst of all worlds in a way.'

As their mug told the country, Labour went into the 2015 General Election promising to 'control immigration'. What that meant in practice ranged from pledging to stop EU migrants from being able to claim benefits for the first two years of their time in the country and introducing 'fair rules' to 'prevent the exploitation of migrant workers, which undercuts local wages and increases demand for further low-skilled migration'.[72] These were ill-informed policies. Research in 2013 found that only 1 per cent of migrants claim benefits, in comparison to 4 per cent of the British population, but this policy gave succour to an anti-migrant rhetoric that was adamant immigrants were merely here to take.[73] The same went for the contradictory policy on employment: there was no robust evidence to show that immigration was causing low pay, yet Miliband divided workers up along national lines, thereby capitulating to pressure from the political right inside and outside his party.

Their immigration election pledge was one of five, all of which were not only printed on the side of mugs but were in the days before the election etched into an eight foot six inch tablet dubbed the 'Ed Stone'.[74] 'The real problem', Abbott said at the time, 'is that immigration controls are one of our five pledges at all.'[75] But Shadow Chancellor Ed Balls disagreed, bluntly claiming there was nothing to be ashamed of. 'I'm hoping after the general election I can do a toast in that mug as we get on and change Britain for the better.'[76] That celebration would never happen; with a net loss of twenty-six, Labour lost forty-eight seats in the election, Balls's among them.

As Patrick Gordon Walker is said to have done in Smethwick decades earlier, Miliband inadvertently reinforced the very rhetoric the far right thrived off. UKIP told the public that immigration was to blame for their falling living standards and the country's creaky public services; Labour and the Conservatives said they were right. Unsurprisingly, people who were significantly motivated by immigration chose the genuine article over the unenthusiastic imitation; UKIP or the Tories rather than Labour.

When I ask Harvey Redgrave, ex-Downing Street staffer and Ed Miliband's former adviser on migration, why Labour didn't robustly challenge anti-immigration messages at the 2015 General Election, he claims that had already been done. 'That is what New Labour did. New Labour's approach on immigration was . . . stop moaning about it, it's good for us, it's good for our economy, there is no upper limit on immigration. I would say we've tested that.'

But New Labour's approach was never that simple or positive. Telling people that immigration is good for the economy and changing the immigration system in line with that, while continuing to implement differential rights for different groups of people, might have initially appeared to be adequate. But after fifty to sixty years of racialised anti-immigration politics, this was never going to be an effective long-term strategy.

Ministers delivered speeches on how to create a national identity that embraced 'diversity' and 'cultural pluralism'. But there was no real substance to what form such a policy might take or how it could possibly be inclusive, particularly since they refused to properly engage with the brutalities of Empire, choosing to eulogise it instead. Whiteness, national identity and belonging remained closely tied together. MPs who engaged in jingoistic nationalism, who implied that people of colour – some of whom were migrants – held different values to white Britons, who talked about and treated refugees as a threat to the UK, and who demanded that migrants and Muslims integrate into society, were in fact asking some of society's most vulnerable people to force themselves into existing racist, exploitative structures and conform to a society that problematises them.

One of the real failures of New Labour was not that they let 'too many' people in. They made the economic case for immigration but they at once failed to mitigate rising racism, xenophobia and inequality, while also creating and enforcing different forms of racism and exploitation. What appeared at first glance like it could be a break with the UK's racist immigration policy turned into an altogether different picture, and nowhere did this look bleaker than in New Labour's approach to asylum. Through draconian policy and degrading rhetoric about asylum they helped to embed anti-immigration ideas into British politics, and then they left them to fester. From Blair through to Miliband, the Labour Party has, in its own unique ways, failed to challenge anti-immigration politics. Playing a corroboratory role, they reinforced myths with machismo, all the while preaching fairness.

4

Legitimate Concerns

how long must we make a case for migration? recount the times it has carried this country on its neck so this nation could bask in the glory of its so called greatness? how loud should we chant our stories of beauty of struggle of grit? write all the ways we are lovely and useful across our faces before we become a hymn sheet singing of desperation?

Selina Nwulu, *The Audacity of Our Skin*

When a Love Productions television crew arrived on Derby Road, Southampton, in spring 2014, it's unlikely they knew their documentary shoot would soon become the focus of a national media storm. As they initially started work for what was a Channel 4 project, more and more locals cottoned on to what the programme was about, and a sense of unease began to rise. Camera-people, producers and residents of the street who had agreed to take part in filming were met with impassioned protest and some isolated threats of violence.

A tumultuous meeting between community members and the production team, which had been organised to dispel growing tensions, ended with no resolution. Some of Derby Road's residents ended up making a trip to London so they could protest outside Channel 4's headquarters. Within months, the crew were forced to abandon filming.

The TV company had been set to make a six-part series that would be an 'honest look at how immigration has changed one street'.[1] But producers were left with only enough footage to make a one-hour documentary, *Immigration Street*, which, following on from the highly controversial *Benefits Street*, was ample reason to explain why residents didn't want the documentary to be made in the first place.

People from all over the world have come to call Derby Road their home. In the 1950s and '60s, new arrivals from India, the Caribbean and parts of the African continent moved onto this one street, and in the past two decades they were joined by people from Lithuania and Romania. It is an ideal place to explore the UK's rich history of immigration. But local councillor Satvir Kaur, who was heavily involved in the protest, explains that the majority of residents were especially opposed to filming because it was a time when 'the debate of immigration was being sensationalised on their doorstep'. Rafique, a shopkeeper on the street who featured significantly in the final cut, cautioned during the one-hour programme, 'The media, the way they portray immigrants coming over, they only talk about the negative side.'[2]

Accustomed to seeing migrants being depicted as untrustworthy, inhuman and unwanted, Derby Road residents didn't trust that their lives would be documented without a side-dish of disparagement. You could catch glimpses of these anxieties in the final cut; fear of how they might be misrepresented seemed to be a driving factor of their protest. These are people too often talked about, not talked to. And even when they are, too rarely are their worries treated as important. Usually it's worries about immigration that are placed at the centre of discussion.

What they called 'genuine feeling' in the '70s has become 'legitimate concerns' in the 2000s. However politicians describe supposed public attitudes towards immigration, they always seem to have a pithy phrase to make negative attitudes appear respectable. Flick through some of the Parliamentary debates and political speeches from then and now and the same words jump out at you: in the '70s you learn that 'ordinary people' were 'genuinely afraid' of immigration. They had a 'genuine feeling' migrants were a problem. Even when it doesn't make an appearance, the idea behind it is still there. 'I acknowledge the doubts and fears about future migration which are felt by many of the majority community,' Labour home secretary Roy Jenkins told the Commons in a July 1976 debate on immigration.[3]

The problem isn't the word 'genuine', which could just be taken as an accurate descriptor, but the subtext. It doesn't matter if 'fears' were a fitting cover for prejudice or racism or if they are misguided and ill-informed – if public discontent is characterised as 'genuine', it becomes unquestionable. This was the same message as at the 2015 General Election, when the phrase 'legitimate concerns' seemed to fall from almost every Labour politician's lips. Whether they thought immigration was bad for the economy or a threat to UK 'culture', the implication was that if people's views are 'legitimate' then there was no reason they should or can be challenged. The approach was embraced enthusiastically by politicians and commentators from different political persuasions. Listening to and acting on those 'concerns' was, and still is, treated as a high priority in the UK. 'We are leaving the EU in part because the left wouldn't take voters' concerns about immigration seriously,' one pollster still claimed not long after the Brexit vote in 2016.[4]

Meanwhile, other politicians have wrapped themselves in 'genuine feeling' and 'legitimate concerns' to tacitly vindicate their own xenophobic politics, purporting to be talking on behalf of the disenfranchised public. For different reasons and with different end goals, politicians on the left and the right agree that peoples' concerns about immigration were legitimate. It's precisely because this thinking shapes the way immigration is understood – and how it is reported – that Derby Road residents' anxiety over how they would be represented was understandable.

Public views are complicated and nuanced, and they certainly aren't static, but there's no point denying there has been 'concern'.[5] A poll before the 2012 London Olympics showed that 53 per cent of people thought 'more often than not immigrants . . . do not bring anything positive, and the likes of the Olympic-winning athletes are an exception.' Another later that year found that 67 per cent of people thought 'immigration over the last decade . . . had been a bad thing for Britain'. Only 11 per cent thought it had been good. In 2014, YouGov revealed in one poll that 26 per cent of respondents thought that the government should encourage immigrants and their families to leave Britain, including family members who were born here – otherwise known as voluntary repatriation.[6]

Politicians read these polls not as a flashing warning sign but as if they were a helpful roadmap for winning popular approval. They have presented themselves as hard-nosed truth talkers, crusading against 'fake news', while quiescently responding to people's 'concerns' about immigration, no matter how misguided. Anti-immigration politics is presented as an unalterable fixture of political life; the 'debate' assumed to flow from the bottom up. What this ignores is how politicians, the media and the UK's imperial history and present help to create and sustain anti-immigration discourse.

There's nothing more patronising – or dangerous – than the assumption that peoples' minds cannot be changed – or that indulging in xenophobia is a politician's only choice if they want to properly represent 'the people'. Views fluctuate, and anti-immigration politics, persistent and deeply embedded though it is, is based on lies. Listen carefully to what people are saying and you might just find those 'concerns' are not 'legitimate' at all.

Three years into the job, Prime Minister David Cameron was on a mission. He wanted to let the public know that, while the UK should welcome migrants who 'come here and work hard', the same open arms should not be offered to people he considered a 'constant drain on our public services'.[7] But he also had another task – to cut the funding for those same public services. Cameron was overseeing the tightest squeeze in public spending in sixty years. Not entirely dissimilar from Harold Macmillan, his predecessor by about fifty years, Cameron positioned himself as defending the welfare state from 'outsiders' while coolly slashing budgets; decimating the very sector he claimed to be protecting from 'foreigners'.[8]

People might look at what is happening in their own work-places and misdiagnose why their wages are falling or why they can't get a job as a consequence of 'too many' migrants. But relentless *Daily Mail* front pages and unfounded claims made by some of our most senior politicians make these conclusions more prevalent and seemingly authoritative. In September 2017, Theresa May declared in the Commons: 'There is a reason for wanting to control migration. It is because of the impact that net migration can have on people, on access to services and on infrastructure. But, crucially, also because it often hits those at the lower end of the income scale hardest.'[9] Since the mid-2000s, it's become common sense to blame migrants from the EU for undercutting wages and making people poorer.

The very same day that May stood at the dispatch box and claimed that migrants were creating a downward pressure on wages, Liberal Democrat and former business secretary Vince Cable revealed that, while in Coalition with the Tories, he witnessed Theresa May's Home Office suppress nine reports which showed that migration was not having a negative impact on wages.[10] 'When it comes to debates on race and immigration,' writes journalist Gary Younge, 'honesty is usually the first casualty.'[11]

Marissa Begonia, a domestic worker and activist for domestic workers' rights, tells me with a mixture of fury and weariness just how frustrating these kinds of claims are. 'They always use migration as the scapegoat, when all their policies, all the things that they're doing failed, in terms of economy, they blame migrants.'

This idea has taken root in the public's consciousness. A Home Affairs Select Committee report published in January 2018 said that the public have 'significant concerns about the impact of migration on public services' and worry that immigrants are coming not to contribute but to play 'the system'. The government, it concluded, must be 'more proactive in challenging myths and inaccuracies' and 'publish more factual information about the costs and benefits of immigration'.[12] But politicians and the media have spent decades giving legitimacy, and contributing, to those inaccuracies, blaming migrants for overstretched public services, housing shortages and low pay.

So what *do* the facts say? Study after study has found that immigration is not a significant causal factor in low wages.[13] There is some evidence that people on low pay have to compete against one another, but nowhere is immigration found to be playing a key role in creating plummeting wages; in contrast, the evidence consistently shows that it is a net positive to the economy. The same was true half a century ago; in the 1960s, when arguments were being made for immigration controls, the Treasury analysed the economic role of people from the Commonwealth and found their work contributed to the economy and that they didn't 'take' jobs from people born in the UK.[14]

Claims that an increase in the number of migrants results in lower wages or fewer jobs available for those already living here is just bad economics. When I put the well-worn argument that migration is damaging to the economy to economist Jonathan Portes, he's not convinced. 'The most important, most basic thing about the economics of immigration in the labour market is that immigrants add to supply and demand,' he says. 'People who say, "They must be taking our jobs, they must be pushing down wages, it's just supply and demand," well they're only looking at supply and not looking at demand.'

No less than anyone else, immigrants work, pay bills and buy goods and services. Through all these everyday acts they grow tax revenues, boost the economy and produce jobs. If simply having more people active in an economy meant fewer jobs, that would give Germany one of the highest unemployment rates in Europe, and Greece one of the lowest.

Singled out from every other political issue and afforded undue attention, immigration is used to explain away our economic problems. If politicians were as concerned as they say they are about the worst off, there's plenty they could do other than to restrict immigration. By directing the blame at people who come into the country, people in power have abandoned or intentionally obscured a thoroughgoing analysis of what causes our deeply unequal economy – a system that thrives off low-paid, increasingly insecure labour that affects so many people, including migrants.

There was never a golden age of work. Poor working conditions, racism, sexism, homophobia and ableism have long shaped peoples' lives. But over the '80s and into the '90s, the economy shifted from an industrial base to a service sector, and cities began to reconstitute themselves to become twenty-four-hour operations with disposable, casualised workers. Thatcher restructured the economy away from the manufacturing sector, dismantled forms of wage protection, privatised and semi-privatised key industries, and oversaw a worsening of pay and conditions, all the while undermining trade union rights. She set out to defeat striking workers and systematically removed employment rights, restricting union activity, including making it illegal to picket away from your own workplace. These changes, paired with economic shifts, brought about the collapse of collective bargaining. The proportion of employees who were members of a trade union plummeted from 56 per cent to 31 per cent under the Conservatives.[15] Rights became less about the collective and more about the individual.

Labour, traditionally the party of the unions, were expected in 1997 to revive what Thatcher had sought to quash. New Labour made some important and necessary changes to the UK's economy: the reduction of child poverty, introduction of the minimum wage and the establishment of Sure Start centres made a fundamental difference to peoples' lives. But armed with their Third Way politics, Labour kept Thatcher's financial approach intact. Housing is a good example of what that meant in practice. As Thatcher sold off council housing through her Right to Buy policy, there was a steady decline in the number of council houses that were built – never fewer than 17,710 a year – and that continued to plummet, dropping to 7,870 under New Labour's entire thirteen years in office.[16] Between 1997 and 2010, for instance, only 0.3 per cent of all the homes that were built were owned by local authorities. Housing became a commodity, not a right, as the crisis of where to live exploded in the UK.

When I ask Mark Serwotka, general secretary of Public and Commercial Services Union (PCS), about New Labour's economic approach, he is visibly unimpressed. 'It was Blair and Brown who announced the biggest job cuts in the civil service that we have ever seen [which were] carried on by the Coalition government,' he says with incredulity, shaking his head. 'You have this whole embracing of the markets.'

New Labour's record on unions wasn't necessarily much better than Thatcher's. They introduced some new rights and reversed some of Thatcher's measures, but those that made striking harder stayed in place and trade union membership continued to decline. This only worsened with the governments that followed. The Trade Union Act 2016 made it more difficult to strike; new rules demanded that a vote for industrial action must have at least 50 per cent turnout and 40 per cent of 'those eligible had to vote "yes"' for it to be lawful, but without any accompanying measures to help make the process more accessible – for example e-balloting, which wasn't allowed. The years in which workers' rights were eroded are often overlooked as people blame migration for falling wages and low-quality jobs, but any cursory review of the labour market shows that work and workplaces have been fundamentally transformed, largely for the worse.

The results of Thatcher's and then New Labour's policies were a lack of affordable housing and a labour market structured around short-term, insecure contracts that meant people could be fired at the drop of a hat. With record levels of home ownership in 2003 and a relatively stable economy, that didn't seem too much of a problem. But around this time, wages began to stagnate for most people, resulting in increased borrowing, and already high levels of private debt exploded. The New Labour government which had been lauded as progressive modernisers ended up overseeing a widening of inequality.[17] Although Gordon Brown helped to salvage the economy when the financial crash came in 2008, the consumer-spending-driven UK economy, which was heavily reliant on the financial sector, was ill-prepared to cope.

All over our newspapers and immortalised in films, we knew who – bankers and financiers – and what – a deregulated financial industry – was to blame for the crash and its aftermath. But when the Coalition imposed austerity onto an already exploitative economy two years after the financial crash, producing a dangerous elixir of plummeting pay, living standards and insecure work, they peddled an already persuasive anti-immigrant narrative further still – and with it, contradictory strategies of blame. Migrants were coming to the country to simultaneously take benefits *and* steal jobs. Immigrants – sometimes the last people through the door – were accused of causing the country's long-term economic problems.

But the Coalition government had another strategy: blaming poor Britons. As they stripped away support for people with disabilities, limited the amount of state support that households could receive and introduced the Bedroom

Tax, they pathologised poverty. They sold spending cuts to the public by declaring that there are two kinds of people in the country: hard-working strivers and lazy skivers, and you choose which one you want to be. State support was cast not as a necessary safety net, but as a system that was being shamelessly abused by people too lazy to find a decent paying job. The problems of a labour market that produced in-work poverty faded into the background, as poverty was imagined as an individual failing.[18] While the Coalition government disparaged people in poverty as 'scroungers' who were cheating the system, a 2015 Citizens UK report found that taxpayers had to top up peoples' low pay to the cost of £11 billion a year.[19] Poor Britons were blamed for gaming the system, just as migrants were accused of bringing about low pay; in this way, both groups were and continue to be dehumanised as a threat to the economy, even as they are increasingly pitted against one another. Far from being rivals, they have a lot in common.

The connection between the two has a long history. 'Migration issues in contemporary Britain', migration scholar Bridget Anderson writes, 'cannot be extricated from centuries of struggle for control of labour and anxiety about the threat of "uncontrolled" masses.' Before people who moved around the globe were known as 'migrants', elites were primarily concerned about the movement of the poor *within* England. To be able to move was to be able to find different people to sell your labour to, and so successive laws stretching back as far as 1349 stigmatised the movement of the poor and criminalised giving money to beggars, people who, like today's 'benefit scroungers', were seen as a threat to social order. As the centuries flew past, laws got more restrictive.[20]

A fixture in British politics since at least the days of Queen Elizabeth I and the Poor Laws,[21] the 'deserving' and 'undeserving' poor have been pitted against each other. Even when the National Assistance Act 1948 introduced universal welfare, an informal distinction continued to exist between worthy white people and people of colour who weren't seen as belonging. Thatcher dismantled welfare provision across the board, believing the market to be the ultimate corrective, and that state support for the unemployed and the ill undermined peoples' desire to work. New Labour, similarly, thought that the way to deal with social problems was to impose a strict order on society; to them, welfare was a crutch that kept people in poverty. Tony Blair described the long-term unemployed as suffering from a 'culture of poverty, drug abuse, low aspirations and family instability'.[22]

Perhaps better than anyone else, Conservative Peter Lilley inadvertently made visible the connection between poor migrants and poor people born in the UK. He took to the stage at the Conservative Party conference in 1992 and to the tune of a song from Gilbert and Sullivan's *The Mikado*, Lilley, secretary of state for social security, sang an attack on people at the margins of society. Like something out of Roald Dahl's *The Witches*, the Conservatives in that room showed their true colours. To rapturous applause and laughter from fellow Tories, Lilley entertained them by outlining his plan to 'close down the something-for-nothing society', listing those in his line of fire: 'benefit offenders', people who make 'bogus claims' and 'young ladies who get pregnant just to jump the housing queue'. He began that speech with an attack on New Age travellers: 'Most people were as sickened as I was with the sight of these spongers descending like locusts,' he said, 'demanding benefits with menaces, we are not in the business of subsidising scroungers.'[23]

At conference the following year, he widened his net further. Swapping his song for casual xenophobia, he attacked migrants as 'people travelling around, pretending to look for work, but really looking for the best benefits'. 'Just imagine the advice you might find in a European phrasebook for benefit tourists': "Wo ist das Hotel?" – Where is the Housing

Department? "Où est le bureau de change?" – Where do I cash my benefit cheque?' he continued. '"Mio bambino e in Italia" – Send child benefit to my family in Italy. "Je suis un citoyen de l'Europe" – Give me benefits or I'll take you to the European Court. But next year's edition will have just one phrase – "Où est la société de something for nothing?" – Sorry, Jacques, Britain's branch is closed.' Lilley announced the government would introduce a residence test people would have to complete before they could claim housing support. 'We have all too many home-grown scroungers,' he claimed. 'But it is beyond the pale when foreigners come here expecting our handouts.'[24]

And, so, just like the concept of benefit scroungers, benefit tourism became a nationally accepted myth. Reinforced by successive governments, it was then placed firmly in the centre of the debate during the EU referendum. Once David Cameron had committed the UK to the referendum – all in the name of keeping together the Conservative Party, which has for decades been deeply divided over Europe – he realised he needed to renegotiate the country's relationship to try and please backbenchers and voters who might otherwise opt to leave.

After decades of accepting and reinforcing that immigration was a problem in the UK, Cameron came to the conclusion that changing freedom of movement was essential to satisfy those potential leavers. When he tried to negotiate an 'emergency brake', which would put a cap on how many EU migrants could work in the UK, German chancellor Angela Merkel pointed out that such a mechanism would only be considered in the event of a social or economic crisis.[25] This simply wasn't the case for the UK; immigration was not causing any of the problems that politicians claimed it was.

So Cameron focused on benefits, striking a deal that would potentially allow the government to stop EU migrants from claiming in-work benefits for their first four years in the country. This had echoes of Tony Blair's hasty decision in 2004 to restrict the social support migrants coming from new EU member states could access. The figures on in-work benefits are difficult to calculate because they're made on the basis of households, which can include people of different nationalities, but the government appeared to be targeting people who needed state support because of pitifully low wages, penalising those suffering from in-work poverty.[26] The idea that 'benefit tourism' was real and concerning was a key part of Cameron's renegotiation with the EU, itself central to the case he made for Remain.

Then, in 2016, Theresa May backed plans to introduce passport checks for pregnant women visiting hospital, claiming that the move was part of an effort to crack down on so-called maternity tourism. Ignoring that it's migrant workers who keep the NHS going and evidence suggests that 'health tourism' barely even makes up 0.3 per cent of NHS spending,[27] the Conservatives attacked migrants coming into the country as abusing the health service.

'Health tourism' and 'benefit tourism' are not an issue in the UK. But what if they were? While politicians regularly claim that huge numbers of people come to the UK 'illegally' to claim benefits or to use the health service for free, there's little interest in considering how desperate you might have to be to move to a different country just to access healthcare or state support. If migrants were coming here to access support, there's barely anyone asking why. The same kinds of questions were startlingly absent in debates about Britons who might have been reliant on state support to get by; instead, they were just dismissed as lazy.

'I've done a lot of reporting on austerity', investigative journalist Rebecca Omonira-Oyekanmi says, 'and what I find talking to people on the ground, is that the same issues affecting white and brown and black British working-class people are the same issues affecting irregular migrants and refugees.

They're rubbing alongside each other in the job centre. They're the ones who are being sanctioned, they're the ones who are turning up to court to be evicted from their social housing because they can't afford to pay the rent.'

One woman tells me about the impact of the complex benefit system. She volunteers in a centre that supported migrants who were undocumented, destitute or in need of help and she encountered people from Eastern Europe who, for all manner of reasons, couldn't access state support; many of them ended up sleeping in parks, toilets and derelict buildings.

The complex, near-impossible-to-navigate asylum and immigration system is evidence of a similar political strategy to that of the minefield of welfare bureaucracy, whereby people who aren't able to work are badgered through fit-to-work tests, and others are 'sanctioned' – another word for being docked state support – for making the smallest mistake. In both systems, it's not uncommon to have to prove 'innocence' from a position of assumed guilt, and in the process, humanity is lost. Citizens can get caught up in the government's immigration net, as they did with Windrush, and immigration policy can be used as a precursor to domestic policy. 'Immigration and welfare reform are two sides of the same coin,' David Cameron admitted in 2011.[28]

The way that citizens and migrants are treated isn't the same, and migrants' humanity should not be dependent upon their proximity to working-class Britons. Still, anti-immigration politics that blames migrants for undercutting wages and draining public services obscures the connections between working-class people, regardless of where they were born. They're told it's simply the way the world works and that they have to compete against one another for a supposed finite number of jobs and access to underfunded public services. If you aren't part of the competition, you're undeserving. But, even then, not everyone is allowed to enter the race. 'On your bike, as Margaret Thatcher's minister Norman Tebbit said, and you are a saint shining with neo-liberal virtues,' writes academic Bob Sutcliffe. 'On your ferry, and you are a demon against whom great European democracies change their constitutions in panic.'[29]

Chuba, spent years trying to secure his status in the UK. He tells me he's sick of seeing migrants portrayed as if they're 'coming here, taking houses, taking benefits', when the truth is they don't have 'power' to 'even take those things'.

We've been left with an economic system in which wealth sloshes around at the top of society and most other people work and struggle to get by. Between 1979 and 1999, work became more polarised, as there was a significant increase in the number of both highest-paying jobs and the lowest-paying.[30] In 2016, the average income of the top fifth of households was fourteen times that of the bottom fifth and while the poorest 10 per cent of households paid on average 46.8 per cent of their income in tax in 2014–15, the richest 10 per cent paid on average 34 per cent. People of colour who experience higher rates of poverty, homelessness and deprivation are disproportionately affected.[31] Meanwhile, between 2006 and 2016, the combined wealth of Britain's 1,000 richest people doubled to £547 billion.[32]

'Frankly, even if you stopped migrants coming into Britain, that is not going to change the conditions in which people work,' Manuel Cortes, general secretary of the Transport Salaried Staffs' Association (TSSA) union, says. 'Only a change in the composition of that labour market, how it's regulated and what wages are paid can change that.' Where Cortes is direct, other parts of the left equivocate. He is one of the only trade union leaders so far to take this unambiguous stance; some would rather dodge this issue than confront it.

While parts of the right scapegoat migrants, there are sections of the left that embrace a nationalistic form of socialism or 'socialism in one country' that's mostly interested in protecting workers at home, not abroad.[33] Ignoring migrants' humanity and their (limited) agency, they say that as part of neoliberalism, immigrants are used to undercut wages, or they argue that the left's focus should be on helping potential migrants in the countries they're already in – an easy political statement to make, but one that rarely has much substance to back it up.[34]

The existence of these nationalists doesn't give the internationalist left a pass to ignore exploitation, which often gets pushed into the shadows of the debate. Immigration doesn't cause low pay, but there *is* an issue of how the economy allows huge companies to seek out the most exploitable workforce in order to pay the least and make the most profits. This isn't confined to migrant workers, it's people who aren't unionised and don't know their rights, and in sectors where labour rights aren't strong enough. These aren't just unhappy accidents in the economy; it's how it's designed.

Perhaps the most extreme example of state-sanctioned exploitation exists in detention centres. Generally, people waiting to hear the outcome of their asylum applications aren't allowed to work, unless that is, they're in one of these liminal spaces, the majority of which are run by private providers like G4S. Detainees are paid a maximum of £1 per hour for routine work, a desultory salary that is marginally increased by a 25p 'bonus' for specified projects.[35] Former detainee Andy only has contempt for the system that left him teetering on the edge of, and sometimes falling into, destitution. 'They're making money on human suffering.'

With few (if any) activities like language or art classes on offer, these jobs, which were introduced under New Labour and called 'paid activities', were justified as a remedy to detainee boredom and frustration. Detainees don't have to be paid any more than they are because they aren't considered workers, which also means they're not entitled to certain rights and protections. Cleaning, cooking, hairdressing – research suggests the jobs detainees do are essential to keeping the centres running, and mean that fewer full-paid staff are needed. Outside detention, migrants and refugees are wrongly accused of 'undercutting' wages; inside they're put to work – often by private companies – for almost no pay.

Discussing the different ways that exploitation operates can be difficult in our polarised political debate because the idea that immigration plays a significant role in driving down wages or creating unemployment is so common that there's a need to challenge it, and yet nuanced arguments are rarely welcomed in these discussions. Campaigners have used studies to point out that migration boosts the economy, showing the reality that people from abroad don't come to claim off the state. An example of this is One Day Without Us, a grassroots movement set up as a response to the Brexit result and the rise in hate crimes that followed. It organises an annual national day of action, celebrating immigrants and immigration in the UK. Part of their strategy is underscoring the contribution migrants make to this country. In 2018, they publicised findings that showed migrants working in the adult social care sector contribute £4.4 billion to the English economy annually. The message: immigrants are essential to the economy.[36]

This is one weapon in campaigners' arsenal – whenever a study is published showing that migration is good for the economy, to highlight it to challenge the kettle logic about immigrants; that they are 'scroungers', after benefits, and that they are taking British people's jobs. Rather than pilfering from the public purse, they show, migrants are contributing to it.

When I meet seasoned campaigner Tatiana Garavito in the British Library, she tells me of her difficulty with the 'economic contributions' strategy. Garavito came to the UK from Colombia over a decade ago; she's a grassroots organiser and a trained immigration legal advisor. 'It seems like we're always apologising for everything, we still have this narrative of "we are contributing, economically, culturally". We're always trying to prove a point.'

Herein lies a conundrum for people trying to diffuse myths about immigration. The evidence that migrants contribute to the economy needs to be repeatedly remade because there's so much disinformation out there that has proved so effective among the general public. For the people who are maligned as a drain on the economy, there is a deeply personal aspect to refuting such a persuasive anti-immigrant narrative that is such a far-cry from the lives they lead.

But the 'contributions' line is a beginning, not an end point. Graphs and data aside, immigrants' worth and right to be in the country shouldn't merely be contingent on their economic contribution. Politicians purport that the UK is a country that believes in mutual respect and that cares about humanity, yet it consistently ascribes value to people's lives primarily in terms of economics.

The argument that immigrants are hardworking relies on its polar opposite to function, the people who supposedly don't deserve to be in the country because they don't contribute in the 'right' way. Not dissimilar from strivers versus skivers, it's precisely the promotion of an active, engaged, exceptional or hardworking immigrant that draws a dividing line between the 'good' and the 'bad', 'deserving' and 'undeserving' migrant, which drives the rationale for a points-based systems and work-related visa regimes.[37]

So how do you effectively challenge misguided public perceptions, reinforced by politicians and the media? It's regularly said that facts won't change peoples' minds, and that a convincing story is more effective. But the lies that assume that migrants are uniquely and specifically an economic burden are symbolic of prejudice. Myths must be debunked – and then migrants' humanity re-centred.

As well as rejecting the old canard that migrants drive down wages, trade unions need to spend more time challenging anti-immigrant narratives, academic Dr Sundari Anitha says. 'What they haven't successfully done is they haven't framed the issue sufficiently as one of workers' rights and wages. And so it allows the right to hijack it as "migrant workers undercutting our wages", rather than making the argument one of living wages for all workers and adequate measures to prevent exploitation.'

While parts of the movement have demanded better protection for migrants, and people have been fighting together for better pay, the nationalistic element of the labour movement also shies away from directly challenging anti-immigrant messages.[38] The leaflet that is regarded by many to be the first ever to oppose immigration controls in the UK demonstrates that this has been a problem for over a century. Written in 1895 by several Jewish trade unions, *A Voice from the Aliens* made an 'appeal to all right-thinking working men of England not to be misled by some leaders who have made it their cause to engender a bitter feeling amongst the British workers against the workers of other countries'. Public opinion had been turned against Jewish refugees fleeing violence in tsarist Russia, and in the early 1890s, the TUC passed a number of resolutions in favour of immigration controls. The leaflet called on workers 'to combine against the common enemy', capitalism, rather 'than fight against us whose interests are identical with theirs'.[39] These words resonate today. The divides created between workers continue to exist, and inadvertently or not, parts of the labour movement prop them up.

Ben Sellers, a former union organiser, tells me he encountered unwillingness in some of the bigger unions to challenge their own members in sectors where organising migrant workers would be wildly unpopular. And when he worked for the TUC, the umbrella organisation for this country's trade unions, Sellers says there was a lack of understanding about dynamic organising. 'There was a patronising attitude that they should be coming to us,' he explains. But it can be done differently.

You wouldn't know it from the way immigration is talked about, but migrants have driven and won fights for better pay and conditions in some of the UK's most affluent institutions. From Harrods to Sotheby's, they have been making change happen. Henry Chango Lopez is President of the Independent Workers Union of Great Britain (IWGB), a small union that has been at the forefront of organising these workers. Over twenty years ago he arrived from Ecuador, where he was studying and working as a taxi driver. Once in the UK, he started working as a cleaner and eventually got a cleaning job at the University of London (UoL). In an almost empty university bar, he tells me he had been living in this country for a long time before he knew that unions existed. 'I didn't even know there was law for the low paid workers and precarious work.' And so he was 'a victim of all this precariousness and exploitation'. When he started working at UoL, he got involved in the trade union, and there learned about what rights he had and how to fight for better pay and conditions.

Many of the union's members are outsourced workers in UoL, which is made up of a number of different colleges and research institutes – from University College London (UCL) to the Royal Veterinary College. They often don't have the same terms and conditions as people who are employed directly by the places that fall under the UoL umbrella. 'In the University of London we have managed to organise a workplace where there is like 400 outsourced staff . . . we have managed to organise most of the outsourced workers that are cleaners, porters, security, maintenance, caterers, gardeners . . . now we are the biggest union on campus.' Organising has paid off: they won the London Living Wage, as well as trade union recognition.

They also run a campaign called 'Tres Cosas', Spanish for three things, which demands sick pay, holiday pay and pensions. When the campaign began, staff could be sacked on the spot, Chango Lopez tells me, and they only had statutory minimum sick pay, statutory minimum holidays and no pension, in comparison to employees' third-plus days of holiday pay, six months' full sick pay, plus half pay for the rest of the year and pension contributions. 'We had nothing basically,' he explains. 'Not just conditions, but we have not ever had respect or dignity in the workplace or security as well.' The campaign won the workers six months of full sick pay, as well as five more days of holiday. They haven't got equality yet, he admits, but they have gained some security.

The public are fed all kinds of stories about migrants who bring down wages by selling off their labour for the cheapest price and who come to take jobs that would otherwise be for Britons. But migrants can be part of the very struggle against low pay and exploitation they are accused of causing. These more complex realities never get a hearing, as those, like Chango Lopez, who spend their time organising workers, fighting for and sometimes winning better wages and conditions are systematically excluded from the debate. Their struggles are inconvenient for people who want to sell anti-immigration politics, regardless of the cost.

On the first day of March 1979, Britain's public broadcaster was taken over by some of its sharpest critics. For just half an hour, academic Stuart Hall and actress Maggie Steed picked apart the BBC's reporting on migration. As part of the *Open Door* series, which gave the public a chance to talk on the airwaves about a subject they cared about with full editorial control, Hall and Steed guided the audience through a swift but incisive tour of how racist attitudes were implicit in the broadcaster's coverage of immigration.

In *It Ain't Half Racist, Mum* – a play on the title of one of the BBC's *It Ain't Half Hot Mum*, notorious for its racism – viewers saw the very specific way that black and brown migrants living in Blackburn, Lancashire, were depicted in television programmes; how anti-migrant voices were centred in analysis and the way white 'intellectuals' were given airtime, unchallenged, to paint a picture of black communities made up of crime, unemployment and family breakdown.

The institutions the programme sought to place under its uncompromising microscope didn't greet the idea warmly. 'The BBC have effectively tried to censor the programme we're making today,' Hall and Steed said. 'The Corporation's news department has denied us access to any of their material. Independent Television News and many commercial companies have been similarly obstructive.'[40] Welcome or not, they made it onto the airwaves.

When I sat down to watch Hall and Steed, I knew there would be similarities between then and now. But as the thirty-minute programme deftly unravelled the multiple layers of reporting on immigration, I was struck by just how much of what the two presenters were attacking is still true today. The way people consume their news has changed, as have some of the certain groups of immigrants that are the focus of reporting, but the *way* immigration is presented remains remarkably similar.

'Whenever a TV programme is made about blacks, the starting point is always numbers,' Hall said. 'A number is a fact, you can't quarrel with it.' But as 'soon as you say numbers, it doesn't matter how you wrap it up – there is only one lesson to be drawn, the numbers are growing. There are too many of them.' As it was in the '80s, so it is now.

Every four months, the Office for National Statistics releases the latest migration statistics, which is invariably reported as news – the BBC, for instance, will run stories declaring a fall or a rise in the numbers, or question what the latest figures tell us. At times, commentators are called upon to talk about what the net migration figures mean for the country. This might not seem like a big issue; there is similar regular, albeit not entirely unproblematic, reporting of crime statistics and NHS statistics, and people might say figures about migration are in the public interest. But such blanket coverage fits too neatly into the already widespread and damaging narratives on immigration. One study indicated the subtle markers that such reporting leaves behind: between 2006 and 2015, the most common adjective used to describe immigration was 'mass' – dehumanising and stigmatising, because this word has now come to suggest that migrants are overwhelming the country.[41]

The public are rarely given a human picture of what immigration means, about the very people the 'debate' refers to and the reality of the system. When migration is reported on, it is often removed from the context of why people move in the first place. 'Too often it's just looked at in isolation,' Rebecca Omonira-Oyekanmi says, 'so it's not ever linked with anything else.' But this is also fuelled by misreporting.

The evening work restrictions were lifted on people from Romania and Bulgaria arriving in the UK, the *Daily Mail* gave a stark warning: 'Sold out! Flights and buses full as Romanians and Bulgarians head for the UK'. But the *Mail's* story wasn't true. In the first four months of 2014, the number of people coming from these so-called A2 countries dropped. The sold-out flights? They were fabricated. Nearly two months later, the newspaper was forced to publish a clarification.[42] These stories are believable because of the broader context of hysteria about numbers. But imagine how different the front pages of the *Sun* and the *Mail* would look if they had to put the retractions in the same sized font, on the same page of the paper as the original story. A petition on the campaign website, 38 Degrees, proposed to make it law.[43]

One of the other reasons these headlines are shared so widely is due to the viral effect of right-wing Facebook groups and Twitter accounts. The *Daily Mail* online has been a go-to site for articles that might be shared on these platforms. One 2016 headline announced that 'Migration "has created 900 no-go areas in EU": Devastating report shows order breaking down – including in London'.[44] In the actual article, it becomes clear the 'report' this supposed evidence came from is actually the website of the Hungarian government, of which far-right politician Viktor Orbán is prime minister. There was and remains no evidence to back up these claims. But this argument – that parts of London are 'no-go areas' because of immigration – is widely circulated and believed in far-right circles, so an article like this just gives further weight to these wildly inaccurate claims.

Newspapers are corporate entities; profit helps shape their agenda. 'Because money is so tight for a lot of publications, they're having to resort to publishing whatever gets the most clicks for ad revenues,' one journalist who has worked at a right-wing tabloid, as well as other less anti-migrant papers, says about alarmist or clickbait reporting. 'Big sensationalist stories that scaremonger obviously will do very well usually and they'll also get a lot of clicks from the other side sharing it saying this is disgusting.' And that's why campaigning group Stop Funding Hate lobbies companies to stop advertising in newspapers like the *Daily Mail* and the *Sun*; their aim is to 'make hate unprofitable'.[45]

In 2014, after being told repeatedly that migrants are over-running the country, polling company Ipsos MORI found British people thought immigrants make up 24.4 per cent of the population. According to the 2011 census, it's more like 13 per cent.[46] This miscalculation is telling; it's a reflection of a society repeatedly told there are 'too many' migrants here and, crucially, that their presence creates problems.

'Floods', 'deluges' and 'swarms'. With their alarmist words, politicians and pundits paint a picture of the UK under constant threat of being overrun by 'outsiders'. This idea that the country is full has snaked itself around British politics, strangling accurate understanding of this vexed terrain.

On an overcast Sunday afternoon a few weeks before the 2016 London mayoral election, I was out on the capital's streets knocking on doors. The campaign had been a tense one, and with the EU referendum just around the corner, people were raising all kinds of issues. 'I won't be voting at all,' one woman said initially peering from around her half-ajar door. When I asked her why, she inched it open to tell me: there are too many immigrants and asylum seekers in this country. Around the corner, another woman explained she was worried about immigration and asylum. It wasn't so long after the 'refugee crisis' had been in the news, and she said she had sympathy with people fleeing conflict and famine, but that the UK couldn't take in more people.

When I sit down with Alp Mehmet, vice chair of the pressure group Migration Watch, which advocates for more restrictive immigration policy, he gives a similar reasoning: 'I don't think migration on the present scale serves interests either of those who are already here or those who are going to come over,' he says. 'You're concerned about the provision of services, be it health, be it welfare, be it schools, be it housing – all these people need all these things to live a civilised existence.' Senior Tory MP and Brexiter Chris Grayling struck the same tone in the run-up to the EU referendum. 'If immigration carries on at this current rate, it is going to put increasing pressure on public services – health and education,' he wrote. 'It is going to mean that we have to build over very large amounts of green belt land to provide extra housing for people moving to the UK. It means we are going to have to build far more roads to cope because we will have gridlock otherwise,' he continued to argue. 'It is going to change the face of our country ... And you, the citizen of the United Kingdom, have no say over that.'[47]

This might seem pragmatic, but the risks Grayling and Mehmet warn of don't add up. 'There's nothing stopping the population of Doncaster moving to Islington tomorrow if they want to, but they won't. So it's not free movement, it's a question of whether you can make reasonable enough predictions and plan for it,' economist Jonathan Portes says, 'particularly because most people who arrive don't immediately use services.'

That's because these people are often young, in good health and don't bring any children; they are therefore less likely to use the NHS or state schools than the average citizen. They also work and pay their taxes, which help to fund public services. Even so, governments can plan for an increased demand in services and immigration should be seen as any other form of population change. This is a point Diane Abbott made as shadow home secretary in 2018: 'Of course,' she said, taking on the usual arguments, 'there is pressure on schools, on the NHS and on housing from a growing population. But these are problems associated with growth, which should be met with investment.'[48] One issue is capitalism's obsession with economic growth on a planet that can only handle so much consumption and destruction, but when it comes to the domestic, population changes can be accommodated, they just take the right planning and investment.

Geographer Danny Dorling has argued that any signs of overpopulation are actually the result of poor use of land, wage compression and the slashing of state support, not immigration. 'We've managed to organise ourselves so that much of our daily lives is crowded,' he said. 'We have the smallest homes in Europe. Meanwhile, there's lots of wasted space.' Our population figures are somewhat out of date because the last UK census was in 2011, but what we can deduce from the information we have is the country isn't even particularly densely populated, despite what we might like to believe. Dorling points out that London is the lowest density mega-city on the planet; 'the densest part of London is four times less dense than Barcelona.'[49] In 2012, it was estimated that just 2.27 per cent of England's landscape was built on.[50]

Population density is usually understood by dividing the number of people in a country by the land area of that same country, but urban studies specialist Alasdair Rae argues that this isn't always the best way to make sense of population density. He makes the case for 'lived density', which allows us to understand how densely populated an area is by looking at the places actually occupied by people. Spain might seem like a sparsely populated country when you divide the number of people by the land, but large swathes of the country are empty. 'Spain contains within it more than 505,000 1km squares. But only 13 per cent of them are lived in.' That means the 'lived density' is much higher than you would think. Under this measure, England still has relatively high population density for Europe but nowhere near as much as other countries.[51] Even for those who remain adamant that population growth can't be handled, it just simply isn't true that the UK is 'full'. Portes points out that population growth can be good for a country, and that it's better than the opposite – population decline. 'Inner London lost a fifth of its population in the 1970s, which is pretty amazing when you think about it,' he explains, 'and . . . at that time if you asked people what's going on, people would say: "cities are dying".'

Population increases aren't in and of themselves a threat to the UK. With an ageing society, this country needs people from outside to come in and do the jobs we simply don't have the workforce for. This reality is a useful corrective to refute the misleading allegation that the number of migrants coming to the UK isn't sustainable. But just like the 'migrants contribute' argument, it shouldn't be used to justify migrants' existence or to prove that they deserve to be here; where's the humanity in that?

In the mid-eighteenth century, it's said people warned that if too many Jewish migrants came into the country, they would turn St Paul's into a synagogue. In 1978, when net migration was zero, 70 per cent of people said they felt the country was being 'swamped' by other cultures. Between 1989 and 2012, Ipsos MORI polled the public eleven times on whether they agree with the statement 'there are too many immigrants in Britain.' The total number of those who agreed to some degree never dipped below 54 per cent.[52] Just as Stuart Hall said forty years ago, if you talk about migration as a question of numbers, it's always threatening, because it's always too much.

Not long after the EU referendum, David Korski, David Cameron's former adviser, made an illuminating admission. When they were trying to negotiate with Brussels before the vote, they couldn't find any suitable evidence that would 'satisfy the European Commission' that immigration put pressure on communities. 'There was no hard evidence,' he confessed. 'That is not to say we didn't perceive immigration as a problem. Cameron was convinced it was a real challenge – if perhaps more of a cultural one than an economic one.'[53]

Often framed in terms of being bad for 'integration' or damaging to 'cohesion', the argument that immigration is a threat to 'culture' comes in different forms. These are slippery words, but what we should understand is that when some people talk about numbers they aren't just worrying about perceived pressure on public services or the economy; they dislike *certain people* coming into the country and it's *certain people* who are bad for the economy. From the local high street, all the way up our conception of national identity, people believe that particular groups of migrants are incompatible with the UK.

With a picture of the Union Jack behind her and the 2015 Conservative Party conference in front of her, Theresa May spoke with certainty on this very issue, the same kind she had when she wrongly told a conference that an undocumented migrant couldn't be deported because of his pet cat. This time she claimed, 'When immigration is too high, when the pace of change is too fast, it's impossible to build a cohesive society.' Only on this occasion, the then home secretary wasn't saying anything the public hadn't heard before; Labour leader Ed Miliband had already made similar comments about immigration in 2012: 'There are issues around the pace of change in communities.'[54] There is a shared assumption in the claims of these political adversaries that, because of 'too much' immigration, people look around them in their communities and feel out of place.

Even if people express their unease in these terms, that doesn't mean this is all that's going on. Research consultant Dr Zubaida Haque doesn't have much time for the 'pace of change' argument. Reflecting on the debate over the past two decades, she says, the problem was technological change, the reduction in manufacturing, the benefits and tax system making people worse off. The restructuring of the state and the economy in order to maintain profit margins and GDP was not an accident; it meant investment in communities was non-existent. Pointing the finger of blame at migrants helped politicians to get away with it.

Place and community have rarely coincided, and we needn't romanticise the past where racism and sexism shaped peoples' lives, alienating them and telling them they don't belong.[55] But over the past fifty years, significant economic change has altered the way people interact with one another. That includes privatisation, a sharp rise in consumerism, ever-more top-down social changes and a steady decline in manufacturing, which has left many people scrambling for work in an un-unionised, low-pay service sector. Corner shops have closed and been replaced by supermarket chains, and where sales clerks once stood, there are machines – people have been left feeling even more powerless and without a voice in the places they live.

These trends have continued apace under austerity: during the five years of the Coalition government seven care homes, twelve day centres, fourteen libraries and two leisure centres closed in the city of Leeds alone. In 2018, the government's own figures showed that since 2010 local councils had closed more than 500 children's centres.[56] There are, quite literally, fewer public spaces for people to coalesce.

When it comes to analysing peoples' sense of social dislocation, politicians tend to push to the sidelines the UK's democratic deficit and all the changes that take place without peoples' input. 'It seems to prove the adage that in order for something to become a big story, it doesn't have to be plausible, it just has to be resonant,' says Benjamin, an activist who helps run a social centre for migrants in London. 'And the idea that migration is bad for "community cohesion" is plausible and it's resonant, but it's not true, and it's been a very convenient way for opportunist politicians . . . to deflect and detract attention from the real problems.'

A lot of people might be happier or more comfortable if I ended the discussion about 'legitimate concerns' with this chapter. Then fears over immigration could be explained by economic anxieties, the depletion of community spaces and worries about whether the country's infrastructure can cope with population growth. It should follow that if the economy is made fairer, anti-immigration views might disappear. This is an analysis some on the left are eager to buy into, but it's woefully incomplete.

If peoples' dislike of immigration could be understood entirely as a by-product of economic concerns, how do we explain the 40 per cent of Leave voters who said in one poll that they would be willing to experience some drop in personal income so long as immigration was reduced. This is surely liable to change, not least depending on the question you ask, but it chimed with an admission Nigel Farage made in 2014. The then UKIP leader said that rather than be 'slightly richer' he would like to reduce immigration to supposedly achieve more 'united communities'.[57] A former commodities broker, Farage isn't what you'd call struggling to get by, but his comments still speak to an important truth: anti-migrant views can't always be passed off as a product of economic anxiety or material change. There is much more to people's 'legitimate concerns'.

5

'It's Not Racist. It's Common Sense'

*But it makes an immigrant laugh to hear the fears of the
nationalist, scared of infection, penetration, miscegenation,
when this is small fry, peanuts, compared to what the immigrant fears – dissolution, disappearance.*

Zadie Smith, *White Teeth*

I have a bad memory. So, true to my bad recall, I don't know
exactly who said it or exactly why, but I do clearly remember
that it was said: 'That's because you're not from here.' Legs
splayed either side of me, sitting on the warm playground
tarmac of the first school I went to in a leafy suburb of
Newcastle, one of my friends had turned to me, casually made
this comment and moved on without skipping a beat. In a
haze of poorly remembered exchanges and recollections
pieced together from other peoples' stories, this is one of those
defining encounters that we all have from childhood, and it's
remained firmly lodged in my mind.

I had citizenship and all of the many privileges that came
with it. But my mum was brown and she was an immigrant,
or at least she'd have been seen as an immigrant by most, even
though she came to the UK with a British passport from a
country that was once considered the jewel in the crown of
the Empire. And, so, I was 'mixed race' and the child of an
immigrant. My mum wasn't 'from here'; neither was I. It's
unlikely my classmate came to this conclusion on their own,
they probably learned it subconsciously from an adult in their
life who had noted our difference and used it to define us.

Low wages or overcrowded public services couldn't entirely explain this throwaway comment. Written into these words was something else altogether.

When people say that the reason they don't like immigration isn't just about or even because of economics, they're being honest. There's little evidence, academics Jens Hainmueller and Daniel J. Hopkins claim, that attitudes on immigration are heavily related to 'personal economic circumstances'. Whether it's largely about economics, culture or a mix of the two, it's 'symbolic concerns' about the nation that matter most.[1] For some people, it's predominantly or exclusively worries about the economy or overpopulation that drive their feelings on immigration, but for others there's something else in the mix: 'culture'. This is what the phrase 'legitimate concerns' covers too. But how can we understand the relationship between immigration and anxieties over cultural change?

This question rarely gets considered because it's assumed that cultural anxiety is normal and natural, that the way to deal with it is to reduce immigration, and that there are two things in particular that it's indisputably not about: race and prejudice.

'There is nothing innately left wing about supporting uncontrolled immigration. In fact, properly managing migration will help build an open and anti-racist society and mean Britain is better able to provide asylum to those in need,' writes the Fabians' deputy general secretary in a post-EU referendum pamphlet that mentioned immigration around eighty times in the space of twenty-nine pages. 'The left must also stop conflating concerns about immigration with racism. While it is vital to challenge the language of hate from UKIP and others, the majority of people who worry about immigration are not intolerant.'[2] It is almost as if the last couple of decades of politics hadn't happened at all.

~

The New Right had no formal ties to the Conservative Party, but they were hardly a fringe group. Their aim was to influence society, and in the 1970s and '80s they gave an intellectual polish to Thatcherism. A disparate coterie of right-wing academics, journalists, writers and politicians, they weren't a strictly unified organisation and they didn't have one cohesive way of understanding the world. But, aside from their fierce belief in the 'free market', what united many of them was a social authoritarianism that fixated on the state of the nation. They attacked multiculturalism as disruptive,[3] anti-racism as divisive and argued it was only natural to think that society needed to be protected from 'too many' migrants coming into the country.

New Right proponents thrashed out their ideas in the *Salisbury Review*, a quarterly magazine of conservative thought which began in 1982 and which was edited by the philosopher Roger Scruton. And in some of the country's biggest newspapers – the *Sunday Telegraph*, *The Times*, the *Daily Mail* and the *Daily Express* – leading New Right academics also used opinion columns to air their views.[4]

Bold and unashamed, in these spaces, the New Right rejected the suggestion that their views on immigration were racist. When asked about racism, Enoch Powell, one of the earliest people to express the politics that would become central to New Right thinking,[5] argued 'if . . . you mean a man who despises a human being because he belongs to another race, or a man who believed that one race is inherently superior to another in civilisation or capability of civilisation, then the answer is emphatically no.'[6]

Rejecting that people of different races were biologically different or inferior to white people, the problem with immigration and a multicultural society, the New Right said, was *cultural* difference. An interconnected society was less about social and economic equality and more about the *values* and *traditions* people held.[7] On these grounds, people of colour and certain groups of migrants were considered a threat to national cohesion; the nation was weak and in decline because of them. Academics who dissected this thinking called it 'the new racism'.[8]

The crux of the New Right argument was, as one of their critics put it, that 'it is in our biology, our instincts, to defend our way of life, traditions and customs against outsiders – not because they are inferior, but because they are part of different cultures.'[9] People's supposedly insurmountable and natural thresholds for difference, they implied, should be respected, otherwise immigration and increasing racial diversity would inevitably lead to racism. So, by the New Right's rationale, the only way to avoid racism was to believe this racist logic and act on it.

By the mid-1990s, the New Right had been sidelined; anti-racist activists had forced positive reforms in the UK, in doing so, changing some of the contours of the debate about immigration. But these ideas about 'difference' and otherness, nurtured and disseminated by the New Right, still thrive in contemporary Britain, as people coming from different political traditions advocate for similar ideas. Journalist and commentator David Goodhart is one of those people.

A self-described former liberal, he presents himself as a 'straight-talker' who is willing to challenge the left when, as he claims, it ignores peoples' concerns about 'mass immigration' and the assumed threat it poses to social democracy and the welfare state. On TV, and in the pages of magazines, newspapers and two books, he's argued that when there are too many new immigrants coming in the UK, the country's bonds of solidarity are weakened because more diversity erodes common culture and undermines what's needed for a cohesive society and welfare state. Even though, immigrants have made and continue to make possible that very welfare state. What exactly 'culture' is and which 'cultures' are similar is never really defined; referencing American academic Robert

Putnam, Goodhart argues that 'absorbing 100,000 Australians is very different to 100,000 Afghans'. The distinctions between the more and the less compatible don't always neatly map onto racial categories, and yet, in a move reminiscent of the New Right, Goodhart has been known to blur the lines between immigration and race by putting statistics about people of colour and people born abroad 'side by side'.[10]

Academic Matthew Goodwin seems to have given intellectual gloss to similar arguments, namely that 'people have strong and entrenched fears about the perceived destruction of national cultures, ways of life and values, amid unprecedented and rapid rates of immigration and ethnic change'. By not situating them in a broader political, social and historical context, this kind of analysis gives the impression that all such fears are natural and inevitable. This thinking has subtly nestled into the mainstream in different but often complementary ways.[11]

Littered across newspapers and TV documentaries is the belief that immigration brings with it too much cultural change. Parts of the left have too readily accepted this vision of the world. One national columnist trying to make sense of anti-immigration views expressed by people up and down the country declared that 'millions of people will always be uneasy about large-scale change. Not because they are racist, or anymore prejudiced than anyone else – but because human beings like a measure of certainty and stability.'[12] This doesn't amount to suggesting that diversity is inherently problematic – the columnist pinpointed a variety of sources for public anxiety and argued immigration is not bad for the economy – but the article didn't engage with how race might be a factor in the debate. Stopped dead in its tracks is the potential for broader discussion about *why* people might dislike immigration.

In January 2017, Labour MP Caroline Flint gave us a glimpse of another meaning the loaded term 'culture' can carry with it when it's used in the context of the immigration debate. Is it fair to say that New Labour ignoring concerns about immigration in the 2000s was not only a mistake 'economically but culturally too?' BBC *Newsnight*'s Kirsty Wark asked Flint. 'I think it's not just about economics,' Flint replied, 'it's about the social atmosphere as well. In Doncaster, for example, Don Valley, in my own constituency, back in '97, it was 99.5 per cent white. In the last few years, "non-British" has gone up to 5 per cent. That may not seem much to places like Leicester, but that's a *big* change in small-town village communities.'

In this statement, 'race' and 'culture' collapsed into one another as 'white' and 'British' seemed to become synonymous. Barely anyone registered the slip, but maybe that's because we're so used to hearing it.

BBC *Panorama*'s 2017 'Life in Immigration Town' was a thirty-minute documentary, following up from a piece made ten years earlier, which looked at changing demographics in Slough. It was billed as seeking to answer the question, 'What happens when a community is changed by immigration?' They zeroed in on one particular statistic: white Brits comprised 34.5 per cent of the population, meaning that 'for the first time in Slough' they were 'a minority'. Similarly, producers of Channel 4's *Immigration Street* claimed they chose to film on Derby Road because 'at the last census 17 per cent of residents described themselves as "White British" against a national average of 86 per cent.' Is it 'that only white people are British and everyone else is an immigrant?' TV reviewer Ellen E. Jones asked.[13]

Programmes like these are spun as if earnest presenters are embarking on a neutral sociological exploration of immigration to hear 'ordinary' people's 'concerns' about immigration. But their very premise sets the tone from the beginning: immigration has diluted the number of white Britons in a given area, which in itself is an issue that deserves special attention.

Documentaries about historically black areas being gentrified by 'white Brits' must surely be in the pipeline.

This particular comparator conjures up the image of white British society being changed by people of colour and immigrants who don't naturally belong in these areas – in the same way the New Right claimed. Here we can also see the messiness of what people might mean when they talk about immigration; referring to people from within the EU as well as outside it, including people of colour, no matter if they were born in the UK.

What can lie behind complaints about immigration was neatly captured by Charles Moore, former editor of the *Daily Telegraph*, the *Sunday Telegraph* and the *Spectator* in a column called 'Time for a more liberal and "racist" immigration policy': 'Britain is basically English-speaking, Christian and white, and if one starts to think it might become basically Urdu-speaking [*sic*] and Muslim and brown, one gets frightened and angry.'[14]

Beyond the fringes of the New Right, the distinction between race and immigration has long been blurred by politicians who have argued that, to preserve British identity and reduce racism, immigration needs to be 'controlled'. In 1967 Conservative Duncan Sandys declared, 'We are determined to preserve the British character of Britain, we welcome other races in reasonable numbers, but we have already admitted more than we can absorb.' And Margaret Thatcher said, 'If you want good race relations, you have got to allay peoples' fears on numbers.' Nearly fifty years later, Labour MP Stephen Kinnock made a strikingly similar argument: 'Nobody is born racist, but immigration that reaches levels beyond a society's capacity to cope can lead, in extremes, to racism.'[15]

Reminiscent of some of the response to racist violence in London's Notting Hill in 1958 and the murder of Kelso Cochrane a year later, at its most basic expression, the rationale of today's politics remains that the numbers of certain migrants coming into a country determines whether there will be a xenophobic or racist response. Once again, a negative reaction to 'too much' change is assumed to be a natural one, and the solution prescribed is to have fewer of 'those' migrants.

But anti-immigration sentiment isn't inevitable, and immigration controls haven't reduced prejudice; racism isn't a mistake or a consequence of demographic change; it is a product of history.[16] Racism is only possible because of the category 'race', which is not a given or a natural way of organising society but was and is created and given meaning by people. Racisms are always changing – but they remain present in the way immigration is talked about and legislated for.

Satvir Kaur is a councillor in Southampton who was heavily involved in the local protests against the television programme *Immigration Street* being made on a street in the city. 'A lot of people in this area are not new immigrants, they're second, third generation, and we felt as though we were being targeted because we were a different religion and a different colour and ate different food and worshipped at a different place,' she says when she explains why residents protested. 'I think that was most upsetting for people. It raises the question: at what point do you stop being considered an immigrant and at what point do you start being classed as British?'

When Enoch Powell gave his infamous 'Rivers of Blood' speech, he fashioned himself as a conduit for 'ordinary' people. Some of his most racist utterances were relayed through a supposed quote from one of his constituents, a middle-aged person who he called 'quite ordinary'. It was this man who delivered one of the most well-known lines of this speech: 'In this country in fifteen or twenty years' time the black man will have the whip hand over the white man.' When Thatcher criticised immigration, she leant on a similar reasoning by talking in class terms. She drew a divide between 'a well-heeled politician' who preached 'the merits of tolerance on a public platform before returning to a comfortable home in a tranquil road in one of the more respectable suburbs' and 'poorer people, who cannot afford to move' and who supposedly watched their neighbourhoods 'changing and the value of their house falling' because of immigration.[17] The prime minister who smashed the miners' strike was claiming concern for the very same communities she helped to destroy. In this moment, what trumped her attacks on the working classes was that white people who didn't otherwise have a choice would be forced to live alongside people of colour.

As the anti-immigrant racism of the supposed 'ordinary' Briton was entertained in popular politics, the impact of these views on people of colour was considered peripheral. Fifty years after Powell made his infamous intervention, Shadow Home Secretary Diane Abbott recalled, 'I remember Enoch Powell's speech, I think I was in primary school, and I wasn't following it in huge detail, but I do remember how I felt. People were talking about it even in school and I felt frightened.'[18]

Whether they're attempting to or not, this continues to be one of the ways that certain politicians, commentators and thinkers obscure the public discussion of what people really mean when they insist that immigration brings too much 'cultural' change to their street, town or country. 'Concern' is packaged up as a working-class phenomenon and the immigration debate is framed as a clash of classes: the 'liberal metropolitan elite' versus the 'left behind'. The former are thought of as champions of 'mass immigration', depicted as colluding with one another to let migrants into the country without the consent of the public, championing 'globalisation' and caring little for the supposed impact of this on the rest of society, namely the 'left behind'. These two categories and how they're applied to the 'debate' relies on a lazy understanding of class. One example of this is the way UKIP positioned themselves and how they subsequently came to be understood.

When they were nearing the height of their success, barrister and the deputy chairperson of the Bermondsey and Old Southwark Conservative Association Rupert Myers sketched an image of a party that could be said to be an archetypal understanding of UKIP. 'This isn't a party fuelled by racism but one that taps into the feeling of disenfranchisement among the less well-off,' he wrote. 'Support for UKIP on the doorstep was voiced as support for a party that understood the concerns of ordinary voters, and the three main parties need to learn this lesson.'[19] Often detoxified and, even when critiqued, presented as part of the norm of politics, anti-migrant politicians like Nigel Farage and parties like UKIP are given an air of respectability: if nothing else, they're understood as voices for the 'left behind'.

This feeds their own narrative. They accuse the establishment of being pro-migrant, pitching themselves as David against a liberal Goliath, claiming that their views are being silenced. This is hardly a new strategy. With ample space to air their views in the UK's newspapers, the New Right claimed there was a 'conspiracy of silence' in the 1970s; the establishment was shutting down discussion about the supposed problems black people brought to country. In the process, they were gagging 'ordinary people'. In 1975 *Times* columnist Roland Butt wrote in a collection of essays that the Tories were listening too much to experts: 'Perhaps the outstanding example of the ignoring of popular opinions was immigration.'[20]

Instead of being shut down by the media, contemporary anti-immigration proponents receive a significant, at times uncritical or even celebratory, platform. In 2014, Farage was given a weekly column in the *Independent* to air his views, and since his first appearance in 2000, he was regularly on the BBC's well-known political debate show *Question Time*.

People say that sunshine is the best disinfectant, but in this case it's acting as a source of nutrition. While he toured TV studios bemoaning that debate on immigration was prohibited, the *Mail*, the *Sun* and the *Express* published anti-migrant views on a regular basis.

Often depicted as an audacious beer-drinking straight-talker, the 'man-of-the-silenced' costume is a fitting one for Farage to wear; it makes him seem like a representative for the 'left behind' and one of the few 'authentic' mouthpieces for the people who have been systematically ignored.

Nevertheless, one of the clearest ways that people could express dislike for immigration in recent years, by voting for UKIP, a significant proportion of the working class didn't do. Disproportionately working class but unlikely to vote UKIP, people of colour were nowhere to be found in this picture. They are not really considered part of the 'left behind', even though race, class and gender structure the economy. In fact, race-making and class-making are mutually constitutive processes; people can be racialised as 'other' because of the jobs they occupy and the jobs they occupy can be decided by how they are racialised.

People of colour have long been at the forefront of the struggle against oppression in the UK, and low-income women of minority background, who are least likely to have a voice in the debate, are the worst affected by austerity.[21] So the idea that anxiety over immigration, economic or social, is a working-class concern crumbles at the slightest challenge.

I'm not 'left behind', but my family history tells a different story. On 21 October 1973, my grandmother stepped foot on the country she would live in for the rest of her life. Arriving with five of her children – including my thirteen-year-old mum – to join my grandfather, who had already moved here with almost no money, she had uprooted them from India, after returning there from Uganda, with the hope that this new place would provide opportunity. A self-taught electrician, until he retired, my grandfather worked in London's St Thomas' Hospital just opposite the Houses of Parliament. My grandmother worked in a laundrette, a short-walk from her flat, located between Peckham and Camberwell, two areas of South-East London. Putting in long hours in physically demanding low-paid jobs, these two committed Labour voters would never have considered voting for a party like UKIP. They did all they could to get by, and for a significant part of their lives, they were part of the 'left behind'. But they would have been unlikely to qualify for membership of that group; they would be regarded first and foremost as 'Indians' or 'immigrants', and in this naming process assumed classless.

There's a similar story in the London borough of Newham, where I currently live. It's one of the most diverse places in the country, but it is also plagued by poverty and inequality. According to the charity Trust for London, 35.6 per cent of employees in Newham are low-paid – the highest in London – and the poverty rate is 37 per cent – ten percentage points higher than the London average. It's also solidly Labour. In the 2018 local elections, the Mayor and every single council-lor was Labour. This is a place where people are consistently *left behind* by government policies, but they don't vote UKIP. At the height of their success in the 2015 General Election, in one of the borough's constituencies, West Ham, UKIP only received 7.5 per cent of the vote.

More often than not, the 'left behind' – the people thought to be most motivated by anti-immigration politics – is code for the 'white working class'. Increasingly used after the 2008 crash, often by people who have previously denounced class or spent their careers describing people in poverty as lazy, this term has no analytical value. There are white people who are working class, who have been systematically ignored, exploited and taken for granted, but there is no widespread anti-white ideology: white people aren't routinely discrimi-nated against on the basis of their race. White people who are working class might be seen by some as 'less than' their upper-class counterparts, but this doesn't amount to any significant structural discrimination that isn't also experienced by the rest of the multiracial working class.[22]

Still it's this group that is assumed to be negatively impacted by immigration – not just economically but socially too. The 'white working class', politicians claim, are some of the people who feel most keenly that their identity and sense of self, which is bound up with patriotism, is under threat.[23] In 2009 Hazel Blears, then New Labour's communities secretary, articulated this view: white people on low incomes had an 'acute fear' of immigration, which politicians were ignoring.[24] The year before, the BBC's series of programmes *White Season* suggested the same. The promotional video showed a white man's face being written on in black permanent marker by a brown hand until he disappeared. It asked, 'Is the white working class becoming invisible?'[25] The UK's national broadcaster was fuelling the idea that white working-class people are 'left behind' because of immigration, racial diversity and politicians' imagined preoccupation with solving racial inequality. The message is regularly that white working-class Britons dislike immigration – and their voices should be heard.

In the immediate scramble to understand how the UK had voted to leave the EU, some left-leaning politicians fumbled around in the new terrain they found themselves on and clutched on to the argument that it was the 'left behind' who drove the Brexit vote. It's not as if deprivation and powerlessness didn't play into the result in a significant way, but polls suggest that Brexit was disproportionately delivered by the home-owning, pension-possessing, wealthy, white middle-class people in southern England – who voted for, or at least hadn't been deterred from voting with, the aggressively anti-immigrant Brexit campaign. In the endless analysis that followed the referendum, there were many fewer vox pops of the 'white middle classes' or 'white upper classes' – terms you rarely hear in this debate – for commentators to pick apart than there were of the 'white working class'.[26]

In a society so heavily structured by class it might seem a good thing not to focus all attention on the (white) middle and upper classes, who are overrepresented in our debates and decision-making processes. But when anti-immigration politics is mapped onto the left behind, the middle and upper classes are overlooked and the 'white working class' becomes a racist, xenophobic and thuggish caricature, while anti-racism is somehow cast as a practice of the 'metropolitan elite'. The 'metropolitan elite' is used to lump together all different kinds of people, from radical anti-racists to liberals. This is misleading, as when liberals have been in positions of power they have often done little to challenge, and instead reinforced, institutional racism. Itself a telling response, popular debate that pits this 'metropolitan elite' against the 'left behind' has obscured any real analysis of what people mean when they talk about 'cultural anxiety' because it's assumed to be a cry of discontent from 'the white working class', who should be uncritically heard. It's decidedly more complicated than that.

Jean Donnachie, a retired shop worker, knows this all too well. Now seventy-six, she has lived on Kingsway Court in Glasgow for over twenty years. Home to six, fifteen-storey tower blocks, the area Donnachie lives in doesn't look too dissimilar from estates across the country. But in 2006 it was transformed into a site of protest.

'When we were told we were getting asylum seekers we were only too happy; we said yes because there was a lot of empty flats,' explains Jean. They welcomed these new people into the small community centre on the estate; it was here they all got to know each other through English lessons and nursery sessions. 'After about a year, when they had settled, one morning myself and a few friends witnessed early morning black vans turning up at the flats and the police jumping out with armour and guns over their shoulders.' From her home in Glasgow, Jean still sounds angry about this. 'And the next thing they brought families down, children were in their pyjamas, men with their hands in handcuffs, the gentlemen were put into one van and the women and children into another and they were taken away.'

With people on the estate, Jean started the campaigning group Kingsway Against Removals and Deportations (KARD). Long-term residents and the new arrivals conducted daily patrols to stop people on the estate being bundled into the backs of vans on government orders. One October morning, they stood defiantly arm in arm forming a human chain to stop immigration officials clad in riot gear from deporting the Uzuns, a family from Turkey.[27] For two years, this dynamic resistance would swing into action when officers descended onto the estate. Until, one day, the vans stopped coming. Not entirely dissimilar from the Lancashire millworkers who in 1862 refused to handle cotton picked by slaves in the US, the community in Kingsway Court rallied together to put a halt to the deportations.

Jean is adamant that it's not inevitable to feel unsettled by new, 'different' people coming into an area. 'You know what? Those people . . . I always say I think our community was better for them coming.' Prejudice and racism are pervasive in the UK, but it's an ordinary feature of social life that all different kinds of people live in working-class areas – loving, liking and disliking each other.[28] It is telling that some of the places with the highest anti-immigration feeling have the lowest number of immigrants; often it's the constructed fear of the 'other', not the everyday interactions with people from different countries, that produces anti-immigration views.

When I talk to forty-five-year-old Jon about his thoughts on immigration, he says he has no problem with it. Working two jobs as an operations manager in a shopping centre and on nightshifts as a door supervisor in the North-East, he explains how his jobs bring him into contact with people from all over the world. It's 'quite amazing to watch', he says, 'because you have Jewish people, Muslim people, Chinese people, never a problem with race or cultures.'

Unlike the rigid picture we're presented with, the groups that are used to make sense of society are internally diverse; it's not only that working-class people of colour and working-class immigrants are absent from the analysis of disenfranchisement; working-class people who resist racism are too. Anti-migrant feeling is not an unstoppable train; peoples' identities are not fixed.

That anti-migrant views are seen as inevitable fits into a belief that there is one inherent form of British 'culture' and one set of British values which migrants must integrate or assimilate into, values so many of us are assumed to have just because we were born here. The story goes that immigrants are a threat to British, English or 'Western' 'ways of life'. Treasured but often vaguely defined, these 'values' are imagined as if they're organic to these parts of the world. Shifting in form depending on the time and place, this kind of chauvinistic nationalism is widespread; in India, proponents of Hindutva believe Muslims will sully 'pure' Indian 'culture'.

Cultures are too varied to fit into the demands governments make for national cohesion. The Coalition government itself struggled to define what the term 'British values' meant. In the foreword to their 2015 counter-extremism strategy, David Cameron vaguely described British values as 'the liberty we cherish, the rights we enjoy and the democratic institutions that help protect them'. And when they announced their plans for a Counter-Extremism and Safeguarding Bill, which would introduce new powers to tackle individuals engaged in 'extremist' behaviour, the Joint Committee on Human Rights came to a damning conclusion. They said the government gave 'no impression of having a coherent or sufficiently precise definition of either "non-violent extremism" or "British values",' making clear their concerns that any legislation would 'likely focus on Muslim communities in a discriminatory fashion or could be used indiscriminately against groups who espouse conservative religious views but who do not encourage any form of violence.'[29]

There is no static national identity or homogenous, hermetically sealed 'culture' that's distinct from all others. The people who migrated to Britain and who the very concept of Englishness comes from – the Angles and Saxons – didn't come to this country until the second half of the fifth century.[30] The Royal Family are from Germany. And the leaves for that supposedly quintessential English drink, tea, academic Stuart Hall reminded us, are grown in India and Sri Lanka. Though some bits are stubborn, culture is always changing.[31]

That change isn't always smooth, but antagonism isn't automatically bad. The violence anti-migrant politics can produce should never be underestimated, but clashes of ideas can be constructive. Whether it's the persistence of racism in the UK or particular manifestations of misogynistic traditions maintained by groups across societies, challenging certain norms is productive and, yes – it can be messy.

The identities people claim are rigid actually gain their meaning from being positioned against an 'other'. When they argue racial or 'cultural' differences are insurmountable, they are trying to maintain that distance because of an anxiety that once people grasp that it is just made up, constructed and not all that real, those fixed ideas of 'us' and 'them' might crumble. Jon in the North-East or Jean and KARD in Glasgow are inconvenient for their analysis. If you peel back the layers of the arguments about 'culture', you find how warped they are. Dislike for immigration on the grounds of 'culture' isn't a *natural* response to immigration expressed by the 'left behind'; it is created by histories, political actions and rhetoric. More often than not, the problem isn't difference, it's that difference is perceived to be a problem at all.

~

Hours before pro-refugee Labour MP Jo Cox was murdered by white supremacist neo-Nazi Thomas Mair as he shouted, 'Britain first,' Nigel Farage was standing proudly in front of one of the defining images of the EU referendum campaign. With one week to go until the vote, the then UKIP leader unveiled a billboard with 'Breaking Point' emblazoned onto it. Pictured above these words was a queue of mostly brown refugees crossing the Croatia–Slovenia border.[32] The image and accompanying words told voters that these people would come into the country and destabilise the nation. Aside from its obviously inflammatory message, there was something peculiar about this billboard: the referendum was supposed to be about EU freedom of movement, not people seeking asylum.

Politicians from the official Vote Leave campaign denounced the poster; Michael Gove said he 'shuddered' when he saw it and Chris Grayling called it 'wrong'.[33] They showed no such squeamishness when it came to their own campaign literature, warning in one leaflet that alongside four other countries, Turkey was set to join the EU.

They produced a bright-red billboard that declared, 'Turkey (population 76 million) is joining the EU.' Next to these words was an image of a trail of footsteps passing through a door that was made to resemble a British passport. They argued that people from Turkey would 'create a number of threats to UK security', and Boris Johnson and Michael Gove wrote a joint letter to David Cameron, warning that 'the public will draw the reasonable conclusion that the only way to avoid having common borders with Turkey is to vote leave and take back control on 23 June.' These pieces of propaganda were not the same as the 'breaking point' poster, but their messages were still deeply racialised.[34]

The country that is the former seat of the Ottoman Empire was not directly described as a predominantly Muslim one, but this fact loomed large in the background of discussion. Though they weren't the only countries mentioned in the leaflets, Turkey, Iraq and Syria – all of which are Muslim majority – were jointly associated in a picture that emphasised Turkey's borders with these countries. That these three places were chosen can only have been to imply that people from these countries would cause havoc in the UK.

Similarly, Tories on the Remain side criticised Farage's poster, but they didn't exactly pour cold water on the core message of some leave campaigners. David Cameron said it wasn't 'remotely on the cards' that Turkey was going to join the EU anytime soon.[35] It was, and remains, unlikely that Turkey will become a member state, but Cameron's comment was representative of a political class entirely uninterested in challenging negative stereotypes about people from Turkey. The official Remain campaign wanted to pivot away from immigration and focus on the economic risks of leaving; they weren't interested in claiming that immigration wasn't a problem.

Political outriders helped pave the way to this point. In the years before the referendum became a serious political possibility, certain Conservative and Labour politicians, as well as UKIP, the BNP and the National Front, have in their own ways dragged national politics even further to the right on immigration. Floating ideas like voluntary repatriation and banning immigrants with HIV from the UK, they have made some extreme suggestions. In the process, they've encouraged and cleared the way for politicians who have already indulged in racism and xenophobia to follow them, if not right to the edge of this anti-migrant cliff, then close enough.

Conversely, there's a dearth of voices with a sizeable platform from which to counter the prevailing discourse. Until Jeremy Corbyn was elected Labour leader, the only significant players who were even arguing that immigration is not an issue were the Scottish National Party (SNP) and the Greens, relatively small parties and new to the subject. This was the context of the EU referendum, whereby even though people like Corbyn refused to give in to anti-migrant messaging, there were far fewer voices defending migrants than there were politicians clamouring over one another to attack them.

People's views aren't merely imposed from above; everyone is capable of forming their own ideas, but that doesn't happen independently from the world around us. Anti-immigrant racism among the electorate is treated either as unavoidable or as a compartmentalised concern of the economically disenfranchised working class who are reduced to a caricature. It's as if these views, which are by no means confined to one class in society, have nothing to do with the history of colonial and anti-migrant politics, or with the role that contemporary politicians and the media have played in promoting xenophobia.[36] MPs consistently stoke the flames of racism before claiming it's an inevitability.

The racialised EU debate is a striking example of a broader phenomenon. It's not uncommon to hear Muslim migrants, as well as Muslims who were born in the UK, described as illiberal and importing dangerous norms and culture into Europe. One particular far-right narrative is that being Muslim equates to being an immigrant. The far-right – among which is Tommy Robinson, former leader of the English Defence League – claims Europe is under threat from Muslims.[37] By opposing Muslims and saying they have no problem with people of colour of other or no faiths, they claim they aren't racist.

Discrimination on religious grounds is not always synonymous with race, but in the nineteenth century, Muslims were imagined as a separate race with a fixed mindset and specific characteristics.[38] Contemporary anti-Muslim politics continues to constitute a form of racism; Islamophobia and the accompanying suggestion that Muslim 'culture' threatens Europe reduces people with diverse and complex views, traditions and understanding of faith to a homogeneous unit. 'Backwards' Islam is positioned in opposition to a 'modern' Europe, racialising a whole religion as one.

The right thrive off this narrative, but it is sanitised and intellectualised by liberals. In the wake of 9/11, the invasion of Iraq and the ensuing War on Terror, commentators and politicians, the UK's prime minister Tony Blair among them, depicted the Western world as engaged in a battle to defend liberal values from encroaching Islam. One study found that between 2000–2008, there was an increasing number of print media news stories related to Muslims and that they centred on terrorism and supposed cultural difference. While the War on Terror depicted Islam as the ultimate enemy, a sprawling security apparatus silenced Muslims, or people assumed to be Muslims, from expressing views that might run counter to the mainstream and, in turn, entrenched social divisions. 'This started long ago, with the Rushdie affair, the Gulf Wars, where people were questioning Muslim loyalties,' media and cultural studies lecturer Naaz Rashid says. The immigration debate, then, hasn't remained static; it has shifted throughout the decades to position different groups into the line of fire. Muslims are lumped together as a menacing group that are the antithesis of 'the West', and imagined as a security risk, as well as a symbol for 'bad migration' and 'bad diversity'.[39]

Lesbian, gay, bisexual, transgender (LGBT+) rights and women's rights are two issues weaponised by anti-migrant proponents to make these arguments. Immigrants – often from countries that form parts of the Middle East and the African continent – are depicted as harbouring homophobic, misogynistic attitudes; they are the anathema to a 'Western' culture under which women and gay people supposedly live discrimination-free.[40]

One night in early November 2017, I meet with Morten and Kennedy, two members of Lesbians and Gays Support the Migrants (LGSMigrant), in east London. They explain to me why they reject this position: homophobia exists in all areas of society, they say, and contrary to anti-migrant discourse, it isn't specific to one group.

Based on Lesbians and Gays Support the Miners – an alliance formed in the mid-1980s when mining communities came under sustained attack from Thatcher, and celebrated in the film *Pride* – LGSMigrant formed in the summer of 2015 while the 'migrant crisis' was regularly being featured in the news; they fundraise and engage in direct action.[41] 'There's an idea that the LGBT community, because of the oppression we are facing and have faced historically, has a responsibility to stand up for people facing state oppression,' Morten, one of the group's founding members says. 'The right were using gay rights as a weapon against Muslims and migrants and we felt like unless we said something about it we were complicit it in.' There may be some communities in which homophobia is more prevalent, Morton says, but 'is the solution to let people drown in the Mediterranean and lock people up in detention?'

They also point out that it's not as if protecting LGBT+ rights is some kind of value intrinsic to the West. It was only towards the end of the 1960s that homosexuality was legalised in the UK, and at the height of Empire one of Britain's exports was laws against homosexuality. 'Their struggle is bound up with ours,' Kennedy says of the people who cross the Mediterranean, 'it wasn't long ago we were considered illegal.'

As for far-right feminism, Nigel Farage, who has since joked about the idea of Donald Trump sexually assaulting Theresa May, declared the Cologne attacks the 'nuclear bomb' of the EU referendum campaign. On New Year's Eve 2015, outside Köln Hauptbahnhof, the main train station of one of Germany's largest cities, at least one hundred women said they had been sexually assaulted. Grabbed, robbed and surrounded by groups of men, they reported what seemed to be a coordinated attack, and the news reports referenced others who claimed the attackers 'looked North African or Arab'.[42]

A *New York Times* editorial warned: 'Europe must . . . find a way to cope with a problem that has been largely ignored until now: sexual aggression by refugees from countries where women do not have the same freedoms as in Europe.'[43] Although it was never uncovered exactly who was responsible for each of the attacks on these women, the reporting read as though the perpetrators were exclusively Syrian men who neither knew nor cared about European social norms. It would be more accurate to view acts of violence committed by men all around the world as a particular manifestations of global patriarchy.[44] But in this case it is racism that gives these claims about difference meaning and a semblance of coherence. Weighed down by colonial narratives, culture is used as a differential marker, drawing a distinction between respectable white men and barbaric brown men; it's precisely the supposed ancestral, innate 'otherness' that is used to explain such behaviour.[45]

Imagine, just for a moment, if this situation were reversed. If sexual violence committed by white or 'Western' men – whether the people we know to be perpetrators because of the MeToo movement or high-profile figures like Jimmy Savile – were to be presented as inherent to *European culture*. Instead they're seen as monsters; deviations from the respectable norm, even when statistics show us the norm is better described as entirely unrespectable.

In England and Wales, an estimated 510,000 women aged sixteen to fifty-nine experienced sexual assault between March 2016 and March 2017. But one 2018 poll found that even if a woman hasn't consented to sex, a third of men believe it wouldn't be rape if she had flirted on the date beforehand; perhaps more revelatory is the statistic that 21 per cent of women believe the same and 24 per cent of people don't think sex without consent in a long-term relationship is rape.[46] For some people, when migrant men are involved, their supposed inherent cultural difference is to blame; when European men are, women are at fault.

Wading into the debate about immigration during the height of press coverage of the 'migrant crisis' in 2015, then foreign secretary Philip Hammond said it would be impossible for Europe to 'preserve its standard of living and social infrastructure if it has to absorb millions of migrants from Africa'.[47] Utterances like this are 'a euphemism', academic Alana Lentin explains, 'for saying . . . these brown people are coming to kill us in our beds and take away our jobs. And so the "pragmatic" solution is often posed as one of reducing migration.'

Muslims, and at different times, black and brown people, are marked out as pollutants, undeserving leeches or security menaces; they're thought to create and exacerbate social problems. Lurking in these ideas is the belief that they threaten what is historically a white, and therefore pure, continent and – in line with the New Right thinking – the response to the difference these migrants are supposed to represent is characterised as only natural. It's on these terms that they're considered a fitting target of resentment.[48]

In the spring of 2007, after just over ten years, Tony Blair announced he would be stepping down as prime minister. He offered one of his final assessments of the nation while still in power. 'The British are special,' he told the audience inside the Trimdon Labour Club, in his constituency, Sedgefield. 'The world knows it; in our innermost thoughts we know it. This is the greatest nation on Earth.' Arguments like this, which rely on notions of civility filtered through this lens of culture and ideas of white superiority, would be a lot easier to buy if the Opium Wars hadn't happened, if over 1,000 people hadn't been killed or injured by British colonialists in the Amritsar Massacre, and if Britain hadn't made large parts of its wealth from its exploitative empire. 'If Western culture were real,' says philosopher Kwame Anthony Appiah, 'we wouldn't spend so much time talking it up.'[49]

When I explain to former Ed Miliband adviser Harvey Redgrave that I think immigration, racism and prejudice are still intimately connected, he challenges me. 'The EU migration that happened mid-2000s was not racialised in the sense that they looked like us, they're white, they're European. It didn't have the same look or feel as some of those earlier waves of migration did.' But people, he says, still 'thought of it as the same phenomenon, but it wasn't'. Here, there's still an image of a white 'us' and a white Europe. But Redgrave hits on something that is worth exploring because there *is* still a political imaginary where Europeans are seen as white, and how this relates to the way people from Eastern Europe are talked about is not straightforward.

One remark you might hear in the immigration 'debate' is that when some people walk down a local high street in the UK they don't recognise what country they are living in. Eastern European shops can spring up where derelict car parks or empty shop windows used to be; places that have helped revive the high street, which has been on life support after small shops were squeezed out by huge supermarket chains.[50] But it's the change we're told people don't like; the different lettering on signs or the languages and accents they hear when they walk down the road. When I speak to one woman from Poland, she says after the referendum there have been moments when she's felt too vulnerable to speak Polish, fearing she'll be marked out as different, so she speaks English to blend in. These are people who are assumed to be white.

But this is the meeting of xenophobia and racism; what intellectual Ambalavaner Sivanandan called xenoracism. Xenophobia might be understood as the 'natural' fear of strangers and racism the discriminatory way whole groups of people who are racialised as inferior to white people – assumed to have some meaningful ancestral difference from one another – are treated. With these two features together, Sivanandan says, xenoracism 'bears all the marks of the old racism except that it is not colour-coded'.[51] Though applicable to different groups and at different times, xenoracism means that people from parts of Europe are dehumanised and 'othered' in ways that wealthy French financiers, Italian businesspeople or Australian bartenders rarely have been.

We know this is possible because skin colour isn't the only marker of race. In the eighteenth and early nineteenth centuries, Irish migrants and working-class people were thought to occupy a degraded whiteness; Thomas Carlyle compared Irish peasants, English seamstresses and English working classes to 'negroes'.[52] How race operates is messy, slippery and changing; whiteness is shifting and hard to pin down. Eastern European migrants who might be considered as having white skin still experience anti-immigrant policies or rhetoric that are reliant on and produce the very idea of them being seen as 'not quite white'.[53]

People from Eastern Europe who tend to be concentrated in 'low-status', badly paid jobs have been the focus of tabloid anti-immigration campaigns which consistently claim that migrants from this part of the world bring crime, discord and 'cultural' change to the UK. One person I speak to from Hungary tells me how he came to the UK after the 2008 crash. He works so many jobs and such long hours that he barely gets any time off. His life here, he says, is really no life at all. It's possible that Eastern European people or particularly their children might be seen as belonging and thus acceptable in a way that people of colour, both migrants and people born in the UK, won't; 'not being white, and being black are two very different things'.[54] But right now, they are also the subjects of anti-immigration politics.

When I ask Alp Mehmet about why people dislike immigration, he argues, 'This isn't just white middle-class Anglo-Saxon people . . . this is migrants as well, and we find as often as not people will come to us from migrant communities and say, "Look you know I am originally from India, from Bangladesh and I'm really not happy with what's going on."' From this point of view, it seems that disliking immigration is less about race or prejudice because there are also immigrants of colour and people of colour born in the UK who dislike immigration.

It shouldn't be a surprise that immigrants or people of colour can be anti-immigration. They exist in the same society as everyone else; they hear the same stereotypes and read the same newspapers. These people's anti-immigration views might not be predominantly a product of racism; they might also arise from a misguided belief that migrants threaten their jobs, public services or security. Or they might have prejudiced views about immigrants from certain parts of the world because they're perceived to be of a 'lower class' or because of the way the media and politicians present the debate.

When Mancherjee Merwanjee Bhownaggree, an Indian immigrant, became the Conservative MP for Bethnal Green North East, a constituency in London, he ran on an anti-immigrant platform. The year was 1895, and one piece of election material in support of Bhownaggree's candidacy, written to the 'members of British Industries, Trade & Labour Defence League' blamed 'foreign pauper aliens' for everything from 'increased house rent in East London' to 'over-crowding and insanitary dwellings'. It listed boot makers, cabinet makers, tailors and cigar makers as having to compete with 'foreign pauper aliens'. To change this, it demanded in black, bold writing: 'VOTE FOR BHOWNAGGREE'. Today's equivalents might be the minority ethnic councillors in Barking and Dagenham who defected to UKIP because they claim there are too many Eastern Europeans in the UK.[55]

'You can't really use people of colour as a pass to say, "We're right,"' campaigner Tatiana Garavito argues. 'We are human beings, we are very complex, we all get fed information by the media, so it's not that if you're a person of colour you will *get* everything.' Some people who are migrants might want to prove their 'insider' status by agreeing with anti-migrant sentiment, they might fear they will be lumped in with newcomers in anti-immigrant backlashes or, until recently, non-EU migrants might have been unhappy with an immigration system that privileged people from Europe.

Even so, a 2015 research project conducted by race equality think tank the Runnymede Trust suggests that people of colour and migrants are more likely than the rest of the population to think that immigration is positive than negative. When headlines about Eastern European migrants adorned newspaper front pages, a lot of the participants of colour 'felt that they were the target of immigration discourse'.

People who experience British racism are more likely to be (though not *bound* to be) better informed about it. They're also far less likely to be mobilised by anti-immigrant politics, be it in the form of the BNP, UKIP or the vote to Leave the EU. So even though there are people of colour who are sceptical about immigration, there's often a major difference in how they behave. 'The debate on immigration is like a cover for another debate on race and racism,' one participant in the study said. 'It's a way to talk about being anti whatever group you're against. That group is usually of colour or [speaks] a different language. [It's] having a way to express some anger about other groups that are perceived as being racially different.'[56]

In 1999, former Tory minister and party chairperson Norman Tebbit confirmed why people of colour might feel the immigration debate is about them. Speaking to the *Los Angeles Times*, he declared that 'a large proportion' of Britain's Asian population would fail to pass what he called the 'cricket test': 'Which side do they cheer for? . . . It's an interesting test. Are you still harking back to where you came from, or where you are? And I think we've got real problems in that regard.'[57] For British Asians, their belonging to the country was contingent on their willingness to show loyalty to it, otherwise could they really be trusted?

From New Labour's reaction to violence in 2001 to the two journalists who complained in the *Daily Mail* that the 'true impact' of immigration wasn't being recorded because the

Office for National Statistics class migrants' children 'as British rather than second or third generation immigrants', citizenship doesn't guarantee belonging. Dormant in some of these assumptions is the thinking summed up by Enoch Powell in 1968: 'The West Indian or Asian does not, by being born in England, become an Englishman. In law he becomes a United Kingdom citizen by birth; in fact he is a West Indian or an Asian still.'[58]

'The link between race and immigration does seem to be missing in our current discourse on immigration policies,' Fizza Qureshi tells me. There is little discussion about how 'the way they're implemented perpetuates a racist discourse'. Preliminary evidence from work on the government's hostile environment policy, which forces landlords and NHS staff to check people's documents before they are leased properties or given certain types of healthcare, showed that people of colour and those deemed to be 'visibly foreign' were more likely to have to prove they have the right documentation to access services than white British people. For example, research conducted by the Joint Council for the Welfare of Immigrants (JCWI) into Right to Rent checks showed that 58 per cent of the time a black and minority ethnic tenant had their inquiry turned down or ignored.[59] Peninah, from the Racial Justice Network, tells me that she has seen from her own work how the hostile environment affects people who have 'an accent', 'a foreign sounding name' or people who are 'black and brown'.

When Abdillaahi Muuse was detained for common assault, he gave his Dutch passport and driving licence as proof that as an EU citizen he couldn't be deported. But officials from what was then the UK Border Agency were reported to have bluntly told Muuse, a Dutch national of Somali origin: 'Look at you, you're African.' They held him for four months and told him they would send him to 'Africa'. He successfully challenged detention, but if immigration had nothing to do with race, why did Muuse, an EU citizen, end up in detention?[60]

Back in a busy, bright North London café, Redgrave still isn't convinced by the way I see racism structuring the debate on immigration. 'So let me ask you a question then,' he says. 'If you said seven or eight out of ten people in this country think European migration is too high, do you think then seven or eight out of ten people in this country are racist?'

If we're not seeing politicians trip over one another to say 'it's not racist to be concerned about immigration', we're caught up in debating whether individual voters, or individual politicians like Nigel Farage, are racist. The conversation moves rapidly away from the reality of immigration and the way racist fears are encouraged or how migrants are used as scapegoats for government policy, and becomes a personalised debate about whether someone using such rhetoric is racist. We all fall down the rabbit hole and politics becomes a game; we can focus on individuals and people can react, be offended or apologise, and we never return to the question of where these ideas come from and how they are used. 'Structural racism does not make of every individual a racist,' academic Robbie Shilliam has succinctly explained, 'but implicates every individual, variously, in the reproduction and/or contestation of racial structures.'[61] Such is the reality for immigration.

When politicians and commentators say that 'it's not racist to be concerned about immigration', they are suggesting that those who claim the contrary are stifling the debate. But shutting down all analysis of how racism shapes and is produced by the way we talk about and treat immigration is a way of sidestepping a discussion that is long overdue. If you spend all your time thinking about the symptoms of an illness and never about the causes, you can never expect to treat it.

~

For a while it felt as though 'legitimate concerns' was a political myth that almost everyone had bought into. One of the core justifications for giving credence to such 'concerns' is that, if the political 'centre' doesn't act on people's worries about immigration, support for the far right will mushroom. It's how David Blunkett defended New Labour's draconian asylum policies, and it's the often-forgotten argument that Thatcher used to prop up her 'swamping speech'.[62]

Years later, in a BBC documentary, then front-bench Labour politician Clare Short described Thatcher's decision to try and take on the National Front in this way as a 'healthy' move. 'There was enough ballast in the Tory Party that was not going to be so vilely, crudely, racist,' she explained. 'It was better to destroy the National Front. I don't know how good her motives were but I think historically it was probably helpful.'[63] At the 1979 General Election the fascist group the National Front put up over three hundred candidates, but their optimism was dashed at the polls; they lost nearly all of their deposits. But this wasn't simply down to Thatcher's supposed pacifying intervention. The National Front had already reached the peak of their success before 1979, and Thatcher in fact helped to further mainstream racist views about immigration. In the February after her comments, public opinion polls suggested the number of people who thought immigration was an urgent issue went from 9 per cent to 21 per cent.[64]

The far right is dangerous and toxic – to peremptorily dismiss it would be to underestimate it. It is not the same as 'the centre'. But aggressive, fascistic groups aren't a peculiarity entirely disconnected from the normal state of affairs and they don't just begin to be a threat when they do well electorally.[65] Moreover, it's not just the far right that produces anti-immigration politics.

People in the so-called centre believe that if they take on some of the far right's arguments, they can control them and make them reasonable. They embrace cheap, jingoistic or unthinking nationalism, which already decorates tabloid front pages, with the claim it will somehow help to address social anxieties. By assuming that they don't reproduce racist politics – by believing that it is only the far right who do this – they would rather issue condemnations than reflect on how their own politics might reinforce or contain within it xenophobic and racist attitudes. The public is their alibi; opinion encourages them to behave this way, even though they help create that very opinion.

The left often fear that, if they don't accept people's 'concerns' about immigration, they will leave a political vacuum that the right will fill. This has been tested to death. Over Ed Miliband's five years as Labour leader, barely a conversation would pass without a front-bench politician asserting they were listening to peoples' concerns and accepting immigration was a 'problem'. They were particularly concerned that they would not secure the (white) 'working-class vote' if they didn't signal that they too believed immigration needed to be reduced. This didn't win them the 2015 general election, and what followed was a rise in anti-immigration sentiment. The role of politicians on the left should be to marginalise far-right or xenophobic politics by proving them false, rather than to help mainstream them by co-opting their messages. Concerns about immigration aren't 'legitimate' and practising anti-immigration politics doesn't destroy it – it strengthens it.

Conclusion

Without new visions we don't know what to build, only what to knock down. We not only end up confused, rudderless, and cynical, but we forget that making a revolution is not a series of clever maneuvers and tactics but a process than can and must transform us.

Robin D. G. Kelley, *Freedom Dreams*

It was 'ordinary' people who suffered in the early hours of 14 June 2017 in Kensington and Chelsea, one of the richest boroughs in the country. The blaze that tore through the twenty-four-storey, west London block snatched away people's homes, their neighbours, their friends, and for some, their family members. Seventy-two people died that summer morning.

In the days following the fire that would simply become known as Grenfell – the name of the tower that had been reduced to a black, hollowed out structure – residents would speak with fury and inconsolable grief about the fact that they had tried repeatedly to prevent something like this from happening; complaints and concerns sent to the organisation responsible for running the block and thousands of others were ignored. In a prescient blog, tenants warned that they would only be heard when an incident happened in which people died.[1] The charred remains of Grenfell Tower stand on the city skyline as a reminder of failed housing policy driven by profit, austerity and corporate greed.

In the days following this atrocity, who this impacted and exactly whose voices had been ignored became clear. The faces of the dead and missing were taped to lamp posts all over west London and appeared on the front pages of national newspapers – people like Ligaya Moore and Khadija Saye and her mother Mary Mendy. Many of them belonged to groups which society likes to malign as a burden, while ignoring the way they're grossly mistreated: Grenfell Tower was the home of migrants from all over the world, refugees and working-class Britons of all races.[2]

Grenfell residents included the people our politicians and media pit against one another when they blame migrants for undercutting wages, putting strain on our public services, taking up scarce housing or destroying 'culture'. But they were all ignored, all overlooked. 'Ordinary' people are concerned about immigration, we're told, but it was 'ordinary' people who died at Grenfell.

For decades, the UK's immigration 'debate' has been anything but. The voices of people who try to challenge the received wisdom that immigration is a problem are stifled. It's run on one-dimensional stereotypes while silencing the very people who are its focus. In a country that boasts mutual respect as one of its core values, human beings have been turned into things.

It's not as if everything has stayed the same during this time. Some governments have expanded the number of immigration routes as others have actively tried to reduce the number of people coming into the country. Certain parts of the UK have been more welcoming than others. Immigration has risen and fallen on the political agenda. Although there's always a migrant to blame, exactly which group of people is marked out as creating social and economic rifts is liable to change.

Yet negative myths about immigration, both pervasive and persuasive, endure in one form or another. Even when politics has been at its most polarised, MPs and commentators who are ideological foes have found common ground in characterising immigration as a problem. Whether applied to the 1960s or 2016, this holds very little truth. Immigrants aren't undercutting wages or ruining public services. Racism and xenophobia are not an unavoidable product of 'too many' migrants of a certain kind arriving in a certain town. Immigrants from particular places don't inevitably disrupt an imagined harmonious, homogenous national culture or identity. People and traditions move and transform, and just like all the other changes that happen in our world, that can be easy and smooth, as well as untidy and antagonistic.

That there's an 'us' and 'them' is not a given; divisions are actively produced and reproduced. But after decades of bad policy and bad politics on immigration, in early September 2015, there was a glimmer of hope in Westminster.

Parliament Square was packed with people when Labour MP Jeremy Corbyn took to the makeshift stage. 'They're human beings, just like you, just like me,' he said, addressing a pro-refugee rally. 'Let's deal with the refugee crisis with humanity, with support, with compassion to try to help people who are trying to get to safety, trying to help people who are stuck in refugee camps, but recognise that going to war creates a legacy of bitterness and problems.'[3]

On 12 September 2015, tens of thousands of people had marched through the streets of Central London in solidarity with refugees, a month after news of the 'refugee crisis' had finally become widely known in the public domain. Had this been any other September in the years before, Corbyn's appearance would have, at most, received a passing mention in newspaper write-ups of the rally. It wasn't surprising he was there. An ally to all sorts of important causes, along with many people on the left, I was used to seeing him at demonstrations, talks and protests; whether speaking in support of the West Papuans who struggle for freedom or demanding the

Chagos Islanders be returned home after being exiled in the 1960s by Harold Wilson's government. But his presence at this event was now newsworthy.

Just hours before, I was sitting in the packed Queen Elizabeth II Centre in Westminster, waiting to hear the results of the Labour leadership contest. By this point, everyone anticipated that Corbyn, a long-time backbencher, would win – but they had underestimated the scale by which he would. When his landslide victory was read out, confirming he had received 59.5 per cent of the vote, the room seemed to operate on two plains: on one level were the stony-faced MPs and perplexed pundits who remained seated, on the other were the elated activists and small minority of Corbyn's Parliamentary colleagues who jumped out of their seats to celebrate; the loud silence existing alongside boisterous cheers. After making a brief acceptance speech, his first act as leader was to speak at the demonstration.

Corbyn's election was substantial and symbolic. It seemed that MPs and technocrats were no longer in control of a top-down party machine, but that power would be given to members, most of whom were to the left of the majority of Labour MPs. The left, which had been sidelined for decades, was on the rise. On so many issues, policy promised to move leftwards in a way it had never done before. For the first time in a long time, there was hope that a break with the status quo was possible in UK Parliamentary politics.

I spent the summer covering the leadership race, reporting on Corbyn's candidacy announcement, in the room where he laid out his anti-austerity economic agenda, and attending his final campaign rally in Islington. I documented how the other MPs in the race quickly became sidelined.

Candidates had dropped out along the way, but by the time members and supporters cast their ballots in the leadership contest, Corbyn had been up against Andy Burnham, Yvette Cooper and Liz Kendall. All three were, in some way, part of the old guard that had plummeted in popularity in the UK and whose social democratic counterparts were experiencing, or would experience, near wipe out in many parts of Western Europe. Their answers to questions during that summer's hustings showed their weakness. Kendall, who became an MP in 2010, was open about her Blairite views, which didn't appeal to many members (she received 4 per cent of the vote). While Burnham and Cooper, both ministers at some point under New Labour, tried hard to fashion themselves as 'sensible', middle-of-the-road politicians. Their strategy was a flop: lacking any real conviction, they gave bland, woolly answers to important political questions.

The long-time backbencher hadn't been the frontrunner when he entered the contest, but over the course of those long July and August days, Corbyn had a profound impact on UK politics. Rallies and meetings he spoke at were packed to the rafters; people spilled out onto the streets wanting to hear from this figure who represented a refreshing change from the Labour front-bench politicians they were used to.

On immigration, Corbyn's rivals offered little more than watered down anti-migrant politics, the kind that had been de rigeur during the Ed Miliband era and which Cooper, as shadow home secretary, had championed. In contrast, Corbyn attacked Labour's 2015 election pledge to 'control immigration' as 'appalling'.[4] As a backbencher, Corbyn voted against the New Labour government's draconian asylum policies and dedicated much of his time to left-wing causes. His record suggested he wasn't a fair-weather friend or a smooth-talker; his election as leader signalled there could be a significant change in how Labour approached immigration.

Over the next two years, amid bitter infighting and a failed leadership challenge headed by MP Owen Smith, Corbyn's Labour decisively rejected the government's austerity package which Ed Miliband had timidly embraced. Front-bench Labour politicians began to talk about ideas that had been exiled from mainstream politics for decades: nationalisation, regulation, collectivism.

Rejecting the usual anti-immigration arguments, Corbyn refused to describe immigration as a numbers question; he wanted to talk about migrants as people. And just over a year into his leadership, the anti-racist, pro-migration and long-time left-wing MP Diane Abbott was appointed shadow home secretary. In post, she has, at the time of writing, demanded Labour change the narrative on immigration, said they would end the much-hated hostile environment, pledged to close down two of the country's detention centres, and suggested they would reform the entire immigration system, including making efforts to scale up the rights of non-EU migrants so they are on par with EU migrants.[5] When the Conservative government was unclear about EU citizens' rights in the Brexit negotiations, Labour promised all EU nationals living in the country before Brexit would have their existing rights guaranteed.

During the 2017 General Election, Corbyn continued to praise immigration and promised to scrap Theresa May's immigration cap. The Conservatives stuck by their commitment to reduce immigration, promising to 'bear down' on non-EU migration and increase earning thresholds, which at the time meant only those people who earned £18,600 or more could bring their non-EU spouses to join them in the UK, the cost was more if they had children they wanted to come too.[6]

But the Opposition's politics can't just be measured against these anti-immigration proposals; they cannot be considered 'good' just because they're an improvement on the government's uncompromisingly xenophobic policies. In ways not entirely dissimilar to the response to scandals over anti-semitism, Labour hasn't always effectively confronted the xenoracism that underlies the discussion. While challenging some of the myths when the opportunity presented itself in moments like Windrush, there hasn't been enough of a sustained, concerted and active attempt to change the public conversation about immigration. At times, it appears peripheral to their agenda.

Written in a short space of time for an early election that few people expected, Labour's 2017 manifesto promised to end freedom of movement and replace the Tory earning thresholds with 'a prohibition on recourse to public funds'.[7] The former policy would likely result in tighter border controls; the latter suggested that immigrants were coming to claim benefits, and compounded the damage inflicted by claiming that they should not be allowed to. Both pledges would serve to continue and even extend a system that dehumanises and mistreats people.

It was as though they hoped the 'debate' on immigration would go away, and in a way it looked like it had. In the 2017 election it seemed to be somewhat less important, as peoples' views evolved, perhaps because the promise of the UK's exit from the EU and its symbolic guarantee that immigration would be reduced at least momentarily had sated some peoples' anti-immigration feeling. Perhaps it was partly also down to Corbyn redirecting the blame elsewhere: at extractive capitalist economics, not immigration. But even this message has been lost in the confusion of the UK's Brexit negotiations.

In the summer of 2017, Corbyn was being quizzed about Brexit on Sunday morning prime-time politics programme *The Andrew Marr Show*. Asked whether a government led by him would allow EU freedom of movement to continue, Corbyn initially didn't buckle. In January of that year he had stuck by his belief that EU immigration wasn't too high.[8] But when pushed by Andrew Marr, he wavered: 'What there wouldn't be is the wholesale importation of underpaid workers from central Europe in order to destroy conditions, particularly in the construction industry,' adding that he would ask agencies to 'advertise in the locality first'.[9]

He appeared to be referring to the EU Posted Workers Directive, whereby an employer who sends an employee to do a job temporarily in another member state does not have to abide by all the local labour laws. Significant though it is, this directive impacts less than 1 per cent of the labour force and when Corbyn made this statement, the EU was in the process of reforming it.[10] But this sort of nuance is lost in the sea of xenophobia that leads people to believe immigrants are causing low pay and where the debate is skewed against immigration. It's not migrants who are the problem, it's the much broader exploitative economy which should be and so often is in Corbyn's line of fire.[11]

Part of the problem has been how Labour has attempted to manoeuvre through Brexit negotiations. Agreeing to end freedom of movement – the only freedom they proposed abandoning of the four that make up the single market – meant they failed to take the lead on anti-immigration politics that undergirded the EU referendum.[12] It's not that free movement in Europe should be protected while non-EU migrants continue to navigate processes that have for decades been exclusionary, racialised and unfair. The focus should be on levelling up non-EU migrant rights, not bringing their European counterparts into an already unjust system. Even if only implicitly, committing to ending freedom of movement feeds anti-immigration politics.

Some Labour members have told me they would rather the immigration question was kicked into the long grass because they believe taking it on would torpedo the party's chances of winning an election. Others are convinced that if Labour gets into power and makes the economy fairer, then everything else will fall into line. And while there are members who are eager to push the party further on this issue, a handful sign up to the nationalistic 'socialism in one country' argument, which has gained increasing purchase in other parts of Europe too. But a left-wing politics must be global in its vision, and any case for economic justice that is concerned with the entirety of the working class must have anti-racism and anti-imperialism at its heart.

Running throughout much of this is an understandable trust that the leadership, which has a long history of standing with migrants, will deliver a better, fairer system on immigration. But the point is not only to get into power so that you can try to implement better policy; it is also to change politics and society as well.

But that isn't just down to the leadership. As well as offering an alternative to the moribund status quo, one of the stated purposes of the Corbyn project was to challenge the way people do Parliamentary politics. Under Corbyn, the Labour Party has, in some ways, given power to members and begun to let go of the reins that previous leaders gripped tightly onto by offering top-down diktats or hoarding power in the centre. Change on immigration can and should come from below; it's up to members to campaign in communities and put pressure on politicians.

Anti-immigration politics does not manifest itself in neat and contained ways, and there are no easy answers for how to challenge it. But considering how people think and talk about immigration is a good starting point.

There can be no caveats when rejecting anti-immigration rhetoric. Migrants aren't causing low pay or poor services, and there aren't too many migrants in this country. Arguments about 'undercutting' have 'never been based on evidence or fact', Petros Elia, general secretary of the small union United Voices of the World, told me a couple of years ago. 'It's always been based on prejudice . . . anyone that advocates that there's a correlation between wage levels is making it up. There isn't a debate to be had. This is not true. How it's managed to remain a debate is beyond me.' His solution is to 'talk about the things that do affect wage levels'. That would include setting the record straight by showing that migrants aren't an economic drain, but not using these arguments to justify peoples' right to be in the UK. It's necessary to debunk the narratives that politicians and the media help keep in circulation because they create new hostilities and keep old ones afloat. But in a truly emancipatory politics peoples' lives matter because they are people, not just because they're workers, 'highly skilled' or the 'best and the brightest', and they matter regardless of where they were born.

Talking about immigration in a sensitive way requires we avoid reductive arguments about how much people contribute economically or 'culturally'. 'Why is it we talk about British rights and not migrant rights?' asks Peninah from Racial Justice Network, which brings together organisations and people who work on race and equity. 'Why don't we have compassion for these people? Who wants to leave their family, their school friends, the place they grew up? Who wants to leave all of that to come here unless you have no other choice?'

Inua Ellams is a writer who has tried to push back against how immigration is distorted in the UK. He wrote and starred in the show *Evening with an Immigrant*, which he toured around the country. The aim, he tells me, was to introduce people with a British passport to an immigrant and create a forum for 'the British public to see the effects of the immigration policies over the last two or three decades in the United Kingdom'. What he wanted to do was to 'put a human face to this big bad word' that newspaper headlines drown in negativity. He found the experience largely positive. By putting a person and history to this dehumanising term, he realised that much of the audience were 'surprised at the effect of the policy' and had 'their stereotypes of immigrants' challenged.

Injecting humanity into the discussion also demands that we expose how controls work. Erin is an activist with Docs Not Cops, who campaign against the Immigration Act 2014 and the discrimination against migrants in healthcare. She conducts workshops with healthcare professionals or third-sector organisations in which she raises awareness about immigration policies the government expects NHS workers to adhere to and their impacts, in the process exposing what

reducing immigration or controlling borders means in practice. 'A lot of it seems like it's not that bad, but when you
dissect it, it becomes really clear just how pernicious and
insidious and awful it is,' she says. People often have no idea
just how cruel the immigration regime is.

There's perhaps no more tricky terrain than 'culture'; on
this the left have usually buried their heads in the sand or
accepted the right's arguments. To some people, migrants are
the cuckoo in the nest, bringing unwanted and incompatible
difference. This can be a euphemism for the racialisation of
people as 'other' whether they're Jewish, Muslim, black or
brown, or considered 'less than white'. We rarely talk about
this country's Anglo-Saxon past as a story of tribes from
Germany and Denmark migrating to this country in search of
a better life. Millions of people move, but not every one of
them is called an 'immigrant'.

Racism and xenophobia are not just individual character
flaws; they are institutionalised constructs that are produced
collectively. The UK's sense of self can't be separated from its
centuries of colonial domination; the racism and ideas of
whiteness that were central to the imperial project. By refusing to face up to the horrors of Empire, the techniques of
control and division, and ongoing imperial forms of power –
the persistence of colonial power structures, including racial
categories – people still claim there is an 'intrinsic' British
culture or value system apparently shared only by people who
are born here, though whether you're able to enter that club
can also depend on your skin colour. Certain immigrants are
assumed to rock the boat. Engaging with the past is not to
self-flagellate but to recognise and understand it. Without
this, it is impossible to even begin to challenge the racialised
'them' and 'us' at the heart of the national identity and
immigration debate.

If race crops up in the discussion, it's usually when people
want to attack wealthy 'foreigners'. 'Russian oligarchs' or

'Saudi billionaires' are denounced for buying up expensive properties from afar, leaving them vacant and selling them on for an enormous profit. The super-rich do exacerbate and help sustain the severe housing crisis; they treat housing like financial assets and help incentivise companies to build luxury, cash-cow apartments which only the very few can afford to live in. But focusing on specific nationalities like this 'others' inequality; rich Britons who play this same property investment game disappear, making it seem like it's primarily outside influence that is the cause of unaffordable house prices. But these people buying and selling homes like they're a commodity aren't the only reason for the housing crisis. Factors such as land values and how planning permission is designed – determined largely by policy decisions – have played a huge part in the lack of affordable homes in the UK. We can learn much more about problems in the world by examining structural inequalities produced by capitalism than we ever will from treating immigrants, rich or poor, as the issue.

But to be able to make sense of how the debate is racialised, people need to get to grips with the past as well as the national present. We need to teach the history of Empire properly in schools, including exactly what race is and how it was created, and provide a detailed understanding of the UK's exclusionary history concerning immigration. Currently, these efforts are piecemeal. There are optional GCSEs on Empire and recent migration history, yet, thanks to Michael Gove's fixation on chronology when he was Conservative secretary of state for education, primary school children miss out on the history that explains how many of the people who came to the UK from the colonies and former colonies arrived as citizens. The risk is that pupils will leave school knowing little about the policies aimed at people coming into the UK in the '60s and '70s, which, as academic Gurminder Bhambra says, were not so much immigration policies, but 'policies of racialisation'. 'If we understood that,' she adds, 'we wouldn't just shift the boundary of citizen and migrant to include people from (former) colonies. To say that I'm not a migrant is not a lack of solidarity with those who are migrants . . . If we were to accept that I am British then that would mean that we would have to think differently about migration in the present.'

The stories we don't tell about immigration – as well as the ones we do – aren't just a matter for schoolbooks, newspaper front pages or Parliamentary politics; they are all around us – both the good and the bad. From the films that forget the complexity of the UK's past, like Christopher Nolan's white-washed *Dunkirk*, to the books that begin to subtly capture its messy present, like Nikesh Shukla's *The Good Immigrant*.[13] The programmes we watch and the literature we devour aren't just peripheral; they help to shape how we understand migration.

If the way people understand and talk about immigration on a day-to-day basis is going to change, then the world around them, and the way immigration is depicted, treated and discussed, has to change too.

'Let's pretend we were inventing the world from scratch today and you decided you were going to have borders,' Benjamin, a migrants' rights activist says. 'On what basis would you make the decision about who gets to move and who doesn't get to move through borders? Surely you wouldn't make them in the way the world is constituted today?' We live in a world where movement of most people is considered a problem in a way that the movement of capital rarely is – even though it creates inequality as it crosses borders.

There is no such thing as a progressive border. As long as there *are* borders, it's hard to see how people won't be divided up, monitored, denied entry, separated from their families and friends, and deported. But if there is going to be an immigration system for the time being, how could it be transformed for the better?

When I ask Kelly, who has been stuck in the system for years, what she would change about the UK's immigration regime, she says she wants a more straightforward process that people can actually afford to move through. 'The fees', she says, have been a big problem for her and so has the lack of help available. She is so used to an unforgiving system that she has no illusions about the likelihood that any meaningful change might occur soon.

And then there's the time – the months and years people never get back and the toll it takes on their mental health, trying to get their papers in order. 'I've worked with people who've been here ten years, thirteen years, even seventeen years and still waiting for their status,' Peninah says. Why would they put someone through all of this waiting 'if they care about the human'? Interminably long waiting periods or deportation without notice or the ability to appeal – these are the hallmarks of a system that is inhumane. People exist in limbo for years, waiting to hear about their claims, battling a woeful lack of support and endless amounts of confusing bureaucracy. Or they are suddenly faced with a cliff edge – flown out of the country under the cover of night with almost no way to stop what's happening to them.

So, if there has to be an immigration system, legal aid must be brought back, as Labour has committed to doing, to support people through the process. There should also be a reduction in the huge administrative costs involved in migrating to the UK and applying to stay here and changes to the system so it is clearer and easier to understand and possible to make sense of why decisions are taking so long. As it stands, the immigration rules are complex and impossible to navigate without money or support, when often neither are available.

Simply making the existing system more efficient or less costly for migrants would only be a limited shift in policy.

After reversing the policies that already exist, many of which Corbyn, Abbott and McDonnell voted against, a left-wing government could accept more refugees into the country and give them the right to work. Instead of trying to close down borders and push people to make dangerous crossings, they could make routes safer and easier to navigate for everyone. They could also devise more straightforward and less lengthy ways to become citizens for people who want to apply, look at alternatives to detaining people so they could close down all detention centres, and grant people the same rights as British citizens as soon as they arrive, from the right to work to state support.

That should also mean an end to an immigration system based simply on economic need. Instead, the aim should be to put humanity at the centre of decision making and rhetoric. As a statement of principle, creating an immigration system driven by economic need – which is how Labour has spoken about it – doesn't take us far enough away from the cold, dehumanising way of talking about migrants as things, rather people. And future governments could, as Omar Khan, the Director of the race equality think tank the Runnymede Trust, has suggested, introduce a system whereby rich countries have to accept a certain number of people each year, alongside refugees and people who come for work.[14]

Operating as they do within a system built on racialised, class-based exclusion, these are far from perfect suggestions. But they could hugely transform some peoples' lives and their experiences of the UK's immigration regime for the better in the immediate future. Changing this, and how people talk about migrants and immigration, remains an urgent task. People have been denied their dignity, their families and years of their lives, and in many cases died, because of immigration regimes.

But thinking about this doesn't mean change can only be achieved through Parliament or policy. Precisely because political parties are primarily concerned with controlling the arms of the national state – and thus borders – it is not the only arena where paradigm shifts on immigration are going to happen. That might seem like an odd claim to make in a book that has documented how poorly politicians and governments have approached immigration in the UK, but we have to understand and learn from these pasts to challenge and transform the world around us.

Power lies in further developing international and grassroots anti-racist movements that will challenge racialised anti-immigration politics, as well as the common myths about immigration, and building solidarity with migrants. There are already groups doing some of this work: campaigners disrupting deportations, pilots refusing to fly with detainees on board, migrants organising against government policy, people on hunger strike in detention centres, others stopping immigration raids, nurses and doctors refusing to comply with immigration rules, people successfully campaigning against the hostile environment and lawyers holding states to account. There is hope for change in these movements, including the people who agitate for no-borders in France by declaring, 'We are all foreigners,' and who all around the world, in multiple languages, announce that 'no one is illegal'.

It was an unusually hot weekend in May when I arrived at Akwaaba, a volunteer-run Sunday social centre for refugees, asylum seekers and migrants set just off a bustling street in East London. In the airy, bright main hall of a building that functions as a school during the week, I found a group of just over thirty volunteers in a circle discussing their roles for the day: there would be around thirty to forty children in the play area and eight birthdays to celebrate, people teaching each other to sew, regulars doing yoga in a darkened classroom upstairs, English lessons and, the main event: lunch.

Run entirely by volunteers and on donations, this is a space where once a week people come to make friends, relax and learn new skills. It doesn't matter what your immigration status is or what country you're from, you'll be welcome. The clock hit two and people began to trickle into the school hall; after about thirty minutes the room started to come alive. Volunteers and visitors greeted each other with hugs before catching up on the ins and outs of what had happened since they last saw each other. People entered the room and, with their friends or family, settled in the same spaces they appeared to have sat in every week.

Walk around and you find the whole building buzzing with activity. An arts and crafts space or a computer workshop – different kinds of activities sit side by side; a space where politics, culture and community meet. One volunteer told me that the aim wasn't to 'give' to others; the volunteers see it instead as a community space for them too. This welcoming, innovative social centre is evidence of the kind of local activities, collective struggles and personal connections suffused with anti-racist sentiment that might challenge the racialised xenophobia that shapes politics in the UK and beyond. That can also mean pushing against and past the parameters of what's possible in Parliamentary politics and popular debate.

Why have anti-racist movements 'so often been content to build . . . alternative conceptions of the world from simply inversions of the dismal powers that confront us', theorist Paul Gilroy asks, 'rather than altogether different conceptions guided by another political morality?' Imagine political, economic and social systems where 'race makes no sense', he urges us.[15] Not always separable from race, why not encourage similar, transformative thinking on immigration. As well as implementing concrete changes to the current system, what would it mean to demolish that system and build something else entirely?

It can feel impossible to think of another world. One without the borders or the immigration controls which give rich people the right to move but treat this same freedom as dangerous in the hands of the poor. A world where race is illogical, and there is no global inequality or capitalism-driven climate change forcing people from their homes.

But we already live in a society where people are trying to achieve their utopias, or what some of us might call dystopias, as Omar Khan, director of the Runnymede Trust pointed out to me during the height of the Windrush affair. People want to fortify hard borders that are supposed to keep out 'unwanted' migrants but that really function to make movement more dangerous – even deadly – for those forced to navigate them. While claiming pragmatism, politicians commit to strong national states, as international capital exercises power across borders, over and beyond the reach of government.

Investing time in thinking about a different, utopian vision of the world might be considered a dangerous distraction when energy should be spent challenging the rising far right and normalised xenophobic, nativist politics. But this political project needn't replace efforts to come up with realisable policies in the near future; it can happen alongside it – the reformist with the revolutionary.

With issues like climate breakdown, where the situation is certainly grave, it needn't involve, as some people are wont to do, making panicked warnings about huge movements of people that feed narratives about migrants arriving as threatening 'floods'. It should be put in context. It's hard to forecast how many and in what ways people will have to move because of the inherent unpredictability of the impacts of climate change and the lack of comprehensive data on climate change-induced migration.[16] But people are already unable to stay in their homes or make a living because of the way the climate is breaking down. A better understanding of why people are driven to migrate would help produce more welcoming and supportive societies, where those arriving are not considered an unwanted burden or valued merely in terms of their economic contribution.

But challenging anti-migrant politics isn't just about changing peoples' minds. It's about building resistance with migrant justice at its heart, where borders are not reinforced but opposed and dismantled. Mobilising people to challenge the existing system requires a long-term vision that can't just be about repudiating the status quo: people need something to fight *for*.

Multinational corporations can move production to whatever country offers the cheapest supply of materials and labour, countries where the vast majority of people are penned in by borders, forced to work for low pay and in poor conditions, and then those corporations export the proceeds of that labour across those same borders to be sold.[17] Migration is connected to global and local inequalities produced by capitalism and imperialism, which are inherently tied up with racial and gender discrimination. Reform of trade agreements, a global living wage, global labour standards, the implementation of workable green economic strategies and direct challenges to imperialism in its many forms – these are just some of the changes we can introduce to improve the way the world works.

A lot of people who move don't want to; if the world were fairer, they wouldn't have to. For the people who do, that movement would and should be easier. But any kind of politics that challenges borders would mean reimagining the world altogether, because denaturalising the border does not guarantee equality. Historically, some anti-colonial movements relied on nationalism and the sanctity of the border to keep out imperial powers. And parts of the planet that have relaxed certain border controls, like the EU, have allowed open movement between citizens of member countries but established stronger, harder walls to keep out the rest of the world.[18]

Belief in nation states is part of the problem. This book hopefully demonstrates that much. The UK's border regime and its toxic way of talking about immigration and immigrants is not an oddity in the world; it is commonplace for countries to scapegoat migrants, racialise them and misrepresent them as disruptive to the stability of the nation.

Even when governments cooperate across borders, they still reify them. Borders are ideological: dividing citizens from non-citizens, laden with racial, class and all other kinds of distinctions, and determining who can and cannot belong. There is nothing natural about them, about the lines drawn between countries, the checks within them or the boundaries we erect between people. This is precisely why there is no need to passively accept their existence.

'Somebody says you have no language and so you spend twenty years proving that you do. Somebody says your head isn't shaped properly so you have scientists working on the fact that it is,' writer Toni Morrison said of racism. 'Somebody says that you have no art so you dredge that up. Somebody says that you have no kingdoms and so you dredge that up. None of that is necessary. There will always be one more thing.'[19] This rings true about the immigration debate. From economic woes to cultural anxiety, there is little in UK life that has not been blamed on immigration. But if you strip down 'legitimate concerns', the question at its core is always what do 'we' do with 'them'.[20] Without rejecting the very premise of the debate, this will always be the case. There will always be one more thing.

Thanks to a failure to understand the UK's past and a political and media class that will, for the most part, happily tout anti-migrant narratives, the outcome of the 'debate' on immigration often feels as if it's decided before it has even begun. But this isn't inevitable. As Bill Morris, former general secretary of the Transport and General Workers' Union, tells me: 'It's a continuous argument: if you go too far there,' gesturing to his left, 'you leave space beside you . . . I don't think so. I think if you have convictions about injustice, about unfairness, you have to be there to defend it. It might not be popular, but it's right.'

Acknowledgements

No piece of work is ever really done alone; it's the product of collaboration and collective labour. This book is testament to that. I want to thank the people who agreed to be interviewed for this book – in particular, those who spoke to me about their experiences of interacting with and moving through the immigration system. I'm extremely grateful for their time but also the energy they spent reliving what are often traumatic times in their lives. I hope that I have accurately portrayed their thoughts and that this book goes some way to changing the system for the better, or at least exposing it for what it is.

Thank you to my editor, Rosie Warren, for showing enthusiasm for this book when it was nothing more than an idea, and for helping me to shape the first draft. Thanks also to Kevin Okoth for his considered feedback and to Mark Martin for all of his edits.

I am lucky to have friends and colleagues who took the time to read drafts, give feedback and discuss my ideas with me. They include Nadia Beard, Brhmie Balaram, K Biswas, Matthew Butcher, Jehanzeb Khan, Sundeep Lidher, Nishit Morsawala, Richard Seymour and David Wearing. My PhD supervisor, Meera Sabaratnam, also challenged, clarified and sharpened my thinking on race – I will always be grateful for her help and support. In particular, thanks to my sister, who read countless iterations of each chapter and gave me invaluable advice.

Many friends gave essential love, support and inspiration when I was writing this book. Among them are Yonca Dege, Shanika Gunasinghe, Ján Michalko, Nithya Natarajan, Selina

Nwulu, Rachel Shabi, Faiza Shaheen, Jo Tomkinson, Hannah Wolkwitz and everyone at book club. Thanks to Rich for reading drafts, listening to my ideas and keeping me going throughout. I'd never have finished it without you.

Finally, I want to thank my parents, whose love and support are the reason I'm able to do the work I do. They are a constant source of encouragement and inspiration. It was my mum's experiences of moving to this country that led me to write about immigration and that will continue to drive my work in the hope that one day we can create a world where books like this one don't need to be written.

Notes

Introduction: An Honest Conversation

1. Alan Travis, 'Immigration Bill: Theresa May Defends Plans to Create "Hostile Environment"', *Guardian*, 10 October 2013.

2. For more information see *A Guide to the Hostile Environment: The Border Controls Dividing Our Communities – And How We Can Bring Them Down*, ed. by Liberty, 2018, available at libertyhumanrights.org.uk, last accessed 10 April 2019.

3. Amelia Gentleman, 'Revealed: Depth of Home Office Failures on Windrush', *Guardian*, 18 July 2018.

4. House of Commons Debate (HC Deb. hereafter), 30 April 2018, vol. 640, col. 35; Sajid Javid, Joint Committee on Human Rights: oral evidence, Detention of Windrush Generation HC 1034, Wednesday 6 June 2018.

5. Amelia Gentleman, 'Windrush Victims Still Prevented from Working, Officials Told', *Guardian*, 6 September 2018; Editorial, 'The *Guardian* View on the Windrush Generation: The Scandal Isn't Over', *Guardian*, 17 October 2018; Amelia Gentleman, '"My Life Is in Ruins": Wrongly Deported Windrush People Facing Fresh Indignity', *Guardian*, 10 September 2018.

6. As academic Bridget Anderson has pointed out, this means, 'as long as this is balanced, the country could have an unsustainable stock of one hundred million migrants, or a "sustainable" stock of five migrants, the net migration figure in both cases would still be zero.' See Bridget Anderson, *Us and Them? The Dangerous Politics of Immigration Controls*, Oxford: Oxford University Press, 2013, p. 51.

7. Hannah Jones, Roiyah Saltus, Sukhwant Dhaliwal, Kirsten Forkert, William Davies, Yasmin Gunaratnam, Gargi Bhattacharyya, Emma Jackson, *Go Home? The Politics of Immigration Controversies*, Manchester: Manchester University Press, 2017, p. 11; 'Immigration statistics, July to September 2013', gov.uk, last accessed 1 February 2019.

8. Decca Aitkenhead, 'Sarah Teather: "I'm Angry There Are no Alternative Voices on Immigration"', *Guardian*, 12 July 2013; 'Windrush: Lord Kerslake Says Policy "Reminiscent of Nazi Germany"', BBC News, 19 April 2018.

9. Heather Stewart and Anushka Asthana, 'Yvette Cooper Calls for National Debate on Immigration as She Launches Inquiry', *Guardian*, 2 February 2017; 'Farage: Migration Has Made Parts of UK "Unrecognisable"', BBC News, 28 February 2014; 'In Full: David Cameron Immigration Speech', BBC News, 14 April 2011.

10. Garvan Walshe, 26 February 2017, available at twitter.com/garvanwalshe/status/835927869478027264?lang=en, last accessed 1 February 2019.

11. 'David Cameron Criticised Over Migrant 'Swarm' Language', BBC News, 30 July 2015; Steve Swinford, 'David Cameron: "Immigration Is Constant Drain on Public Services"', *Daily Telegraph*, 23 July 2013.

12. See for instance Rose Meleady, Charles R. Seger and Marieke Vermue, 'Examining the Role of Positive and Negative Intergroup Contact and Anti-immigrant Prejudice in Brexit,' *The British Journal of Social Psychology*, vol. 56, issue 4, 2017, pp. 799–808.

13. Sebastian Whale, 'Andy Burnham's Full Speech to Labour Party Conference', PoliticsHome.com, 28 September 2016, last accessed 24 June 2019.

14. Home Office, 'Hate Crime, England and Wales, 2017/18', gov.uk, last accessed 9 April 2019; Helen Pidd, 'Immigrants Must Not Lead "Parallel Lives" in UK, Says Chuka Umunna', *Guardian*, 25 September 2016.

1 The Cost of It All

1. The names of certain people interviewed for this book have been changed to protect their identity. Other identifying features may also have been changed.

2. Amnesty International UK, *Cuts That Hurt: The Impact of Legal Aid Cuts in England on Access to Justice*, London: Amnesty International UK, pp. 3, 9. This money was cut under the Legal Aid, Sentencing and Punishment of Offenders Act 2012 (LAPSO).

3. 'Legal Services Commission has closed', gov.uk, last accessed 30 July 2018; 'Migrant Charity in Administration Amid Cash Problem', BBC News, 15 June 2010. It was replaced by the Legal Aid Agency, an executive agency of the Ministry of Justice.

4. 'New Immigration and Nationality Fees for 2016 to 2017', gov.uk, last accessed 6 August 2018; 'Apply to settle in the UK: long residence', gov.uk, last accessed 30 July 2018.

5. Lyn Gardner, 'An Evening with an Immigration Review – How Poetry Saved Inua Ellams's Life', *Guardian*, 23 August 2017.

6. 'Custom enquiry service changes', gov.uk, last accessed 6 August 2018.

7. 'Investor Visa (Tier 1)', gov.uk, last accessed 1 February 2019.

8. 'Apply to settle in the UK: long residence', gov.uk, last accessed 30 July 2018.

9. *Harsh, Unjust, Unnecessary: Report on the Impact of the Adult Dependent Relative Rules on Families and Children*, London: Joint Council for the Welfare of Immigrants and BritCits, 2014; Marinella Marmo and Evan Smith, *Race, Gender and the Body in Immigration Control*, Basingstoke: Palgrave Macmillan, 2014.

10. 'Andrea Gada's Family Granted Visas for Funeral', BBC News, 6 February 2015; James Baldwin, *Nobody Knows My Name: More Notes of a Native Son*, New York: Vintage International, 1993 (1961), p. 106.

11. Alex Balch, *Immigration and the State: Fear, Greed and Hospitality*, Basingstoke: Palgrave Macmillan, 2016, p. 33.

12. *Campaigning on the Immigration Act 2016*, London: Liberty, available at libertyhumanrights.org.uk, last accessed 4 April 2019.

13. See for instance the Asylum and Immigration Act 1996 and the Immigration and Asylum Act 1999, the Nationality, Immigration and Asylum Act 2002 and the Asylum and Immigration Act 2004.

14. Before dispersal was introduced, 90 per cent of asylum seekers would have been given homes in London; it tended to be in places where other people from their country of origin lived. For further discussion see Arun Kundnani, *The End of Tolerance: Racism in 21st Century Britain*, London: Pluto Press, 2007, pp. 45–6; Frances Webber, *Borderline Justice: The Fight for Refugee and Migrant Rights*, London: Pluto Press, 2012, p. 95; and Liza Schuster and John Solomos, 'Race, Immigration and Asylum New Labour's Agenda and Its Consequences', *Ethnicity*, vol. 4, issue 2, 2004, p. 277.

15. Home Affairs Committee, *Asylum Accommodation*, London: House of Commons, HC 637, 31 January 2017.

16. Birgit Glorius, Jeroen Doonmernik and Jonathan Darling, 'Asylum in Austere Times: Instability, Privatization and Experimentation within the UK Asylum Dispersal System', *Journal of Refugee Studies*, vol. 294, issue 4, 2016, pp. 483–505.

17. Emine Saner, 'Jimmy Mubenga's Widow: "We Never Forget Him"', *Guardian*, 12 July 2013.

18. Karon Monaghan QC, *Report by the Assistant Deputy Coroner: Inquest into the Death of Jimmy Kelenda Mubenga*, 2013, p. 17, available at iapdeathsincustody.independent.gov.uk, last accessed 4 April 2019.

19. Home Affairs Committee, *Asylum Accommodation*, London: House of Commons, HC 637, 31 January 2017, p. 35; John Grayson, 'Red Doors for Asylum Seekers: MPs Grill One of Britain's Richest Landlords', *OpenDemocracy*, 1 February 2016.

20. Diane Taylor, 'Home Office Official Tells Man Facing Deportation: "My Job Is to Piss You Off"', *Guardian*, 3 May 2018.

21. The dates have been changed to preserve the interviewee's anonymity.

22. Stephanie J. Silverman and Melanie E.B. Griffiths, *Immigration Detention in the UK*. Oxford: Migration Observatory, 2018.

23. HM Chief Inspector of Prisons, *Yarl's Wood Immigration Removal Centre*, London: Her Majesty's Inspectorate of Prisons, 2015, p. 6.

24. Alice Bloch and Liza Schuster, 'At the Extremes of Exclusion: Deportation, Detention and Dispersal', *Ethnic and Racial Studies*, vol. 28, issue 3, 2005, p. 501; Stephanie J. Silverman and Melanie E.B. Griffiths, *Immigration Detention in the UK*, Oxford: Migration Observatory, 2018. See also barbedwirebritain.org.uk.

25. Amelia Hill, 'Vulnerable Women "Still Locked Up in Yarl's Wood Immigration Centre"', *Guardian*, 1 November 2017; Radhika Sanghani, 'Home Office Refuses to Reveal if Women in Yarl's Wood Immigration Centre Have Been Raped', *Telegraph*, 14 June 2016; Rowena Mason, 'Theresa May "Allowed State-Sanctioned Abuse of Women" at Yarl's Wood', *Guardian*, 3 March 2015; May Bulman, 'More than 100 Women in Yarl's Wood Detention Centre Go on Hunger Strike Over "Inhumane" Conditions', *Independent*, 22 February 2017; Siobhan Fenton, 'Home Office Refuses To Reveal Whether Women in Yarl's Wood Have Been Raped in Case it "Damages the Commercial Interests" of Companies', *Independent*, 12 June 2016.

26. 'ABCs: National Daily Newspaper Circulation December 2011', *Guardian*, 13 January 2012.

27. Richard Peppiatt, 'Richard Peppiatt's Letter to *Daily Star* proprietor Richard Desmond', *Guardian*, 4 March 2011.

28. The *Sun* article that Peppiatt's editor referred to contained a short quote from the father saying, 'I don't know what all the fuss is about.' Harry Miller, 'Asylum Family in £2m Pad', *The Sun*, 12 July 2010.

29. Charles Husband and Paul Hartmann, *Racism and the Mass Media*, London: HarperCollins, 1974, p. 208.

30. Josie Ensor, ' "Photo of my Dead Son Has Changed Nothing", Says Father of Drowned Syrian Refugee Boy Alan Kurdi', *Daily Telegraph*, 3 September 2016.

31. 'Full Text: Tony Blair's Speech on Asylum and Immigration', *Guardian*, 22 April 2005.

32. Chitra Nagarajan, 'How Politicians and the Media Made Us Hate Immigrants', openDemocracy.net, 20 September 2013, last accessed 24 June 2019.

33. HC Deb., 20 April 1995, vol. 258, col. 329; 'Full text: Tony Blair's Speech on Asylum and Immigration', *Guardian*, 22 April 2005. Labour's 1998 White Paper *Fairer, Firmer, Faster* opened by praising immigration but claimed 'many' asylum applications were based on 'a tissue of lies'. See Home Office, *Fairer, Faster, and Firmer – A Modern Approach to Immigration and Asylum, White Paper*, London: HMSO, 1998, 1.14.

34. Michael White, 'Series of Political Knocks Took Toll on Loyal Brownite, Tom Watson', *Guardian*, 2 June 2009.

35. William Allen and Scott Blinder, *Migration in the News: Portrayals of Immigrants, Migrants, Asylum Seekers and Refugees in National British Newspapers, 2010 to 2012*, Oxford: Migration Observatory, 2013, p. 3.

36. 'Asylum in the UK', unhcr.org, last accessed 1 February 2019; Alice Bloch, 'The Importance of Convention Status: A Case Study of the UK', *Sociological Research Online*, vol. 6, issue 1, 2001, pp. 1–10.

37. 'Convention and Protocol Relating to the Status of Refugees', unhcr.org, last accessed 1 February 2019.

38. In 1948 the UK signed up to the Universal Declaration of Human Rights, which gives everyone the right to seek asylum from persecution, although this is a declaration that isn't binding in law. The 1951 refugee convention only covered people in Europe, it wasn't until the 1967 protocol was introduced that all other international contexts were included.

39. Baroness Anelay of St Johns, Mediterranean Sea: Written Question, HL1977, 15 October 2014.

40. Vaughan Robinson and Jeremy Segrott, *Understanding the Decision-Making of Asylum Seekers,* Home Office Research Study, vol. 243, London: Home Office Research, Development

and Statistics Directorate, 2002, p. viii; Heaven Crawley, *Change or Choice? Understanding Why Asylum Seekers Come to the UK*, London: Refugee Council, 2010.

41. Nicholas De Genova, 'The "Migrant Crisis'" as Racial Crisis: Do Black Lives Matter in Europe?', *Ethnic and Racial Studies*, vol. 41, issue 10, 2018, pp. 1765–82.

42. For instance, see Harmit Athwal, 'Roll Call of Deaths of Asylum Seekers and Undocumented Migrants, 2005 Onwards', irr.org. uk, 29 October 2010, last accessed 24 June 2019.

43. 'Nottingham Asylum Seeker Fell from Balcony "After Taunts"', BBC News, 5 October 2011; Corin Faife, 'Modern Times: Osman Rasul – In Memory', *Ceasefire*, 3 August 2010.

44. Bridget Anderson, *Us and Them? The Dangerous Politics of Immigration Controls*, Oxford: Oxford University Press, 2013.

45. See Bridget Anderson and Scott Blinder, *Who Counts as a Migrant? Definitions and their Consequences*, 4th ed. Oxford: Migration Observatory, 2015; Scott Blinder, 'Imagined Immigration: The Impact of Different Meanings of "Immigrants" in Public Opinion and Policy Debates in Britain', *Political Studies*, vol. 63, issue 1, 2015, pp. 80–100.

46. Liz Gerard, 'A Year of Immigration in the White-Tops', *SubScribe: For Journalists and Everyone Who Cares about Journalism*, no date, available at sub-scribe2015.co.uk, last accessed 10 April 2019.

47. Bridget Anderson, *Us and Them? The Dangerous Politics of Immigration Controls*, Oxford: Oxford University Press, 2013, p. 51.

48. Heaven Crawley and Dimitris Skleparis, 'Refugees, Migrants, Neither, Both: Categorical Fetishism and the Politics of Bounding in Europe's "Migration Crisis"', *Journal of Ethnic and Migration Studies*, vol. 44, issue 1, 2018, pp. 48–64.

49. Arun Kundnani, *The End of Tolerance: Racism in Twenty-First-Century Britain*, London: Pluto Press, 2007, pp. 66–7.

50. Gareth Dale, 'Leaving the Fortresses: Between Class Internationalism and Nativist Social Democracy', *ViewPoint Magazine*, 30 November 2017; United Nations Department of Economic

and Social Affairs and the Organisation for Economic Co-operation and Development, *World Migration Figures*, 2013.

51. Mathias Czaika and Hein de Haas, 'The Globalization of Migration: Has the World Become More Migratory?' *International Migration Review*, vol. 48, issue 2, 2014, pp. 283–323.

52. Phillip Connor, 'International Migration: Key Findings from the US, Europe and the World', pewresearch.org, 15 December 2016, last accessed 24 June 2019.

53. Gary Younge, 'For 50 Years Voters Have Been Denied a Genuine Debate on Immigration. Now We're Paying the Price', *Guardian*, 15 June 2016.

54. Satnam Virdee, *Racism, Class and the Racialized Outsider*, Basingstoke: Palgrave MacMillan, 2014.

55. Stuart Hall, *The Fateful Triangle: Race, Ethnicity Nation*, Cambridge, MA: Harvard University Press, 2017, p. 149; Jayati Ghosh, 'Towards a Policy Framework for Reducing Inequalities', *Development*, vol. 56, issue 2, pp. 218–22; David Harvey, 'Neoliberalism as Creative Destruction', *The ANNALS of the American Academy of Political and Social Science*, vol. 610, issue 1, pp. 21–44. As anthropologist Jason Hickel points out, it's poor countries that are developing rich ones. In 2012 'developing' countries received $1.3 trillion in aid, investment and income, but $3.3 trillion left those same countries to go to the 'developed' world in the form of interest payments, investment returns and capital flight. Jason Hickel, 'Aid in Reverse: How Poor Countries Develop Rich Countries', *Guardian*, 14 January 2017. And Jason Hickel, *The Divide: A Brief Guide to Global Inequality and Its Solutions*, London: William Heinemann, 2017.

56. Angel Gurría, 'The Global Dodgers', *Guardian*, 27 November 2008.

57. Marissa Begonia, 'Cry of a Migrant', openDemocracy.net, 17 March 2010, last accessed 24 June 2019.

58. The World Bank, 'CO2 emissions (metric tons per capita)', data.worldbank.org, last accessed 1 February 2019.

59. Bridget Anderson, introduction to *Better Off with Us: Voice of Migrant Domestic Workers in the UK*, ed. by Bridget Anderson,

Margaret Healy and Vanessa Hughes, London: United the Union and KopyKat, 2017, pp. 5–6; Annie Kelly and Harriet Grant, 'Absolutely Unacceptable: UK Accused of Failing to Protect Domestic Workers', *Guardian*, 19 October 2017.

60. Robert MacKenzie and Chris Forde, 'The Rhetoric of the "Good Worker" Versus the Realities of Employers' Use and the Experiences of Migrant Workers', *Work, Employment, Society*, vol. 23, issue 1, 2009, p. 143.

61. Massimo Frigo, *Migration and International Human Rights Law: A Practitioners' Guide*, Geneva: International Commission of Jurists, 2014, p. 37, available at icj.org, last accessed 1 April 2019. Also see Alex Balch, *Immigration and the State: Fear, Greed and Hospitality*, Basingstoke: Palgrave Macmillan, 2016, pp. 101–6; United Nations Human Rights Office of the High Commissioner, *International Convention on the Protection of the Rights of All Migrant Workers and Members of Their Families*, 18 December 1990, available at ohchr.org, last accessed 1 April 2019; United Nations Human Rights Office of the High Commissioner, *Status of Ratification Interactive Dashboard: International Convention on the Protection of the Rights of All Migrant Workers and Members of their Families*, available at indicators.ohchr.org, last accessed 1 April 2019.

62. 'Call for Immigration Rethink', BBC News, 12 September 2000.

63. Bridget Anderson, *Us and Them? The Dangerous Politics of Immigration Controls*, Oxford: Oxford University Press, 2013, p. 88.

64. Max Frisch, foreword to *Siamo Italiani – The Italians. Conversations with Italian workers in Switzerland* by Alexander J. Seiler, Zurich: EVZ, 1965, pp. 7–11, translated for the author by Yonca Dege.

65. Esther Addley and Rory McCarthy, 'The Man Who Fell to Earth', *Guardian*, 18 July 2001.

66. See for instance May Bulman, 'Number of People Granted Asylum in UK Plummets by 26% in a Year', *Independent*, 26 August 2018.

67. 'Syria emergency', unhcr.org, last accessed 1 February 2019.

68. Refugee Council, 'Helping Others is Part of the British DNA', refugeecouncil.org.uk, 2011, last accessed 1 February 2019.

69. Louise London, *Whitehall and the Jews: British Immigration Policy, Jewish Refugees and the Holocaust*, Cambridge: Cambridge University Press, 2008, p. 13.

2 'Keeping' the Country White

1. *Moral Maze*, 'Virtue Signalling', BBC Radio 4, available at bbc.co.uk/sounds/play/bo8gy87z, last accessed 10 April 2019.

2. Sarah Boseley, 'Mary Beard Abused Twitter Over Roman Britain's Ethnic Diversity', *Guardian*, 6 August 2017.

3. Peter Fryer, *Staying Power: The History of Black People in Britain*, London: Pluto Press, 1984.

4. *Our Migration Story* is an Arts and Humanities Research Council-funded collaboration between the Runnymede Trust, University of Cambridge and University of Manchester, available at ourmigrationstory.org.uk.

5. Kojo Koram and Kerem Nişancıoğlu, 'Brexit: The Empire That Never Was', *Critical Legal Thinking: Law and the Political*, criticallegalthinking.com, 31 October 2017, last accessed 10 April 2019.

6. Gurminder K. Bhambra, 'Viewpoint: Brexit, Class and British "National" Identity', discoversociety.org, 5 July 2016, last accessed 10 April 2019.

7. Lucy Mayblin, *Asylum after Empire: Colonial Legacies in the Politics of Asylum Seeking*, London: Roman & Littlefield International, 2017.

8. 'David Cameron's Immigration Speech', gov.uk, 25 March 2013.

9. Peter Hennessy, *The Prime Minister: The Office and Its Holders Since 1945*, London: Penguin, 2001, p. 205; Harold Macmillan, *The Macmillan Diaries: The Cabinet Years, 1950–1957*, edited by Peter Catterall, London: Pan Books, 2004, p. 382.

10. Shashi Tharoor, *Inglorious Empire: What the British Did to*

India, London: Penguin, 2018; cited in Ian Gilmour, *Inside Right: A Study of Conservatism*, London: Hutchinson, 1977, p. 134.

11. Cited in Randall Hansen, *Citizenship and Immigration in Post-War Britain: The Institutional Origins of the Multicultural Nation*, Oxford: Oxford University Press, 2000, p. 3.

12. Kwame Anthony Appiah, 'Mistaken Identities: Color', BBC Radio 4, Reith Lectures, 2016, available at bbc.co.uk, last accessed 10 April 2019.

13. Cited in Kenan Malik, *The Meaning of Race: Race, History and Culture in Western Society*, Basingstoke: Palgrave Macmillan, 1996, p. 93.

14. Kwame Anthony Appiah, 'Mistaken Identities: Color', BBC Radio 4, Reith Lectures, 2016, available at bbc.co.uk, last accessed 10 April 2019; Robert Knox, *The Races of Men: A Fragment*, London: Henry Renshaw, 356, Strand 1850, p. v.

15. Ottobah Cugoano, *Thoughts and Sentiments on the Evil and Wicked Traffic of the Slavery and Commerse of the Human Species*, Cambridge: Cambridge University Press, 2013 (1787), p. 312.

16. Akala, *Natives: Race and Class in the Ruins of Empire*, London: Two Roads, 2018, p. 132. Also see UCL History Department, *Legacies of British Slave-Ownership*, available at ucl.ac.uk, last accessed 1 February 2019; and Catherine Hall, Nicholas Draper, Keith McClelland, Katie Donington and Rachel Long, *Legacies of British Slave-Ownership: Colonial Slavery and the Formation of Victorian Britain*, Cambridge: Cambridge University Press, 2014.

17. Lucy Mayblin, *Asylum after Empire: Colonial Legacies in the Politics of Asylum Seeking*, London: Roman & Littlefield International, 2017, p. 88.

18. Uma Kothari, 'Trade, Consumption and Development Alliances: The Historical Legacy of the Empire Marketing Board Poster Campaign', *Third World Quarterly*, vol. 35, issue 1, 2014, pp. 43–64; Anne McClintock, 'Soft-Soaping Empire: Commodity Racism and Imperial Advertising', in *The Visual Culture*

Reader, ed. by Nicholas Mirzoeff, 2nd ed., London: Routledge, 2001, pp. 506–18.

19. W.E.B. Du Bois (1952), 'The Negro and the Warsaw Ghetto', in *The Social Theory of W. E. B. Du Bois*, ed. by Phil Zuckerman, California: SAGE Publications, 2004, p. 46.

20. Panikos Panayi, *An Immigration History of Modern Britain: Multicultural Racism Since 1800*, London: Longman, 2010, p. 208.

21. David Feldman, *Englishmen and Jews: Social Relations and Political Culture 1840–1914*, New Haven: Yale University Press, 1994, p. 1.

22. Satnam Virdee, *Racism, Class and the Racialized Outsider*, Basingstoke: Palgrave Macmillan, 2014, p. 48.

23. 'Jews in the East End', *East London Advertiser*, 6 May 1899, p. 5; cited in Colin Holmes, *Anti-Semitism in British Society, 1876–1939*, London and New York: Routledge, p. 23. Holmes argues the remark was a general anti-alien comment.

24. In addition to this, Troup does not pass judgement on the policies implemented in the 1905 Act, but says it was 'from the administrative point of view one of the worst ever passed'. Edward Troup, *The Home Office*, 2nd rev. ed., London and New York: G.P. Putnam's Son, 1926, p. 143.

25. Panikos Panayi, *An Immigration History of Modern Britain: Multicultural Racism Since 1800*, London: Longman, 2010, p. 211.

26. British Nationality and Status of Aliens Act 1914, 7 August 1948, available at: legislation.gov.uk/ukpga/Geo5/4-5/17/enacted, last accessed 22 June 2019; Steven Cohen, 'Anti-Semitism, Immigration Controls and the Welfare States', *Critical Social Policy*, vol. 13, p. 76.

27. Ian R. G. Spencer, *British Immigration Policy Since 1939: The Making of Multi-Racial Britain*, London: Routledge, pp. 8, 32; Kathleen Paul, *Whitewashing Britain: Race and Citizenship in the Postwar Era*, Ithaca: Cornell University Press, 1997, p. 152.

28. Elizabeth Buettner, *Europe after Empire: Decolonization, Soci-*

ety, and Culture, Cambridge: Cambridge University, pp. 38, 46.

29. Randall Hansen, *Citizenship and Immigration in Post-war Britain: The Institutional Origins of the Multicultural Nation*, Oxford: Oxford University Press, 2000, p. 67.

30. For further discussion see Robbie Shilliam, *Race and the Undeserving Poor*, Newcastle upon Tyne: Agenda Publishing, 2018, p. 53 and Randall Hansen, *Citizenship and Immigration in Post-war Britain: The Institutional Origins of the Multicultural Nation*, Oxford: Oxford University Press, 2000, p. 56.

31. Cited in Bob Carter, Clive Harris and Shirley Joshi, *The 1951–55 Conservative Government and the Racialisation of Black Immigration*, Coventry: University of Warwick, 1987; Robbie Shilliam, *Race and the Undeserving Poor*, Newcastle upon Tyne: Agenda Publishing, 2018, p. 55.

32. Ian R.G. Spencer, *British Immigration Policy Since 1939: The Making of Multi-Racial Britain*, London: Routledge, pp. 32, 30.

33. Cited in Tony Kushner, *The Battle of Britishness: Migrant Journeys, 1685 to Present*, Manchester: Manchester University Press, p. 175. For personal accounts of arrival, see *Forty Winters on: Memories of Britain's Post-War Caribbean Immigrants*, London: South London Press, The Voice and Lambeth Council, 1988, p. 8.

34. HC Deb., 17 February 1961, vol. 634, col. 1933. See Randall Hansen, *Citizenship and Immigration in Post-War Britain: The Institutional Origins of the Multicultural Nation*, Oxford: Oxford University Press, 2000, p. 18 for further discussion.

35. David Watson, 'Black Workers in London in the 1940s', *Historical Studies in Industrial Relations,* issue 1, 1996, pp. 149–58, 154–5.

36. Bridget Anderson, *Us and Them?: The Dangerous Politics of Immigration Controls*, Oxford: Oxford University Press, 2013, p. 54.

37. *Political and Economic Planning, Population Policy in Great Britain: A Report*, London: Political and Economic Planning, 1948, p. 114. A Royal Commission on Population set up in

1944 considered 'immigration on a large scale into a fully established society like ours could only be welcomed without reserve if immigrants were of good human stock and were not prevented by their religion or race from intermarrying with the host population and becoming merged with it.' Cited in Zig Layton-Henry, *The Politics of Immigration: Race and Race Relations in Postwar Britain*, Oxford: Blackwell, 1992, pp. 27–8.

38. In one well-known case, the British Hotels and Restaurants Association had an active drive to recruit staff from the colonies.

39. Quotes taken from *Black Nurses: The Women Who Saved the NHS*, BBC, 2016, 1:40–1:52; 19:32–19:52; 15:58–16:08. Bruce Paice, head of immigration for the Home Office between 1955 and 1966, said: 'the population of this country, in general, were all in favour of the British empire as long as it stayed where it was. They didn't want it here.' 'Looking back at race relations', BBC News, 23 October 1999.

40. Denise Noble, 'Decolonizing Britain and Domesticating Women: Race, Gender, and Women's Work in Post-1945 British Decolonial and Metropolitan Liberal Reform Discourses', *Meridians: Feminism, Race, Transnationalism*, vol. 13, issue 1, 2015, pp. 53–77.

41. A.S. Jouhl, 'Facing the Facts', *Smethwick Telephone*, 9 June 1961, p. 7.

42. Jordanna Bailkin, *The Afterlife of Empire*, London: University of California Press, 2012, p. 32.

43. Cited in Bob Carter, Clive Harris and Shirley Joshi, *The 1951–55 Conservative Government and the Racialisation of Black Immigration*, Coventry: University of Warwick, 1987, p. 5.

44. Special Correspondent, 'British Workers See Ghosts of Their Past in Immigrants' Trials', *The Times*, 23 January 1965, p. 7.

45. Shohei Sato, '"Operation Legacy": Britain's Destruction and Concealment of Colonial Records Worldwide', *The Journal of Imperial and Commonwealth History*, vol. 45, issue 4, 2017, pp. 697–719.

46. Cited in David Kynaston, *Modernity Britain: Book One: Opening the Box, 1957–1959*, London: Bloomsbury, 2013, p. 176.

47. Cited in Ann Dummett, *A Portrait of English Racism*, London: Penguin Books Ltd., 1984, p. 11.

48. Cited in Ian R.G. Spencer, *British Immigration Policy Since 1939: The Making of Multi-Racial Britain*, London: Routledge, 1997, pp. 109–10.

49. Randall Hansen, *Citizenship and Immigration in Post-War Britain: The Institutional Origins of a Multicultural Nation*, Oxford: Oxford University Press, 2000, pp. 92–3.

50. HC Deb., vol. 648, col. 43, 31 October 1961.

51. Bridget Anderson, *Us and Them? The Dangerous Politics of Immigration Controls*, Oxford: Oxford University Press, 2013, p. 39; Andrew Geddes, *The Politics of Migration and Immigration in Europe*, California: SAGE Publications, 2003, p. 35.

52. For instance, in 1951 around 750,000 Irish people lived in Britain. By 1961 that figure had neared 1 million. In 1959, roughly 65,000 Irish workers migrated to Britain, whereas 31,000 came from the colonies, 35,000 from the Commonwealth and 47,000 from elsewhere. See Ian R.G. Spencer, *British Immigration Policy Since 1939: The Making of Multi-Racial Britain*, London: Routledge, 1997, pp. 90–1; Kathleen Paul, *Whitewashing Britain: Race and Citizenship in the Postwar Era*, Ithaca: Cornell University Press, 1997, pp. 132–3. However, it is worth noting that, between 1962 and 1969, 60 per cent of deportees from Britain were citizens of the Republic of Ireland. For more on this see Jordanna Bailkin, *The Afterlife of Empire*, London: University of California Press, 2012.

53. Benjamin Disraeli, *The Letters of Runnymede*, London: John Macrone, St. James's Square, 1836, pp. 145–6.

54. John Solomos, *Race and Racism in Britain*, Basingstoke: Palgrave Macmillan, 2003, p. 38.

55. William Deedes, *Race Without Rancour*, London: Conservative Political Centre, 1968, p. 10.

56. Liam Fox, 4 March 2016, twitter.com/liamfox/status/705674061016387584, last accessed 22 May 2019.

57. Paul Foot, 'Obituary: Pipe Dreams', *Socialist Review*, issue 187, 1995. See also Gary Younge, 'For 50 Years Voters Have Been Denied a Genuine Debate on Immigration. Now We're Paying the Price', *Guardian*, 15 June 2016.

58. Cited in David Russell, '"The Jolly Old Empire": Labour, the Commonwealth and Europe, 1945–51', in *Britain, the Commonwealth and Europe: The Commonwealth and Britain's Applications to Join the European Communities*, ed. by Alex May, Basingstoke: Palgrave Macmillan, 2001, p. 9; Alexander Kenworthy, 'EMPIRE FIRST – Gaitskell', *Daily Express*, 16 July 1962, p. 1.

59. Labour Party, *Let's Go with Labour for the New Britain: The Labour Party Manifesto for the 1964 General Election*, London: Labour Party, 1964, p. 19.

60. Midland Correspondent, 'Immigrants Main Election Issue at Smethwick', *The Times*, 9 March 1964, p. 6.

61. Cited in Elizabeth Buettner, '"This Is Staffordshire Not Alabama": Racial Geographies of Commonwealth Immigration in Early 1960s Britain', *Journal of Imperial and Commonwealth History*, vol. 42, issue 4, 2014, p. 716; Peter H. S. Griffiths, *A Question of Colour?*, London: Frewin, 1966.

62. Cited in Paul Foot, *Immigration and Race in British Politics*, London: Penguin Books, 1965, p. 49; Randall Hansen, *Citizenship and Immigration in Post-War Britain: The Institutional Origins of a Multicultural Nation*, Oxford: Oxford University Press, 2000, pp. 132, 141.

63. Zig Layton-Henry, *The Politics of Immigration: Race and Race Relations in Postwar Britain*, Oxford: Blackwell, 1992, p. 49.

64. HC Deb., 23 March 1965, vol. 709, col. 380; Richard Crossman, *The Crossman Diaries: Selections from the Diaries of a Cabinet Minister, 1964–1970*, edited by Anthony Howard, London: Mandarin, 1991, p. 73.

65. HC Deb., 3 November 1964, vol. 701, col. 701.

66. Conservative Party, *Action Not Words: The New Conservative Programme*, London: Conservative and Unionist Party, 1966.

67. *Playing the Race Card, Part I*, BBC, 1999, 17:30–18:10.

68. Cited in Zig Layton-Henry, *The Politics of Immigration: Race and Race Relations in Postwar Britain*, Oxford: Blackwell, 1992, p. 76.

69. Cited in Elizabeth Buettner, '"This is Staffordshire not Alabama": Racial Geographies of Commonwealth Immigration in Early 1960s Britain', *The Journal of Imperial and Commonwealth History*, vol. 42, issue 4, 2014, p. 728.

70. C. Russell and H. S. Lewis, *The Jews in London: A Study of Racial Character and Present-Day Conditions*, London: T. Fisher Unwin, 1900, p. 198.

71. For discussion of racism and anti-racism on the left, see Satnam Virdee, *Racism, Class and the Racialized Outsider*, Basingstoke: Palgrave Macmillan, 2014.

72. See, for instance, National Union of Seamen, *The Seamen*, vol. 1, issue 40, London: National Sailors' and Firemen's Union, 1 May 1914, available at cdm21047.contentdm.oclc.org, last accessed 9 April 2019; Satnam Virdee, *Racism, Class and the Racialized Outsider*, Basingstoke: Palgrave Macmillan, pp. 78, 82; 'Hero Shinwell "Incited Racist Clydeside Mob"', *Scotsman*, 3 October 2009; David Parker, 'Chinese People in Britain: Histories, Futures and Identities', in *The Chinese in Europe*, ed. by Gregor Benton and Frank N. Pieke, Basingstoke: Palgrave Macmillan, 1997, p. 68; Panikos Panayi, *An Immigration History of Modern Britain: Multicultural Racism Since 1800*, London: Longman, 2010, p. 229.

73. Amrit Wilson, *Finding A Voice: Asian Women in Britain*, London: Virago, 1978; Marinella Marmo and Evan Smith, *Race, Gender and the Body in British Immigration Control: Subject to Examination*, Basingstoke: Palgrave Macmillan, 2014, p. 4.

74. Randall Hansen, *Citizenship and Immigration in Post-War Britain: The Institutional Origins of a Multicultural Nation*, Oxford: Oxford University Press, 2000, pp. 153–63; Satnam Virdee, *Racism, Class and the Racialized Outsider*, Basingstoke: Palgrave Macmillan, 2014, p. 112.

75. HC Deb., 27 February 1968, vol. 759, col. 1258; Mark Lattimer,

'When Labour Played the Racist Card', *New Statesman*, 22 January 1999.

76. Mark Lattimer, 'When Labour Played the Racist Card', *New Statesman*, 22 January 1999; 'Panic and Prejudice', *The Times*, 27 February 1968, p. 9.

77. Although not everyone remembers this government fondly, Ken Livingstone for instance criticised Wilson's 'support for the American bombing of Vietnam, racist immigration legislation, a wage freeze, cuts in the National Health Service and housing programmes, as well as anti-trade union laws'. See Ken Livingstone, *If Voting Changed Anything, They'd Abolish It*, London: Collins, 1987, p. 11.

78. Stephen Howe, *Anticolonialism in British Politics*, Oxford: Oxford University Press, 1993, p. 233; Ebere Nwaubani, 'Getting Behind a Myth: The British Labour Party and Decolonisation in Africa, 1945–1951', *Australian Journal of Politics and History*, vol. 39, issue 2, 1993, pp. 197–216; Casper Sylvest, 'Interwar Internationalism, the British Labour Party and the Historiography of International Relations', *International Studies Quarterly*, vol. 48, issue 2, 2004, pp. 409–32.

79. For further discussion see Alana Lentin, *Racism and Anti-Racism in Europe*, London: Pluto Press, 2004, pp. 130–1 and Nydia A. Swaby, ' "Disparate in Voice, Sympathetic in Direction": Gendered Political Blackness and the Politics of Solidarity', *Feminist Review*, vol. 108, 2014, pp. 11–25.

80. Teresa Hayter, *Open Borders: The Case Against Immigration Control*, London: Pluto Press, 2000, pp. 135, 141.

81. Teresa Hayter, *Open Borders: The Case Against Immigration Control*, London: Pluto Press, 2000, pp. 135, 141.

82. Andrew Geddes, *The Politics of Migration and Immigration in Europe*, California: SAGE Publications, 2003, p. 45.

83. See for further discussion Runnmyede Trust, *How Far Have We Come? Lessons from the 1965 Race Relations Act*, ed. by Omar Khan, London: Runnymede Trust, 2015.

84. Iyiola Solanke, 'The Race Relations Act @ 50 conference: Where

Were You?', thebritishacademy.ac.uk, 2015, last accessed 3 August 2018.

85. Philip N. Sooben, *The Origins of the Race Relations Act*, Warwick: University of Warwick, 1990, p. 6.

86. Dilip Hiro, *Black British, White British: A History of Race Relations in Britain*, London: Grafton, 1991.

87. Sarfraz Manzoor, 'Black Britain's Darkest Hour', *Guardian*, 24 February 2008.

88. 'Enoch Powell's "Rivers of Blood" Speech', *Daily Telegraph*, 6 November 2007.

89. Amy Whipple, 'Revisiting the "Rivers of Blood" Controversy: Letters to Enoch Powell', *Journal of British Studies*, vol. 48, issue 3, 2009, pp. 717–35.

90. Zig Layton-Henry, *The Politics of Immigration: Race and Race Relations in Postwar Britain*, Oxford: Blackwell, 1992, pp. 81–2.

91. Daniel McGeachie, 'New Asian Threat', *Daily Express*, 5 August 1972, p. 1.

92. Randall Hansen, *Citizenship and Immigration in Post-War Britain: The Institutional Origins of a Multicultural Nation*, Oxford: Oxford University Press, 2000, p. 197.

93. Kathleen Paul, *Whitewashing Britain: Race and Citizenship in the Postwar Era*, Ithaca: Cornell University Press, 1997, p. 182.

94. Daniel Trilling, 'Thatcher: The PM who brought racism in from the cold', versobooks.com, 10 April 2013, last accessed 10 April 2019; Stan Taylor, *The National Front in English Politics*, Basingstoke: Palgrave Macmillan, 1982, pp. 102–3.

95. Hansard, *Official Report*, 4 March 1976, vol. 906, col. 1548; Zig Layton-Henry, *The Politics of Immigration: Race and Race Relations in Postwar Britain*, Oxford: Blackwell, 1992, pp. 87, 154–6.

96. Satnam Virdee, *Racism, Class and the Radicalised Outsider*, Basingstoke: Palgrave Macmillan, 2014, p. 130; Ambalavaner Sivanandan, *A Different Hunger*, London: Pluto Press, 1982.

97. Bethnal Green and Stepney Trades Council, *Blood on the Streets*, London: Bethnal Green and Stepney Trades Council, 1978.

98. Sundari Anitha and Ruth Pearson, *Striking Women: Struggles and Strategies of South Asian Women Workers from Grunwick to Gate Gourmet*, London: Lawrence and Wishart, 2018, p. 101.

99. Bethan Bell and Shabnam Mahmood, 'Grunwick Dispute: What did the "Strikers in Saris" Achieve?', BBC News, 10 September 2016; 'Strikers in Saris', *Guardian*, 20 January 2010.

100. Cited in Keith Teare, *Under Siege: Racial Violence in Britain Today*, London: Penguin Books, 1988, p. 73.

101. Zig Layton-Henry, *The Politics of Immigration: Race and Race Relations in Postwar Britain*, Oxford: Blackwell, 1992, pp. 45–6.

102. Annie Phizacklea and Robert Miles, *Labour and Racism*, London: Routledge and Kegan Paul, 1980, pp. 18–19; cited in Elizabeth Buettner, *Europe after Empire: Decolonization, Society, and Culture*, Cambridge: Cambridge University Press, p. 258.

103. Anandi Ramamurthy, 'Families Divided: The Campaign for Anwar Ditta and Her Children', OurMigrationStory.org.uk, last accessed 1 February 2019.

104. Cited in Charles Husband and Jagdish M. Chouhan, 'Local Radio in Communication Environment of Ethnic Minorities in Britain', in *Discourse and Communication: New Approaches to the Analysis of Mass Media*, ed. by Teun A. van Dijk, Berlin: Walter de Gruyter, 1985, pp. 270, 294, 276.

105. Commission for Racial Equality, *Immigration Control Procedures: Report of a Formal Investigation*, London: The Commission for Racial Equality, 1985, p. 78.

106. Stuart Hall, 'The Great Moving Right Show', *Marxism Today*, January 1979, pp. 14–20.

107. 'An Oral History: British Nationality Act 1981', *The Struggle for Race Equality: An Oral History of the Runnymede Trust, 1968–1988*, available at runnymedetrust.org, last accessed 1 August 2018; Randall Hansen, *Citizenship and Immigration in Post*

-war Britain: *The Institutional Origins of the Multicultural Nation*, Oxford: Oxford University Press, 2000, p. 168.

108. Stuart Hall, Brian Roberts, John Clarke, Tony Jefferson and Chas Critcher, *Policing the Crisis: Mugging, the State, and Law and Order*, London: Macmillan, 1978.

109. Zig Layton-Henry, *The Politics of Immigration: Race and Race Relations in Postwar Britain*, Oxford: Blackwell, 1992, pp. 163, 170; also see for an example of newspaper reporting Fiona Millar, 'Black Power Struggle That Is Tearing Labour in Two', *Daily Express*, 9 April 1987, p. 7.

110. HC Deb., 23 July 1985, vol. 83, col. 910.

111. An inquiry into the report – the Macdonald Inquiry – found that Darren Coulburn, who murdered Ullah, had not done so because he was Asian but stated that it would not have happened if Ullah had been white. See Ian Macdonald, Reena Bhavnani, Lily Khan and Gus John, *Murder in the Playground: The Report of the Macdonald Inquiry into Racism and Racial Violence in Manchester Schools*, Burnage Report, London: Longsight Press, 1989.

112. Zig Layton-Henry, *Politics of Immigration: Race and Race Relations in Postwar Britain*, Oxford: Blackwell, 1992, p. 205.

113. Alex Balch, *Immigration and the State: Fear, Greed and Hospitality*, Basingstoke: Palgrave Macmillan, 2016, pp. 332, 334, 335–6.

114. B. S. Chimni, 'The Geopolitics of Refugee Studies: A View from the South', *Journal of Refugee Studies*, vol. 11, issue 4, 1998, pp. 350–74.

115. Lucy Mayblin, *Asylum after Empire: Colonial Legacies in the Politics of Asylum Seeking*, London: Roman & Littlefield International, 2017.

116. Marinella Marmo and Evan Smith, *Race, Gender and the Body in British Immigration Control: Subject to Examination*, Basingstoke: Palgrave Macmillan, 2014, p. 170.

3 New Labour: Things Can Only Get Better?

1. Philip Johnston, 'Straw Wants to Rewrite our History', *Daily*

Telegraph, 10 October 2000; Stewart Whittingham, 'Now It's Racist to Use Word "British"', *Sun*, 10 October 2000.

2. Runnymede Trust, *The Future of Multi-Ethnic Britain: Report of the Commission on the Future of Multi-Ethnic Britain*, London: Profile Books, 2000, p. xiii. For discussion of the report's flaws, see Claire Alexander, 'Imagining the Asian Gang: Ethnicity, Masculinity, and Youth after "Riots"', *Critical Social Policy*, 2004, vol. 24, issue 4, pp. 526–49.

3. The Human Right Act 1998 incorporated the rights laid out in the European Convention on Human Rights into domestic law and the Race Relations (Amendment) Act 2000 extended existing race equality law to public authorities and, crucially, the police. The Stephen Lawrence Inquiry found in 1999 that the London Metropolitan Police's handling of the investigation into the murder of the teenager six years earlier was 'marred' by incompetence, failure and most importantly institutional racism. See William Macpherson of Cluny, *The Stephen Lawrence Inquiry: Report of an Inquiry by Sir William Macpherson of Cluny*, London: The Stationary Office, 46.1, available at assets.publishing.service.gov.uk, last accessed 1 February 2019.

4. David Gillborn, 'Tony Blair and the Politics of Race in Education: Whiteness, Doublethink and New Labour', *Oxford Review of Education*, vol. 34, issue 6, 2008, p. 722.

5. Runnymede Trust, *The Future of Multi-Ethnic Britain: Report of the Commission on the Future of Multi-Ethnic Britain*, London: Profile Books, 2000, p. 25.

6. Alan Travis, 'Be Proud to Be British, Straw Tells Left', *Guardian*, 12 October 2000.

7. Les Back, Michael Keith, Azra Khan, Kalbir Shukra and John Solomos, 'The Return of Assimilationism: Race, Multiculturalism and New Labour', *Sociological Research Online*, vol. 7, issue 2, 2002, pp. 1–13.

8. John Palmer, 'Eurosceptic', *New Statesman and Society*, 3 March 1995. In this same article, Straw is also reported to have

said, 'Our position has always been that the issue of border controls and immigration policy must be for the UK government to determine and not for the European institutions.'

9. Ann Dummett, *Ministerial statements: The Immigration Exemption in the Race Relations (Amendment) Act 2000*, London: Immigration Law Practitioners' Association, 2001; Richard Seymour, 'The changing face of racism', *International Socialism*, issue 126, 15 April 2010, available at isj.org.uk, last accessed 10 April 2019.

10. Andrew Neather, 'Don't Listen to the Whingers – London Needs Immigrants', *Evening Standard*, 23 October 2009, p. 14.

11. Erica Consterdine, *Labour's Immigration Policy: The Making of the Migration State*, London: Palgrave Macmillan, 2018, p. 6; Philip Martin, *Merchants of Labour: Recruiters and International Labour Migration*, Oxford: Oxford University Press, 2017, p. 32.

12. Scott Blinder, *Briefing: UK Public Opinion toward Immigration: Overall Attitudes and Level of Concern*, Oxford: The Migration Observatory, 2011, p. 5.

13. Stephen Ashe, 'The Rise of UKIP: Challenges for Anti-Racism', in *Race and Elections*, ed. by Omar Khan and Kjartan Sveinsson, London: Runnymede Trust, 2015, pp. 15–17.

14. Jason Burt, 'The Dover Deluge; Pleas for Action as Port Is Flooded by Gipsy Asylum Seekers', *Daily Mail*, 20 October 1997; David Pilditch, 'CRISIS TALKS ON GYPSIES', *Daily Mirror*, 20 October 1997; Kathy Marks, 'Gypsies Invade Dover, Hoping for a Handout', *Independent*, 20 October 1997; Lin Jenkins, 'Dover Overwhelmed by Gypsy Asylum-Seekers', *The Times*, 20 October 1997; Alex Bellos, 'Tide of Gypsy Asylum Ebbs', *Guardian*, 20 October 1997.

15. Emma McClune and Kate O'Brien, 'Immigration: The lure of Promised Lands', *Independent*, 20 October 1997.

16. Jason Burt, 'Minister Warns Slovak Gipsies: Keep Out', *Daily Mail*, 22 October 1997; Steve Crawshaw, 'Gypsies Left to Face Chilly Welcome at the Cliffs of Dover', *Independent*, 21 October 1997.

17. Cited in Jason Bennetto, 'Warning to Editors on "Racist Reports"', *Independent*, 17 December 1998. See also Richard Power Sayeed, *1997: The Future That Never Happened*, London: Zed Books, 2018, pp. 31–46.

18. Colin Clark and Elaine Campbell, '"Gypsy Invasion": A Critical Analysis of Newspaper Reaction to Czech and Slovak Romani Asylum-Seekers in Britain', *Romani Studies*, vol. 10, issue 1, pp. 27–8, 32–3.

19. Celia Donert, *The Rights of the Roma: Struggle for Citizenship in Postwar Czechoslovakia*, Cambridge: Cambridge University Press, p. 145.

20. Panikos Panayi, *An Immigration History of Modern Britain: Multicultural Racism Since 1800*, London: Longman, 2010, p. 18.

21. Stuart Millar, 'Straw's Travellers Gaffe "Misconstrued"', *Guardian*, 20 August 1999.

22. Home Office, *Fairer, Faster, Firmer: A Modern Approach to Immigration and Asylum*, London: Stationery Office, 1998; Kamal Ahmed and Jason Burkey, 'Hard New Straw Line on Asylum', *Guardian*, 20 May 2001; Michael White and Alan Travis, 'Blunkett Defends "Swamping" Remark', *Guardian*, 25 April 2002.

23. Liza Schuster and Alice Bloch, 'Asylum Policy under New Labour', *Benefits*, vol. 13, issue 2, 2005, pp. 115–18; Martin Wainwright, 'Asylum Seeker and Refugee Destitution Has Doubled, Says Trust', *Guardian*, 24 July 2008.

24. MORI, 'Attitudes toward Asylum Seekers for "Refugee Week"', 17 June 2002.

25. Also see Don Flynn, 'New Borders, New Management: The Dilemmas of Modern Immigration Policies', *Ethnic and Racial Studies*, vol. 28, issue 3, 2005, pp. 463–90.

26. Erica Consterdine, *Labour's Immigration Policy: The Making of the Migration State*, London: Palgrave Macmillan, 2018, pp. 2, 63. The International Passenger Survey estimates that non-EU migration into the country increased from 19,000 in 1991 to a

peak in 113,000 in 2004, declining in the mid-2000s to 44,000, and increasing again to 73,000 by 2015. For an overview of some of New Labour's immigration policies between 1997 and 2007, also see Will Somerville, *Immigration under New Labour*, Bristol: Policy Press, 2007.

27. Angelia R. Wilson, 'New Labour and "Lesbian- and Gay-Friendly" Policy', in *Women and New Labour: Engendering politics and policy?*, ed. by Claire Annesley, Francesa Gains and Kirstein Rummery, Bristol: Policy Press, 2007, p. 195.

28. Alex Balch, *Immigration and the State: Fear, Greed and Hospitality*, Basingstoke: Palgrave Macmillan, 2016, pp. 337-8.

29. Writing in his 2006 memoirs, Philip Gould, one of the architects of the New Labour project, remembers how 'concern about immigration continued to heighten, and it was increasingly seen as a primary cause of other problems. People saw Labour as out of touch, not listening and dogged by sleaze and infighting.' See Philip Gould, *The Unfinished Revolution: How New Labour Changed British Politics Forever*, London: Abacus, 2011, p. 493.

30. Erica Consterdine, *Labour's Immigration Policy: The Making of the Migration State*, London: Palgrave Macmillan, 2018, p. 7; Alex Balch, *Immigration and the State: Fear, Greed and Hospitality*, Basingstoke: Palgrave Macmillan, 2016, pp. 378-9.

31. Stephen Castles, 'Guestworkers in Europe: A Resurrection?', *International Migration Review*, vol. 40, issue 4, 2006, pp. 741-66. For discussion on New Labour's immigration regime in detail see Alex Balch, *Managing Labour Migration in Europe: Ideas, Knowledge and Policy Change*, Manchester: Manchester University Press, 2010, p. 151; Erica Consterdine, *Labour's Immigration Policy: The Making of the Migration State*, London: Palgrave Macmillan, 2018, p. 72; Yara Evans, Joanna Herbert, Kavita Datta, Jon May, Cathy McIlwaine and Jane Wills, *Making the City Work: Low-Paid Employment in London*, London: Queen Mary, University of London, 2005.

32. 'Tony Blair: "My Job Was to Build on Some Thatcher Policies"', BBC News, 8 April 2013.

33. Stuart Hall, 'The Neoliberal Revolution', *Cultural Studies*, vol. 25, issue 6, 2011, pp. 105–28; Will Hutton, Patrick Wintour and Andrew Adonis, 'Blair in 1997 "I Am Going to Be a Lot More Radical in Government than People Think"', *Observer*, 27 April 1997; Richard Seymour, *Corbyn: The Strange Rebirth of Radical Politics*, London: Verso, p. 146.

34. Alex Balch, *Immigration and the State: Fear, Greed and Hospitality*, Basingstoke: Palgrave Macmillan, 2010, pp. 379–80; 'Blunkett: No Limit on Migration', BBC News, 13 November 2003.

35. House of Commons, Written Answers, 13 September 2004, Column 1406W; Alice Bloch and Liza Schuster, 'At the Extremes of Exclusion: Deportation, Detention and Dispersal', *Ethnic and Racial Studies*, vol. 28, issue, 3, p. 497.

36. 'Blunkett Accused Over Race', BBC News, 22 February 2003.

37. Benedict Brogan, 'It's Time to Celebrate the Empire, Says Brown', *Daily Mail*, 15 January 2005.

38. Sarah Lyall, 'The World: Why Are You Here? Britain's Race Problem', *New York Times*, 3 June 2001.

39. Ash Amin, 'Unruly Strangers? The 2001 Urban Riots in Britain', *International Journal of Urban and Regional Research*, vol. 27, issue 2, 2003, pp. 460–3; Arun Kundnani, 'From Oldham to Bradford: The Violence of the Violated', London: Institute of Race Relations, 1 October 2001; James Rhodes, 'Revisiting the 2001 Riots: New Labour and the Rise of "Colour Blind Racism"', *Sociological Research Online*, vol. 14, issue 5, 2009. See also Daniel Trilling, *Bloody Nasty People: The Rise of Britain's Far Right*, London: Verso, 2013, pp. 103–8.

40. Derek McGhee, 'The Paths to Citizenship: A Critical Examination of Immigration Policy in Britain Since 2001', *Patterns of Prejudice*, vol. 43, issue 1, 2009, pp. 47–8.

41. 'Text of David Blunkett's Speech', *Guardian*, 11 December, 2001; Andrew Grice, 'Blunkett under Fire for Backing "British norms"', *Independent*, 10 December 2001; Ted Cantle, *Community Cohesion: A Report of the Independent Review Team*, London: Home Office, 2001.

42. 'Hague's "Foreign Land" Speech', *Guardian*, 4 March 2001; Les Back, Michael Keith, Azra Khan, Kalbir Shukra and John Solomos, 'New Labour's White Heart: Politics, Multiculturalism and the Return of Assimilation', *Political Quarterly*, vol. 73, issue 4, 2002, pp. 445–54.

43. Hannah Jones, Yasmin Gunaratnam, Gargi Bhattacharyya, William Davies, Sukhwant Dhaliwal, Kirsten Forkert, Emma Jackson and Roiyah Saltus, *Go Home? The Politics of Immigration Controversies*, Manchester: Manchester University Press, 2017, p. 50.

44. For instance, Minister of State for Immigration, Citizenship and Counterterrorism Beverley Hughes resigned in 2004 over a visa 'scam' scandal and Home Secretary Charles Clarke in 2006 over the so-called foreign prisoners scandal.

45. Labour Party, *The Labour Party Manifesto 2005: Britain forward Not Back*, London: Labour Party, 2005; Labour Party, *The Labour Party Manifesto 2010: A Future Fair for All*, London: Labour Party, 2010. This was also noted in Daniel Trilling, *Bloody Nasty People: The Rise of Britain's Far Right*, London: Verso, 2013, p. 178.

46. Jonathan Freedland, ' "What Do We Do Now?": The New Labour Landslide, 20 Years on', *Guardian*, 29 April 2017.

47. For analysis of the anti-deportation movement and the broader resistance movement, see Teresa Hayter, *Open Borders: The Case Against Immigration Control*, London: Pluto Press, 2000, pp. 134–48. For information on the Campsfield Nine trial, see Louise Pirouet, *Whatever Happened to Asylum in Britain? A Tale of Two Walls*, New York: Berghahn Books, 2001, p. 91.

48. Derek Brown, 'Asylum Seekers' Vouchers', *Guardian*, 28 September 200; HC Deb., 16 June 1999, vol. 333, col. 450.

49. The Immigration Law Practitioners' Association, 'Asylum and Immigration (Treatment of Claimants, etc.) Bill Clause 110: An End to the Rule of Law?', available at ilpa.org.uk, last accessed 1 February 2019; Joshua Rozenberg, 'Labour U-Turn on Asylum

Bill', *Daily Telegraph*, 16 March 2004; see also Will Somerville, *Immigration under New Labour*, Bristol: Policy Press, 2007, pp. 95–101.

50. Patrick Hennessy, 'Howard Puts Immigration at Heart of Election Battle', *Daily Telegraph*, 23 January 2005.

51. Gary Younge, 'The Boundaries of Race in Britain Today', *Guardian*, 25 April 2005.

52. 'European Election: United Kingdom Result', BBC News, 14 June 2004.

53. Daniel Trilling, *Bloody Nasty People: The Rise of Britain's Far Right*, London: Verso, 2013, pp. 127–50.

54. Melissa Kite, 'White Voters Are Deserting Us for BNP, Says Blair Ally', *Daily Telegraph*, 16 April 2006; Daniel Trilling, 'Gone to the Dogs', *New Statesman*, 16 April 2010; 'Call for Migrant Housing Rethink', BBC News, 21 May 2007; 'MP "Should Go" over BNP Comments', BBC News, 24 May 2006; 'Hodge attacked for "BNP Language"', BBC News, 25 May 2007.

55. Ewen MacAskill, 'White Cliffs, White Faces for Blair Speech', *Guardian*, 23 April 2005; Paul Gilroy, *There Ain't No Black in the Union Jack: The Cultural Politics of Race and Nation*, London: Routledge, 2002, p. xxxi.

56. Daniel Trilling, *Bloody Nasty People: The Rise of Britain's Far Right*, London: Verso, 2013, p. 119.

57. Will Woodward, 'Radical Muslims Must Integrate, Says Blair', *Guardian*, 9 December 2006.

58. Patrick Wintour, 'English Tests to Be Part of a Tougher New Strategy on Immigration', *Guardian*, 24 February 2007.

59. Bridget Anderson, *Us and Them? The Dangerous Politics of Immigration Control*, Oxford: Oxford University Press, 2013, p. 106; Frances Webber, *Borderline Justice: The Fight for Refugee and Migrant Rights*, London: Pluto Press, 2012, p. 107.

60. Jonathan Brown and David Langton, 'Pakistani Doctor's Suicide Highlights Plight of Unemployment Immigrants', *Independent*, 19 February 2007.

61. 'Brown's Speech: Full Text Part Two', *Guardian*, 24 September 2007; Gaby Hinsliff and Toby Helm, 'BNP Exploit Public's Fury at Politicians', *Guardian*, 3 May 2009.

62. Alan Travis, 'Foreign Workers Could Be Barred from Entering UK', *Guardian*, 22 February 2009.

63. Labour Party, *The Labour Party Manifesto 2010: A Fair Future for All*, London: Labour Party, 2010.

64. Derek McGhee, 'The Paths to Citizenship: A Critical Examination of Immigration Policy in Britain Since 2001', *Patterns of Prejudice*, vol. 43, issue 1, 2009, pp. 43, 55–6.

65. Colin Brown, 'Brown Calls for National Day to Enjoy "Britishness"', *Independent*, 14 January 2006.

66. Matthew Weaver, 'The Gordon Brown and Gillian Duffy transcript', *Guardian*, 28 April 2010.

67. Frances Perraudin, 'Diane Abbott: Labour's "Controls on Immigration" Mugs Are Shameful', *Guardian*, 29 March 2015; Maya Goodfellow, 'I Hate Labour's Immigration Mug – but I Hate Their Immigration Pledge Even More', *LabourList*, 29 March 2015.

68. 'Labour Conference: Ed Miliband Speech in Full', *Guardian*, 28 September 2010.

69. Richard Seymour, 'Brexit and the "White Working Class"', patreon.com, 5 February 2019, last accessed 10 April 2019.

70. Rob Ford and Matthew Goodwin, *Revolt on the Right: Explaining Support for the Radical Right in Britain*, London: Routledge, 2014, p. 9.

71. Richard Seymour, 'They're Not Racist, But: UKIP and the Crisis of Britain', *Salvage*, 12 October 2015, available at: salvage.zone, last accessed 10 April 2019; UK Independence Party, *Believe in Britain: UKIP Manifesto 2015*, London UK Independence Party, 2015, p. 10.

72. Labour Party, *The Labour Party Manifesto 2015*, London: Labour Party, 2015, pp. 65–7.

73. 'Changing the Debate on Migration: Brexit Update', Centre for Labour and Social Studies in association with Migrants' Rights Network, September 2016.

74. In addition to the five pledges Labour had announced in March 2015, the Ed Stone included a sixth: 'homes to buy and action on rents'.

75. Frances Perraudin, 'Diane Abbott: Labour's "Controls on Immigration" Mugs Are Shameful', *Guardian*, 29 March 2015.

76. Ned Simons, 'Ed Balls Defends Immigration Mug as Shadow Treasury Minister Distances Herself from It', *Huffington Post*, 31 March 2015.

4 Legitimate Concerns

1. 'Immigration Street Protestors Gather Outside Channel 4 Offices', BBC News, 31 January 2015; Homa Khaleeli, 'Immigration Street: the Road That Sent Channel 4 Packing', *Guardian*, 8 February 2015.

2. *Immigration Street*, London: Love Productions, 2015.

3. HC Deb., 5 July 1976, vol. 914, col. 985.

4. James Morris, 'We Must Respect People's Desire for Control', in *Facing the Unknown: Building a Progressive response to Brexit*, ed. by Olivia Bailey, London: FEPS-Europe and Fabian Society, 2016.

5. Alex Balch, *Immigration and the State: Fear, Greed and Hospitality*, Basingstoke: Palgrave Macmillan, 2016; Scott Blinder, *UK public Opinion Toward Immigration: Overall Attitudes and Level of Concern*, Oxford: Migration Observatory, 2nd revision, updated 3 July 2014.

6. Tom Clark and Owen Gibson, 'London 2012's Team GB Success Sparks Feelgood Factor', *Guardian*, 10 August 2012. This poll also found that 47 per cent of people didn't agree with the statement 'more often than not immigrants . . . do not bring anything positive, and the likes of the Olympic-winning athletes are an exception'. But the majority, 53 per cent still agreed with it; 'YouGov/SundayTimes Survey Results', 1–14 December 2012, available at cdn.yougov.com, last accessed 6 April 2019; 'YouGov poll', 6 May 2014, available at twitter.com/JoeTwyman/

status/466510114376400896/photo/1, last accessed 6 April 2019. For the problem with polls, see Mona Chalabi, 'After this General Election Is It Time to Downgrade Opinion Polls?', *Guardian*, 10 June 2017.

7. Steve Swinford, 'David Cameron: "Immigration Is Constant Drain on Public Services"', *Daily Telegraph*, 23 July 2013.

8. Paul explains that 'even as Macmillan's Cabinet discussed the social and economic problems caused by "immigration", they authorized a cut of between £25 and £30 million in the budget for "social investment"'. Paul says this might not have 'deliberately' intensified grassroots hostility, but that inattention to the likely consequences of the cuts facilitated a growth in racial hostility. See Kathleen Paul, *Whitewashing Britain: Race and Citizenship in the Postwar Era*, Ithaca: Cornell University Press, 1997, p. 157.

9. HC Deb., 6 September 2017, vol. 628, col. 151.

10. Philip Inman, 'The Truth About Wages and Immigration Emerges at Last', *Guardian*, 6 September 2017; Ian R.G. Spencer, *British Immigration Policy Since 1939: The Making of Multi-Racial Britain*, London: Routledge, 1997, pp. 79–80.

11. Gary Younge, 'Bitter White Whine', *Guardian*, 26 February 2004.

12. Home Affairs Select Committee, *Immigration Policy: Basis for Building Consensus*, London: House of Commons, 15 January 2018, para. 8, para. 31.

13. Jonathan Wadsworth, Swati Dhingra, Gianmarco Ottaviano and John Van Reenen, *Brexit and the Impact of Immigration on the UK*, London: Centre for Economic Performance, 2016; OECD, *The Fiscal and Economic Impact of Migration*, Paris: Organisation for Economic Co-operation and Development, May 2014; Jonathan Portes, *How Small Is Small? The Impact of Immigration on UK Wages*, London: National Institute of Economic and Social Research, 17 January 2016.

14. Ian R. G. Spencer, *British Immigration Policy Since 1939: The Making of Multi-Racial Britain*, London: Routledge, 1997, p. 115.

15. William Brown, 'Industrial Relations in Britain under New Labour, 1997–2010: A Post Mortem', *Journal of Industrial Relations*, vol. 53, issue 3, 2011, pp. 402–13.

16. Alex Balch, *Managing Labour Migration in Europe: Ideas, Knowledge and Policy Change*, Manchester: Manchester University Press, 2010, p. 111; 'Who Built More Council Houses – Margaret Thatcher or New Labour?', fullfact.org, 12 November 2013.

17. Danny Dorling, 'New Labour and Inequality: Thatcherism Continued?', *Local Economy*, vol. 25, issues 5–6, 2010, pp. 397–413.

18. Carys Afoko, *Framing the Economy: The Austerity Story*, London: New Economics Foundation, 2013; Sally Gainsbury and Sarah Neville, 'Austerity's £18bn Impact on Local Services', *Financial Times*, 19 July 2015. Between 2010 and 2015, a quarter of the Home Office budget was cut by around 24.9 per cent and there were £18 billion cuts to local authority budgets, amounting to authorities having to get rid of key services for 150,000 pensioners and cutting child protection spending by 8 per cent.

19. Owen Jones, *Chavs: The Demonisation of the Working Class*, London: Verso, 2011, p. 196; Citizens UK, *The Public Subsidy to Low Wage Employers*, London: Citizens UK, 2015.

20. Bridget Anderson, 'Migration: Controlling the Unsettled Poor', openDemocracy.net, 1 August 2011 last accessed 24 June 2019.

21. Robbie Shilliam, *Race and the Undeserving Poor*, Newcastle upon Tyne: Agenda Publishing, 2018, p. 9.

22. Joel Krieger, 'The Political Economy of New Labour: The Failure of a Success Story?', *New Political Economy*, vol. 12, issue 3, 2007, pp. 421–32; Tony Blair, 'Values and the Power of Community', 2000, p. 5 , available at global-ethic-now.de, last accessed 5 April 2019; 'Welfare Set for Reform', BBC News, 10 February 1999.

23. John Deans, 'End of the "Something for Nothing Society"; Lilley's £500m Crackdown on Benefit Fiddlers', *Daily Mail*, 8 October 1992; also see Jon Craig, 'Lilley Tackles Dole Cheats in Effort to Save £500m a Year', *Daily Express*, 8 October 1992, pp. 6–7.

24. Richard Cracknell, *The Habitual Residence Test: Research Paper 95/25*, London: House of Commons Library, 1995, pp. 4–5; Patrick Hennessy, 'Scroungers to Face a Hammering', *Daily Express*, 7 October 1993, pp. 12–13.

25. *Inside Europe: Ten Years of Turmoil*, 'We Quit' (episode 1), BBC News, 30:48–31:42.

26. Alex Balch, *Managing Labour Migration in Europe: Ideas, Knowledge and Policy Change*, Manchester: Manchester University Press, 2010, p. 134; Madeleine Sumption and William Allen, *Election 2015 Briefing – Migration and Welfare Benefits*, Oxford: Migration Observatory, 5 May 2015.

27. Rob Merrick, 'Theresa May Backs Passport Checks on Pregnant Women at Hospitals in 'Maternity Tourism' Crackdown', *Independent*, 12 October 2016; 'Health Tourism: What's the Cost?', fullfact.org, 21 December 2016.

28. 'In Full: David Cameron Immigration Speech', BBC News, 14 April 2011.

29. Bridget Anderson, *Us and Them? The Dangerous Politics of Immigration Controls*, Oxford: Oxford University Press, 2013, p. 4; Bob Sutcliffe, 'Migration, Rights and Illogic', *Index on Censorship*, issue 3, 1994, p. 32.

30. Maarten Goos and Alan Manning, *Lousy and Lovely Jobs: The Rising Polarization of Work in Britain*, Working Paper, London: London School of Economics, 2003.

31. 'Ethnicity facts and figures', gov.uk, last accessed 5 August 2018; Deborah Garvie, *BAME Homelessness Matters and Is Disproportionately Rising – Time for Government to Act*, Shelter, 11 October 2017; Matthew Taylor, '50% Rise in Long-Term Unemployment for Young Ethnic Minority People in UK', *Guardian*, 10 March 2015.

32. Centre for Labour and Social Studies, *How Unequal Is the UK?*, London: Centre for Labour and Social Studies, n.d., last accessed 6 August 2018.

33. Barnaby Raine, 'Socialist for Jingoes', *Salvage*, 12 September 2017, available at salvage.zone, last accessed 10 April 2019.

34. Luke de Noronha, 'There Is no Such Thing as a "Left" Case for Borders', *Red Pepper*, 3 December 2018.

35. Home Office UK Border Agency, *Detention Services Order 01/2013: Paid Work*, London: Home Office, 26 March 2013.

36. Katie Bales and Lucy Mayblin, 'Unfree Labour in Immigration Detention: Exploitation and Coercion of a Captive Immigration Workforce', *Economy and Society*, vol. 47, issue 2, 2018, pp. 1–23; Bridget Anderson, *Us and Them? The Dangerous Politics of Immigration Controls*, Oxford: Oxford University Press, 2013, p. 78; Diane Taylor, 'Migrant Adult Social Care Staff Add £44bn to English Economy', *Guardian*, 17 February 2018.

37. William Davies, 'What Is "Neo" About Neoliberalism', *New Republic*, 13 July 2017, available at newrepublic.com, last accessed 10 April 2019; Hannah Jones, Yasmin Gunaratnam, Gargi Bhattacharyya, William Davies, Sukhwant Dhaliwal, Kirsten Forkert, Emma Jackson and Roiyah Saltus, *Go Home? The Politics of Immigration Controversies*, Manchester: Manchester University Press, 2017.

38. Robert MacKenzie and Chris Forde, 'The Rhetoric of the "Good Worker" Versus the Realities of Employers' Use and the Experiences of Migrant Workers', *Work, Employment and Society*, vol. 23, issue 1, p. 144.

39. Jewish Workers Defence Committee, *A Voice from the Aliens: About the Anti-Alien Resolution of the Cardiff Trade Union Congress*, Clerkenwell Green: Twentieth Century Press, 1895, pp. 7–8.

40. Campaign Against Racism in the Media, *It Ain't Half Racist, Mum*, BBC, 1979, available at youtube.com/watch?v=gy57O9Z-MENA, last accessed 5 April 2019.

41. William L. Allen, *A Decade of Immigration in the British Press*, Oxford: Migration Observatory, 2016. Representations of the UK as overwhelmed by migration have become commonplace. In 2006, an ITV News report suggested that Britain had poor immigration control and that the country had witnessed 'another day of immigration chaos'. The banner headline that ran

underneath asked, 'Immigration chaos?', a question the reporter turned into a statement when he said the immigration system was one 'that I think genuinely is in chaos . . . people watching . . . will be profoundly disturbed'. Cited in Greg Philo, Emma Briant and Pauline Donald, *Bad News for Refugees*, London: Pluto Press, 2013.

42. Arthur Martin and John Stevens, 'Sold out! Flights and Buses Full as Romanians and Bulgarians Head for the UK', *MailOnline*, 21 February 2014; Roy Greenslade, 'How the Daily Mail Escaped Censure for its False Immigration Story', *Guardian*, 17 March 2014.

43. Lisa Whalley, 'Newspaper Corrections Should Be the Same Size as the Mistake!', 38 Degrees, available at home.38degrees.org. uk, last accessed 5 April 2019.

44. Larisa Brown and Corey Charlton, 'Migration "Has Created 900 No-Go Areas in EU": Devastating Report Shows Order Breaking Down – Including in London', *Daily Mail*, 2 April 2016.

45. Terry Threadgold, *The Media and Migration in the United Kingdom, 1999 to 2009*, Washington, DC: Migration Policy Institute; Stop Funding Hate, available at stopfundinghate.info, last accessed 6 February 2019.

46. Alberto Nardelli and George Arnett, 'Today's Key Fact: You Are probably Wrong About Almost Everything', *Guardian*, 29 October 2014.

47. Tim Ross, 'Britain's Green Fields Will Have to Be Built over to Provide New Homes for Migrants, Warns Chris Grayling', *Daily Telegraph*, 29 May 2016.

48. Michael Chessum, 'Diane Abbott Has Shown She Wants to Change Labour's Conversation About Immigration', *New Statesman*, 21 February 2018.

49. Andy Beckett, 'Is Britain Full? Home truths About the Population Panic', *Guardian*, 9 February 2016.

50. Mark Easton, 'The Great Myth of Urban Britain', BBC News, 28 June 2012.

51. Alasdair Rae, 'Think Your Country Is Crowded? These Maps Reveal the Truth About Population Density Across Europe', *Conversation*, 23 January 2018, available at theconversation.com, last accessed 1 April 2019.

52. Marcus Collins, 'Immigration and Opinion Polls in Postwar Britain', *Modern History Review*, vol. 18, issue 4, 2016, pp. 8–13; Scott Blinder, *Briefing: UK Public Opinion Toward Immigration: Overall Attitudes and Level of Concern*, Oxford: The Migration Observatory, 2011; Ipsos MORI, 'Too Many immigrants in Britain?', ipsos.com, 28 February 2012, last accessed 24 June 2019.

53. Daniel Korski, 'Why We Lost the Brexit Vote', politico.eu, 20 October 2016, last accessed 24 June 2019.

54. Dominic Casciani, 'The Case of the Cat Deportation Tale', BBC News, 6 October 2011; 'Theresa May Pledges Asylum Reform and Immigration Crackdown', BBC News, 6 October 2015; Patrick Wintour and Alexandra Topping, 'Change Rules on Migrant Workers, Says Ed Miliband', *Guardian*, 21 June 2012.

55. Doreen Massey, *Space, Place and Gender*, Minnesota: University of Minnesota, 1994, pp. 173–4.

56. Damien Gayle, 'More than 500 Children's Centres Have Closed in England Since 2010', *Guardian*, 20 February 2018.

57. YouGov/Policy Exchange/Birkbeck University Survey Results, 16–17 August 2016, available at d25d2506sfb94s.cloudfront. net/cumulus_uploads/document/u12mloq9ox/PolicyExchang-eResults_160907_Authoritarianism_UK.pdf, last accessed 6 April 2019; Patrick Wintour, 'Ukip Wants a Five-Year Ban on New Migrants, Says Nigel Farage', *Guardian*, 7 January 2014.

5 'It's Not Racist. It's Common Sense'

1. Jens Hainmueller and Daniel J. Hopkins, 'Public Attitudes Toward Immigration', *Annual Review of Political Science*, vol. 17, pp. 225–49.

2. Olivia Bailey, 'Introduction: Facing the Unknown', in *Facing the Unknown: Building a Progressive Response to Brexit*, ed. by

Olivia Bailey, London: FEPS-Europe and Fabian Society, 2016, p. 23.

3. In its most helpful form, multiculturalism is a challenge to the notion that there ever was or should be a racially homogenous white nation. Its basic premise is that diverse groups of people can form a common present and future, and in fact, people are already living the reality of a multicultural and multiracial UK on a daily basis.

   But through state-led attempts under Thatcher and then New Labour, multiculturalism became an institutional tool to strip anti-racism of its radical edges and try to bring some of the people agitating for change on the streets into the structures of government. It broke down ethnic groups into separate 'cultural blocks' and treated willing individuals as if they were spokespeople for a whole, supposedly unified, community. Focused on 'ethnic' and 'cultural' projects, it did little to deal with racial inequalities in jobs, housing and wider society; anti-racism became about representation not material changes.

   But the major shortcomings of these incarnations of multiculturalism aside, the New Right railed against the very notion of a multicultural, multiracial society, considering it detrimental to national cohesion, an idea revived by people like David Cameron when he was prime minister, and that anti-racism was damaging British society. In the mid-1980s, it seems the New Right's *cause du jour* was making sure that as many people as possible heard their seething criticism of anti-racism. Through newspapers columns they claimed that people of colour resisting and challenging racism were threatening 'British culture'. In 1984–85, when the left-wing-controlled Greater London Council had an 'anti-racist year', there were reams of articles criticising it from New Right figures.

4. Francesca Klug and Paul Gordon, *New Right New Racism*, London: Searchlight Productions, 1986, p. 7.

5. Satnam Virdee, *Racism, Class and Racialized Outsider*, Basingstoke: Palgrave Macmillan, 2014, p. 117.

6. Cited in Francesca Klug and Paul Gordon, *New Right New Racism*, London: Searchlight Productions, 1986, p. 20.

7. Liz Fekete, *Europe's Fault Lines: Racism and the Rise of the Right*, London: Verso, 2018, p. 32.

8. Martin Barker, *The New Racism: Conservative and the Ideology of the Tribe*, London: Junction Books, 1981, pp. 23–4; also see Etienne Balibar, 'Is There a "Neo-Racism"?', in *Race, Nation, Class: Ambiguous Identities*, ed. by Etienne Balibar and Immanuel Wallerstein, translation by Chris Turner, London: Verso, 1988, pp. 17–28. The uncoupling of race and culture wasn't and isn't unique to the UK. In 1987, Jean-Marie Le Pen, leader of the fascistic, anti-migrant Front National, declared: 'I love North Africans, but their place is in the Maghreb . . . I am not a racist, but a national . . . For a nation to be harmonious, it must have a certain ethnic and spiritual homogeneity.' Cited in Maxim Silverman, *Deconstructing the Nation: Immigration, Racism and Citizenship in Modern France*, London and New York: Routledge, 2003 (1992), p. 167.

9. Martin Barker, *The New Racism: Conservative and the Ideology of the Tribe*, London: Junction Books, 1981, pp. 23–4.

10. David Goodhart, *The Road to Somewhere: The Populist Revolt and the Future of Politics*, London: Hurst & Company, 2017, p. 22; David Goodhart, 'Why I Left my Liberal London Tribe', *Financial Times*, 16 March 2017; David Goodhart, *The British Dream: Successes and Failures of Post-war Immigration*, London: Atlantic Books, 2013, p. 112. With regards to the argument that there is a blurring of race and immigration, see K. Biswas, 'Notoriously Clannish', *Times Literary Supplement*, 16 August 2013. Also see Ben Rogaly, 'Brexit Writings and the War of Position Over Migration, "Race" and "Class"', *Environment and Planning C: Politics and Space*, vol. 37, issue 1, pp. 26–38.

11. Matthew Goodwin, 'National Populism Is Unstoppable – and the Left Still Doesn't Understand it', *Guardian*, 8 November 2018.

12. John Harris, 'It's Not Racist to Be Anxious Over Large-Scale Immigration', *Guardian*, 23 December 2013.

13. I watched the original of the Wark–Flint interviews. For the transcript, see Dan Hancox, 11 January 2017, available at twitter.com/danhancox/status/819225721184030725, last accessed 20 June 2019; *Panorama*, 'Life in Immigration Town', BBC, 2017; *Immigration Street*, London: Love Production, 2015; Ellen E. Jones, 'Immigration Street, Review: There Is Such a Thing as Society – Just as the Residents of Derby Road, Southampton', *Independent*, 25 February 2015.

14. Charles Moore, 'Time for a More Liberal and "Racist" Immigration Policy', *Spectator*, 19 October 1991, p. 7.

15. *The Conservative Conference 1967: The Guardian Report*, Manchester: Manchester Guardian, 1967, p. 34; cited in Jonathan Aitken, *Margaret Thatcher: Power and Personality*, London: Bloomsbury, p. 200; Stephen Kinnock, 'My Cure for a Divided Britain? A Programme of Managed Immigration', *Guardian*, 19 September 2016.

16. Omar Khan and Nissa Finney, *Unnamed Letter to Louise Casey*, London: Runnymede Trust, 22 January 2016.

17. Enoch Powell, 'Enoch Powell's "Rivers of Blood" Speech', *Daily Telegraph*, 12 December 2007; Thatcher quote cited in Randall Hansen, *Citizenship and Immigration in Post-War Britain: The Institutional Origins of a Multicultural Nation*, Oxford: Oxford University Press, 2000, p. 209.

18. Jessica Elgot, 'Some Use Immigration as Euphemism for Race, Says Diane Abbott', *Guardian*, 21 February 2018.

19. Rupert Myers, 'Ukip Supporters I met Weren't Racist – They Felt Disenfranchised and Frustrated', *Guardian*, 26 May 2014.

20. Cited in Roland Butt, 'The Conservative Party in Democracy', in *An Escape from Orwell's 1984*, edited by Rhodes Boyson, Middlesex: Churchill Press, 1975, pp. 82–95, 85. See also Nancy Murray, 'Anti-Racists and Other Demons: The Press and Ideology in Thatcher's Britain', *Race and Class*, vol. 27, issue 3, 1986; Gill Seidel, 'The White Discursive Order: The British New Right's Discourse on Cultural Racism', in *Approaches to Discourse, Poetics and Psychiatry: Papers from*

the 1985 Utrecht Summer School of Critical Theory, ed. by Iris M. Zaval, Teun A. van Dijk and Myriam Díaz-Diocaretz, Amsterdam: John Benjamins Publishing, 1988, pp. 39–66.

21. Akwugo Emejulu and Leah Bassel, *Minority Women and Austerity: Survival and Resistance in France and Britain*, Bristol: Policy Press, 2017; 'New Research Shows that Poverty, Ethnicity and Gender Magnify the Impact of Austerity of BME Women', Women's Budget Group and Runnymede Trust, 28 November 2016.

22. Lisa Tilley, 'The Making of the "White Working Class": Where Fascist Resurgence Meets Leftist White Anxiety', *Wildcat Dispatches*, 28 November 2016, available at wildcatdispatches.org, last accessed 10 April 2019; Shirin Hirsch, 'From Powell to Casey: the Mythical White Working Class', *DiscoverSociety*, 1 February 2017, available at discoversociety.org, last accessed 10 April 2019.

23. Arshad Isakjee and Colin Lorne, 'Bad News from Nowhere: Race, Class and the "Left Behind"', *Environment and Planning C: Politics and Space*, 20 December 2018, pp. 5–6.

24. Deborah Summers, 'White Working Class Feels Ignored over Immigration, Says Hazel Blears', *Guardian*, 2 January 2009.

25. See 'BBC Two Winter/Spring 2008', BBC, 20 November 2007; Owen Jones, *Chavs: The Demonisation of the Working Class*, London: Verso, 2011, p. 117.

26. Danny Dorling, 'Brexit: The Decision of a Divided Country', *BMJ*, 2016, 354; Michael Ashcroft, 'How the United Kingdom Voted on Thursday . . . and Why', 24 June 2016, available at lordashcroftpolls.com, last accessed 6 August 2018.

27. 'Grandmothers Who Tend Their Flock of Asylum Seekers Against Dawn Raids', *The Scotsman*, 26 December 2006.

28. This is what Paul Gilroy calls 'conviviality'. See Paul Gilroy, *Postcolonial Melancholia*, Columbia: Columbia University Press, 2004, p. xv.

29. Home Office, *Counter-Extremism Strategy*, London: Home Office, 2015; Joint Select Committee on Human Rights, Counter-extremism, p. 108, available at publications.Parliament.uk/pa/

jt201617/jtselect/jtrights/105/10507.htm#_idTextAnchor028, last accessed 10 February 2019.

30. Panikos Panayi, *An Immigration History of Modern Britain: Multicultural Racism Since 1800*, London: Longman, 2010, p. 13; Peter Fryer, *Staying Power: The History of Black People in Britain*, London: Pluto Press, 1984.

31. Or, as Stuart Hall put it, 'cultural identity is always something but it is never one thing'. Stuart Hall, *The Fateful Triangle: Race, Ethnicity, Nation*, Cambridge, MA: Harvard University Press, 2017, pp. 173-4. Also see Andrew Lorde, 'Age, Race, Class and Sex: Women Redefining Different', in *Sister Outsider: Essays and Speeches*, Berkeley: Crossing Press, 2007, pp. 114-23, 109.

32. Ian Cobain, Nazia Parveen and Matthew Taylor, 'The Slow-Burning Hatred that Led Thomas Mair to Murder Jo Cox', *Guardian*, 23 November 2016; Ben Beaumont-Thomas, 'Jeff Mitchell's Best Photograph: "These People Have Been Betrayed by Ukip"', *Guardian*, 22 June 2016.

33. 'Michael Gove "Shuddered" at UKIP Migrants Poster', BBC News, 19 June 2016.

34. Daniel Boffey and Toby Helm, 'Vote Leave Embroiled in Race Row over Turkey Security Threat Claims', *Observer*, 22 May 2016. See also Paul Stocker, *English Uprising: Brexit and the Mainstreaming of the far-right*, London: Melville House UK, 2017.

35. Adam Withnall, 'EU Referendum: David Cameron Questions Penny Mordaunt's Judgement over Turkey Veto Claim', *Independent*, 22 May 2016.

36. Paul Gilroy, ' "My Britain Is Fuck All" Zombie Multiculturalism and the Race Politics of Citizenship', *Identities*, vol. 19, issue 4, 2012, p. 394.

37. Daniel Trilling, 'Tommy Robinson and the Far-Right's New Playbook', *Guardian*, 25 October 2018.

38. See Zachary Lockman, *Contending Visions of the Middle East: The History and Politics of Orientalism*, 2nd ed., Cambridge: Cambridge University, 2010, pp. 66-99.

39. Alana Lentin and Gavan Titley, *The Crises of Multiculturalism Racism in a Neoliberal Age*, London: Zed Books, 2011, p. 35; Runnymede Trust, *Islamophobia: Still a Challenge for Us All*, ed. by Farah Elahi and Omar Khan, London: Runnymede Trust, 2018; Runnymede Trust, *Islamophobia: A Challenge for Us All*, London: Runnymede Trust, 1997; Arun Kundnani, *The Muslims Are Coming!: Islamophobia, Extremism, and the Domestic War on Terror*, London: Verso, 2015; Kerry Moore, Paul Mason and Justin Lewis, *Images of Islam in the UK: The Representation of British Muslims in the National Print News Media 2000–2008*, Cardiff: Cardiff School of Journalism, Media and Cultural Studies, 2008.

40. In 2010, a *Financial Times* editorial argued, 'A strong emphasis on cultural assimilation is also justified. This includes an insistence that new immigrants should learn the language of their new countries and robust defence of Western values, such as women's and gay rights. This will make liberals squeamish. But ignoring the warnings sent by the rising far right would be far more dangerous.' See '*Financial Times* Opinion: UK Schools, Europeans Backlash Against Immigrants', *Financial Times*, 4 April 2010.

41. In March 2017, they made headlines when they joined forces with two other campaign groups to close down London Stansted Airport in a bid to stop the deportation of eight people on a late-night chartered flight. Chris Johnston, 'Stansted Runway Closed after Anti-Deportation Protesters Block Flight', *Guardian*, 28 March 2017.

42. 'Cologne Sex Attacks: Women Describe "Terrible" Assaults', BBC News, 7 January 2016.

43. Editorial, 'Lessons From the Cologne Assaults', *New York Times*, 13 January 2016.

44. Sara R. Farris, 'MeToo Shows Sexism Is Not Men of Colour's Prerogative', Al Jazeera, 10 February 2018; Brian Bell and Stephen Machin, *The Impact of Migration on Crime and Victimisation*, London: London School of Economics, 2011.

45. See Frantz Fanon, *Black Skin, White Masks*, London: Pluto Press, 1986, p. 170.

46. Crime Survey for England and Wales cited at Office for National Statistics, available at ons.gov.uk, last accessed 1 February 2019; End Violence Against Women, *Attitudes to Sexual Consent: Research for the End Violence Against Women Coalition by YouGov*, London: End Violence Against Women, 2018, p. 2.

47. Frances Perraudin, '"Marauding" Migrants Threaten Standard of Living, Says Foreign Secretary', *Guardian*, 10 August 2015.

48. Etienne Balibar, 'Racism and Crisis', in *Race Nation, Class: Ambiguous Identities*, ed. by Etienne Balibar and Immanuel Wallerstein, London: Verso, 1993 reprint, pp. 217–27, 219–20.

49. 'Key Quotes from the Blair Speech', BBC News, 10 May 2007; Kwame Anthony Appiah, 'Mistaken Identities: Culture', *Reith Lectures*, BBC Radio 4, 2016, available at bbc.co.uk, last accessed 10 April 2019.

50. Caroline Lowbridge, 'Romanian and Bulgarian Immigration: Boston Families Give their View', BBC News, 2 December 2013.

51. Cited in Liz Fekete, 'The Emergence of Xeno-Racism', *Race and Class*, vol. 43, issue 2, 2001.

52. Cited in Bridget Anderson, *Us and Them? The Dangerous Politics of Immigration Controls*, Oxford: Oxford University Press, 2013, p. 36; Luke de Noronha, 'Race, Class and Brexit: Thinking from Detention', versobooks.com, 9 March 2018, last accessed 10 April 2019.

53. Katherine Botterill and Kathy Burrell, '(In)visibility, Privilege and the Performance of Whiteness in Brexit Britain: Polish Migrants in Britain's Shifting Migration Regime', *Environment and Planning C: Politics and Space*, 20 December 2018, pp. 21–5.

54. Steve Garner, *Whiteness: An Introduction*, London: Routledge, 2007, p. 66.

55. T. J. Ewing, *Vote for Bhownaggree*, H. White, 180 Cambridge Road, N.E., 1895; Hannah Jones, Yasmin Gunaratnam, Gargi Bhattacharyya, William Davies, Sukhwant Dhaliwal, Kirsten Forkert, Emma Jackson and Roiyah Saltus, *Go Home? The Politics of Immigration Controversies*, Manchester: Manchester University Press, 2017, p. 76.

56. Omar Khan and Debbie Weekes-Bernard, *This Is Still about Us: Why Ethnic Minorities See Immigration Differently*, London: the Runnymede Trust, 2015, p. 19.

57. Dan Fisher, 'Split Between Britain, US Seen as "Inevitable"', *Los Angeles Times*, 19 April 1990, p. 10.

58. Steve Doughty and James Slack, 'One in Every Nine People in Britain Was Born Overseas', *Daily Mail*, 25 February 2009; cited in Randall Hansen, *Citizenship and Immigration in Post-War Britain: The Institutional Origins of a Multicultural Nation*, Oxford: Oxford University Press, 2000, p. 188.

59. Chai Patel and Charlotte Peel, *Passport Please: The Impact of the Right to Rent Checks on Migrants and Ethnic Minorities in England*, London: Joint Council for the Welfare of Immigrants, 2017.

60. Frances Webber, *Borderline Justice: The Fight for Refugee and Migrant Rights*, London: Pluto Press, 2012, pp. 141–2.

61. Robbie Shilliam, *Racism, Multiculturalism and Brexit*, robbieshilliam.wordpress.com, 4 July 2016, last accessed 10 April 2019.

62. David Blunkett, 'I Can't Back Down on Asylum', *Guardian*, 14 December 2003. Thatcher argued, 'Now, we are a big political party. If we do not want people to go to extremes, and I do not, we ourselves must talk about this problem and we must show that we are prepared to deal with it.' When she was asked by a caller on BBC Radio 4 to withdraw her statement months later, she refused. The exchange made it onto the front page of the *Sun*, which also praised the government's plans as ones 'no reasonable person – black or white – could quarrel' with, and dismissed the far-right National Front as 'twisted little men'. Cited in Mohan Ambikaipaker, *Political Blackness in Multiracial Britain*, Philadelphia: University of Pennsylvania Press, 2018, p. 204 and Martin Barker, *The New Racism: Conservative and the Ideology of the Tribe*, London: Junction Books, 1981, p. 1.

63. *Playing the Race Card Part II*, BBC, 1999, 47:21–47:34.

64. Daniel Trilling, 'Thatcher: The PM Who Brought Racism in from the Cold', versobooks.com, 10 April 2013, last accessed

10 April 2019; Teresa Hayter, *Open Borders: The Case against Immigration Control*, London: Pluto Press, 2000, p. 164.

65. Journalist Daniel Trilling has made this important distinction between the far right and the centre. Also see Paul Gilroy, *There Ain't No Black in the Union Jack: The Cultural Politics of Race and Nation*, London: Routledge, 1991, p. 119.

Conclusion

1. They wrote on the blog: 'unfortunately, the Grenfell Action Group have reached the conclusion that only an incident that results in serious loss of life . . . will allow the external scrutiny to occur that will shine a light on the practices that characterise the malign governance of this non-functioning organisation'. See Grenfell Action Group, 'KCTMO – Playing with Fire!', grenfellactiongroup. wordpress.com, 20 November 2016, last accessed 6 August 2018.

2. Robbie Shilliam, *Race and the Undeserving Poor*, Newcastle upon Tyne: Agenda Publishing, 2018, pp. 165–81.

3. Nadia Khomami and Chris Johnston, 'Thousands Join Solidarity with Refugees Rally in London', *Guardian*, 12 September 2015.

4. Macer Hall, 'Corbyn Attacks Own Party: Labour's Anti-Asylum Election Stance "Was Appalling"', *Sunday Express*, 27 August 2015.

5. Jamie Grierson, 'UK Visa System Should Treat Eu and Non-Eu Citizens Alike, Says Labour', *Guardian*, 13 September 2018.

6. Conservative Party, *Forward, Together: Our Plan for a Stronger Britain and a Prosperous Future*, London: Conservative Party, p. 54.

7. Labour Party, *For the Many Not the Few: The Labour Party Manifesto 2017*, London: Labour Party, 2017, p. 28.

8. 'Jeremy Corbyn: I've Not Changed my Mind on Immigration', BBC News, 10 January 2017.

9. Helen Lewis, 'Jeremy Corbyn: "Wholesale" EU Immigration Has Destroyed Conditions for British Workers', *New Statesman*, 23 July 2017.

10. Mehreen Khan, 'Posted Worker Problems', *Financial Times*, 24 October 2017.

11. Gareth Dale, 'Leaving the Fortresses: Between Class Inter-nationalism and Nativist Social Democracy', *Viewpoint Magazine*, 30 November 2017.

12. Richard Seymour, 'The danger of racial opportunism', patreon. com, 1 April 2019, last accessed 2 April 2019.

13. Nikesh Shukla, *The Good Immigrant*, London: Unbound, 2016; Sunny Singh, 'Why the Lack of Indian and African Faces in Dunkirk Matters', *Guardian*, 1 August 2017.

14. See *Dinghies, Warships and Windrush: The Politics of Migration in 2019*, Novara Media, available at youtube.com/watch?v=A-ocLc73j1TA, last accessed 2 April 2019.

15. Paul Gilroy, *After Empire: Melancholia or Convivial Culture*, London: Routledge, 2004, p. 61.

16. Cecilia Tacoli, 'Crisis of Adaptation? Migration and Climate Change in a Context of High Mobility', *Environment and Urbanisation*, vol. 21, issue 2, pp. 513–25.

17. Reece Jones, *Refugees Borders: Refugees and the Right to Move*, London: Verso, 2016, pp. 126–7; Bridget Anderson, Nandita Sharma and Cynthia Wright, 'We Are All Foreigners – No Borders as a Practical Political Project', in *Citizenship Migrant Activism and the Politics of Movement*, ed. by Peter Nyers and Kim Rygiel, London: Routledge, 2014, p. 73.

18. Farzana Khan, 'Moving from "No Borders" to Broaderland for the Borderless', *New Internationalist*, 17 December 2015. When I interviewed Professor Gurminder Bhambra she made this point about the relationship between borders and anti-colonial movement.

19. Toni Morrison, Black Studies Center public dialogue, Portland State, Special Collection: Oregon Public Speakers, 30 May 1975, available at pdxscholar.library.pdx.edu/orspeakers/90/, last accessed 25 May 2019.

20. Nicholas de Genova, 'The "Migrant Crisis" as Racial Crisis: Do Black Lives Matter in Europe?', *Ethnic and Racial Studies*, vol. 41, issue 10, p. 1778.

Printed by Printforce, United Kingdom